ST IVES

THE STORY OF PORTHMEOR STUDIOS

ST IVES
THE STORY OF PORTHMEOR STUDIOS

THE WORLD OF ARTISTS AND MARINERS

Marion Whybrow

BORLASE SMART JOHN WELLS TRUST
Studios for Artists in Cornwall

HALSTAR

First published in Great Britain in 2013

British Library Cataloguing-in-Publication Data
A CIP record for this title is available from the British Library

ISBN 978 1 906690 50 2

HALSTAR
Halsgrove House,
Ryelands Business Park,
Bagley Road, Wellington, Somerset TA21 9PZ
Tel: 01823 653777 Fax: 01823 216796
email: sales@halsgrove.com

Part of the Halsgrove group of companies
Information on all Halsgrove titles is available at:
www.halsgrove.com

Printed in China by Everbest Printing Co Ltd

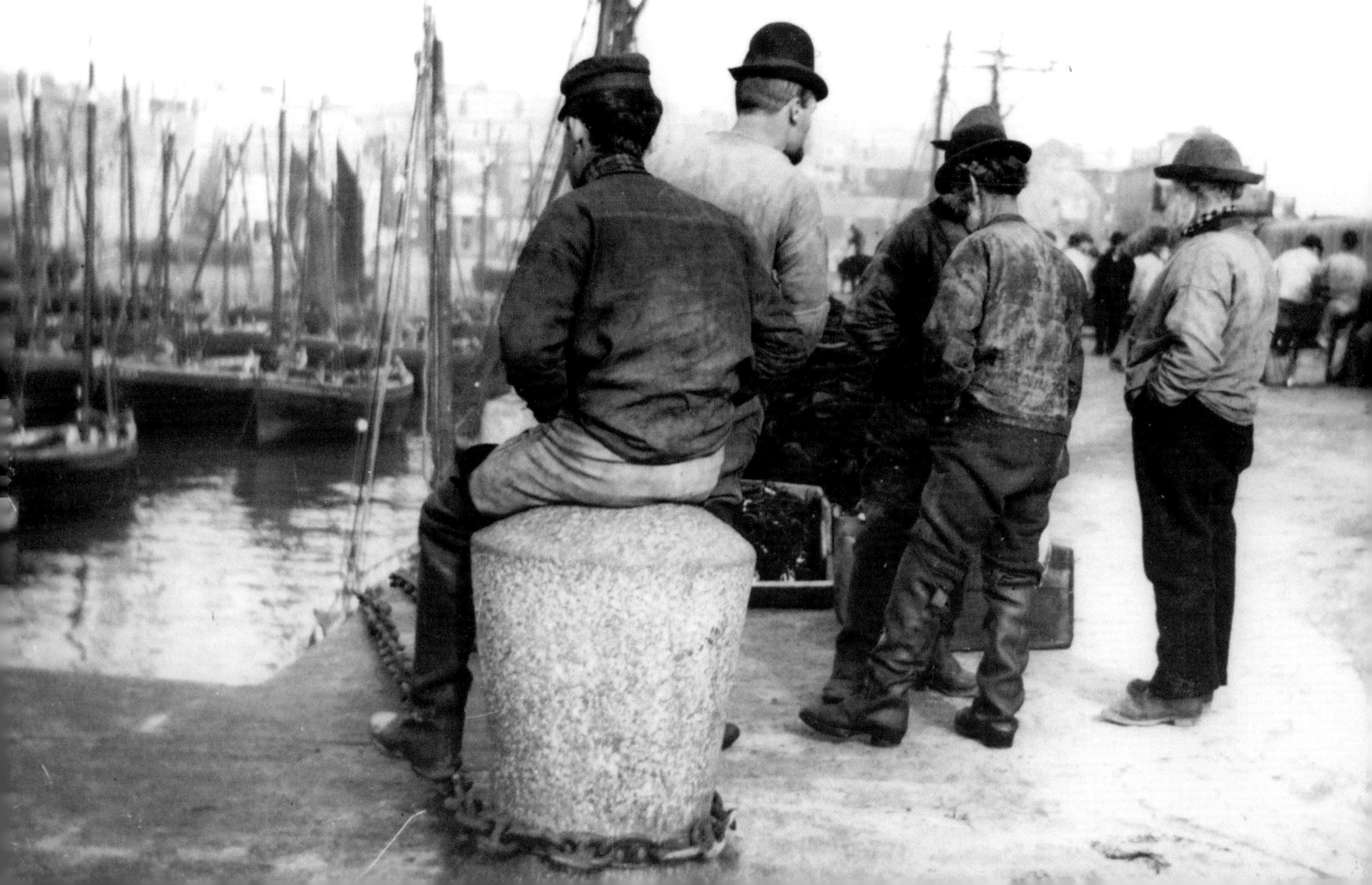

FOREWORD

By Frank Ruhrmund

BEING ASKED TO write this is rather like being asked to walk across St Ives Bay or the harbour at high tide without getting my feet wet. Something only He who could walk on water could manage. Having been born and bred on the other side of the hill, a good ten miles or so away in Newlyn, I'm very much aware of how careful I must be regarding what I might say or even think about St Ives.

Fortunately, although a 'bucca' and not a 'hake', (for readers not from this part of the world, 'bucca' and 'hake' are the age-old nicknames of natives of Newlyn and St Ives respectively), I was young at a time when the parallels between both places were close. In Newlyn we had a 'Downalong', and an 'Upalong', just as St Ives did, even an 'Outalong' and an 'Inalong' as well, and the cobbled streets in 'Downalong', where I lived, reeked, as they once did in both places, with the smell of fish.

It was an age of tight, not to say watertight, communities, when in my family, as they did in most families in Newlyn and St Ives, Mackerel, Mother and Methodism reigned, and everybody knew everyone. Then, too, there were the artists, at least one of whom with his easel seemed a permanent fixture at the bottom of our street. To be honest, we had little or nothing to do with them, they dressed differently, spoke a different language, and smelled of money rather than fish.

Years later, I often wondered if Stanhope Forbes had been among them. The doyen of the Newlyn School of Artists, which came into being, grew up and flourished in the late nineteenth century almost in tandem with the St Ives School, he had close connections with St Ives. He visited the St Ives Arts Club as early as 1890, and his wife Elizabeth even had a studio in the town. Worth remembering that Thomas Cooper Gotch lived in St Ives at that time, and that Forbes would be then meeting such luminaries of the St Ives School as Julius Olsson, Louis Grier, Moffat Lindner, Borlase Smart and Adrian Stokes the first president of the St Ives Arts Club.

All of this was happening, of course, when fishing was declining. Looking at the St Ives of today, it is hard to imagine that it was once a busy thriving fishing port and that, reportedly, some thirty million pilchards were once landed there in an hour. Sadly, such a wealth of fish was soon to be no more but, happily, the town was able to look toward pictures and tourists rather than pilchards for its future. The coming of the railway in 1877 was a help, so too were its magnificent sandy beaches but, above all, unlike Newlyn it was spared the savage slum clearances of the 1930s enabling John Betjeman to state in his *Shell Guide to Cornwall* that 'the granite setts and cobbles have been kept in many of the alleys: the granite outside steps survive to first floors, and the old grey-white grouted roofs remain and so does much of the silver-blue hanging and the granite stone walls of houses and chapels.'

That was written in the 1960s and, while there were changes before this and have been since, the town is lucky in having 'powers that be' who have kept a watchful eye upon its development and, for the most part, have been successful in the battle to keep its former fishing quarter, Downalong, relatively unchanged and a reminder of what used to be.

It was this quarter which housed the fishing families that, along with the quality of light found in St Ives, attracted the artists several of whom were able to buy or rent as studios the fish cellars or lofts the fishermen no longer needed. Talking of studios, the first one I ever visited in St Ives was that of the sculptor Denis Mitchell. I was taken to meet him by the Mousehole painter Jack Pender and, although it was a long time ago, I still remember the thrill, the tingle and buzz, of the occasion. For me, the artist's studio had been, and still is, the 'holy of holies', the place where it all happens, and I could hardly believe that I was sitting there, drinking tea and talking about everything under the sun except art with one who, like all artists, probably spent more time there than he did in his home. I know I came away feeling what a privilege it had been. Although I've been to umpteen artists' studios since then, I think how lucky I've been and still regard each visit I make as a privilege.

Denis Mitchell, 'Dear Denis' as Breon O'Casey always called him, was a founder member of the breakaway group of artists that set up the Penwith Society of Arts in 1949. An action which crystallized the importance of the influx of the young 'Moderns', of the whole post-war avant garde art movement in St Ives, although no one could have even dreamt of it at the time, it was to lead eventually to the opening of Tate St Ives in 1993, and a couple of decades later to the 'regeneration' of the Porthmeor studios and cellars.

Thinking of privilege and studios, I've spent many happy hours, crouched around the stoves in several of the old Porthmeor studios wondering whether the windows might blow out and the sea would come in before I left. Such was the state of their stoves that I often left them feeling amazed that the studios hadn't gone up in smoke long before their 'regeneration' began.

That St Ives now has such a splendid regenerated block of studios and cellars is, in more ways than one, something of a miracle and an event which owes a lot to such believers in the town and to the environment as Dame Barbara Hepworth and Patrick Heron in particular.

Having got this far and survived, I hope, walking on the hake-infested water without being eaten alive or drowned, I must add, the town is also fortunate in having such a recorder of its artists and mariners as St Ives-based author Marion Whybrow. She already has several books about the art and artists of the town to her credit, among them the excellent and definitive *St.Ives 1883-1993: Portrait of an Art Colony*, and I can think of no one better to write the story of the people, past and present, artists and fishermen, architects, builders and trustees, involved in the miraculous 'regeneration of the Porthmeor Studios' – an informative and inspired story for which she will surely be acclaimed yet again.

Frank Ruhrmund

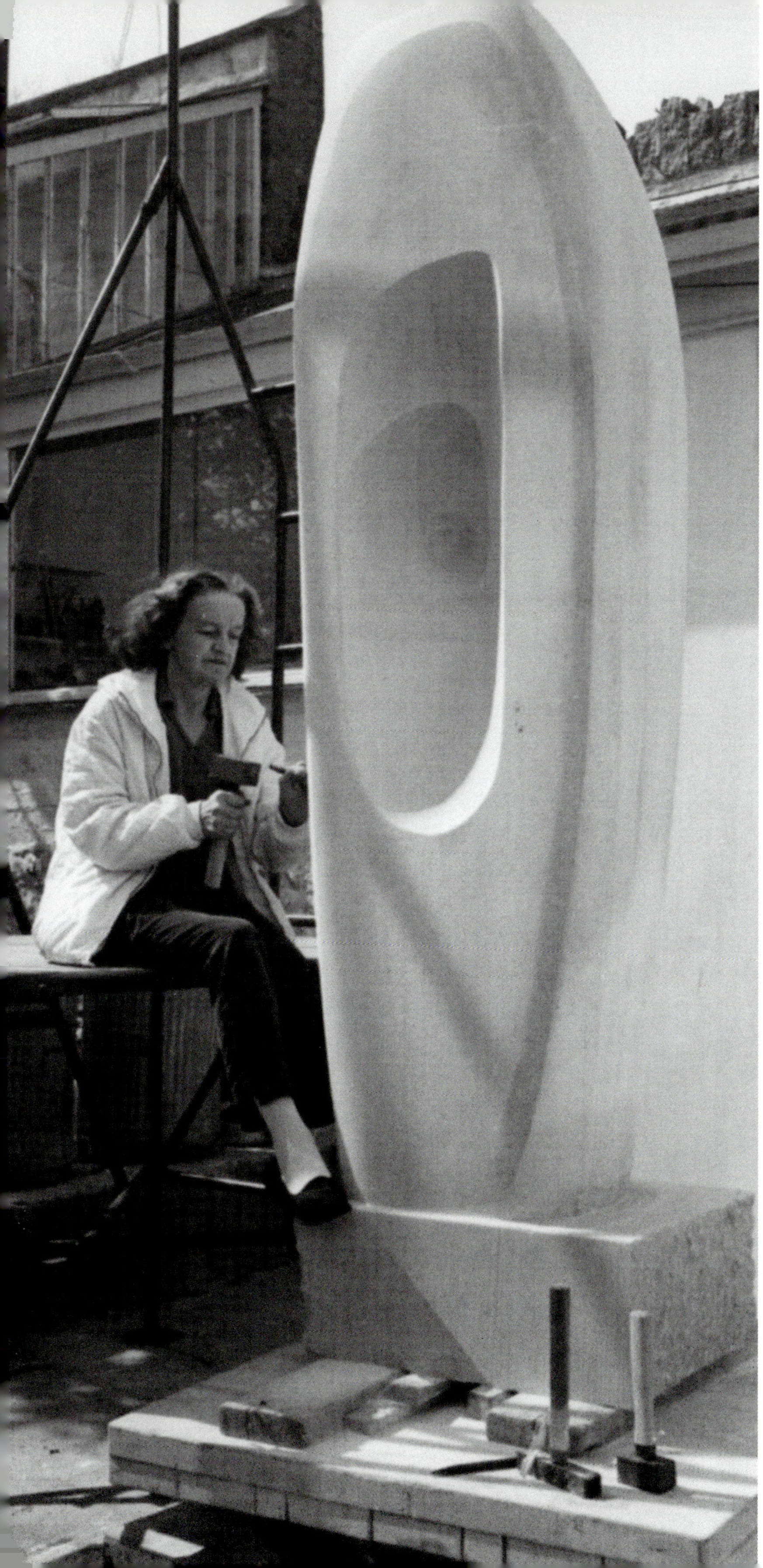

CONTENTS

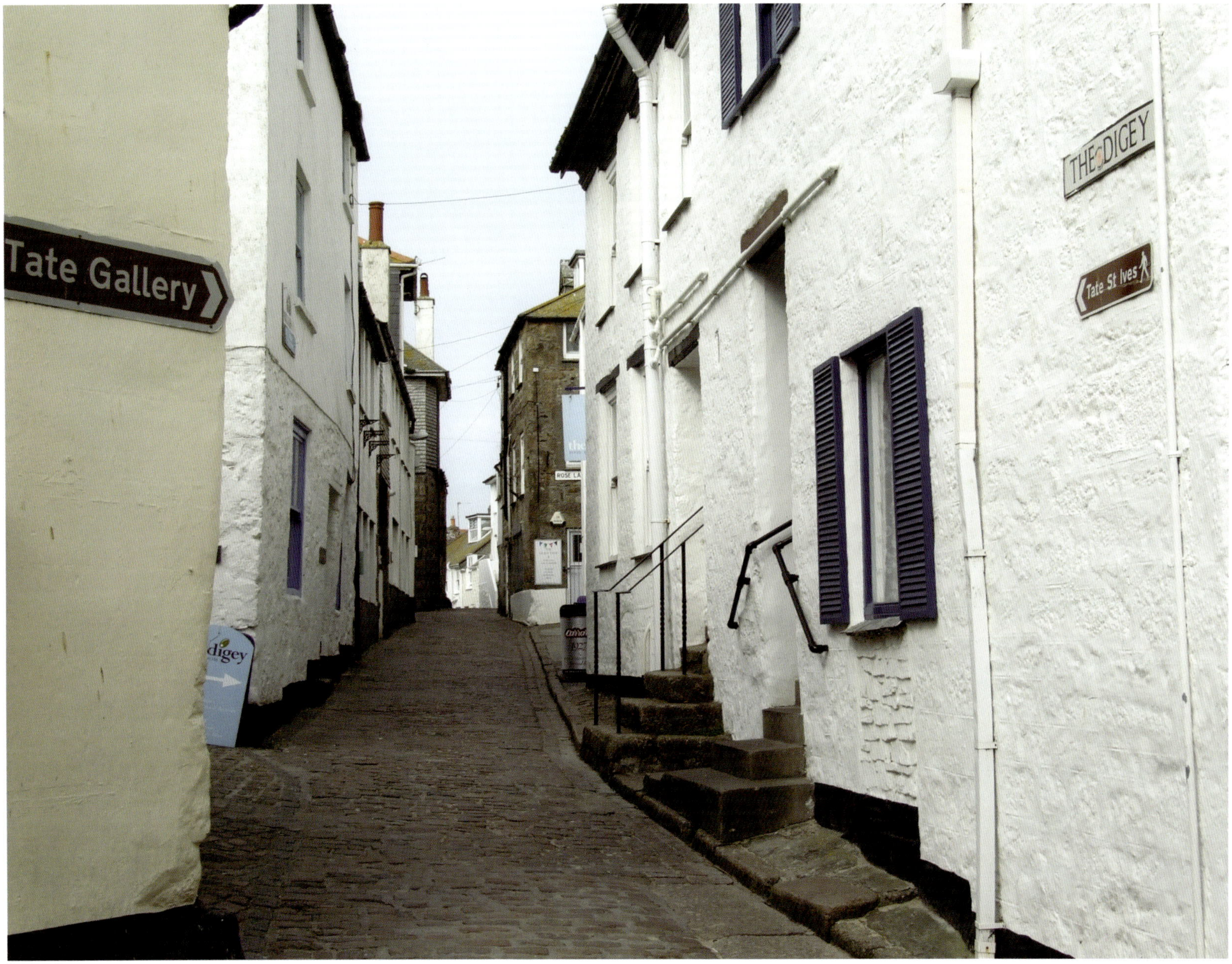

The Digey

ST IVES

Artists and Fishermen have worked together in harmony for 120 years [1]

WALK ALONG THE Harbour or Fore Street in St Ives and you will enjoy a gentle welcome to the town from a warm south-westerly but this is not invariably so; when the wind blows from the east, boats in the harbour suffer a battering from wind and tide. However, if you walk for five minutes towards the Atlantic beach to the north of this isthmus, you will find a tranquil scene, with a mild, warm breeze, blowing from the south-west. These two extreme conditions are often reversed. When the big north-easterly howls along the coast from Land's End to Porthmeor Beach, it is difficult to stand on your feet.

To learn something of the history of the town you can walk up the cobbled lane called The Digey, from Fore Street, and come to a full stop when you reach the wall that prevents you falling on to

Below left: 'Man's Head', James Lynn Pitt

Below right: 'The Island', James Lynn Pitt

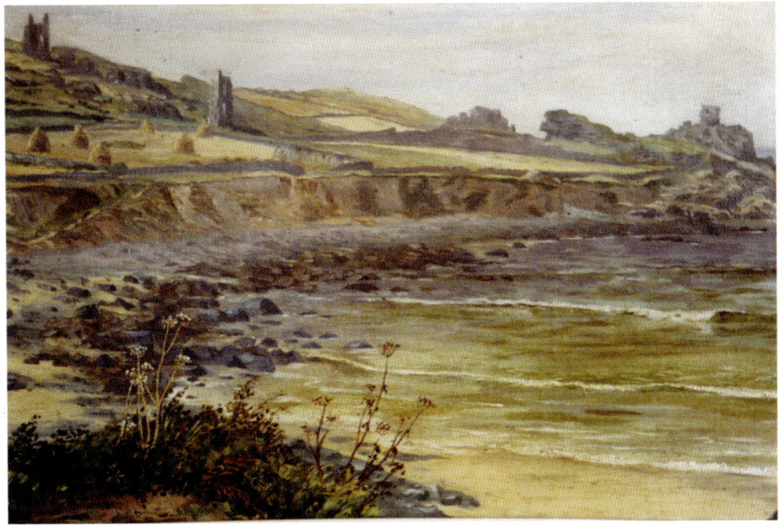

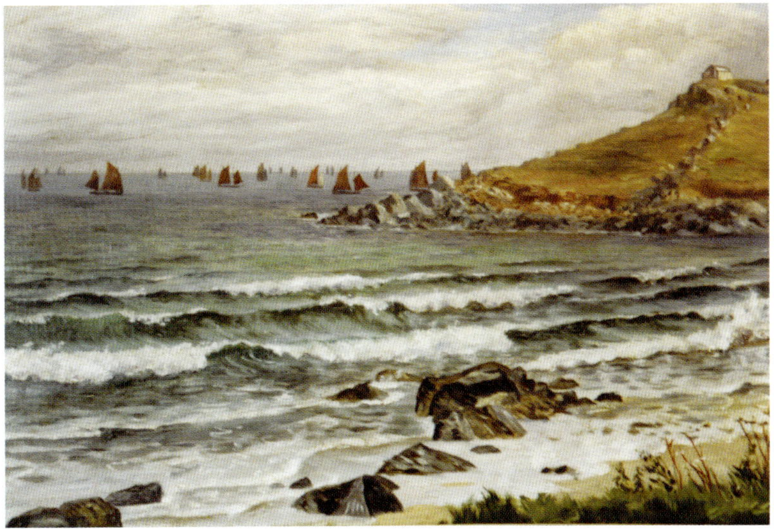

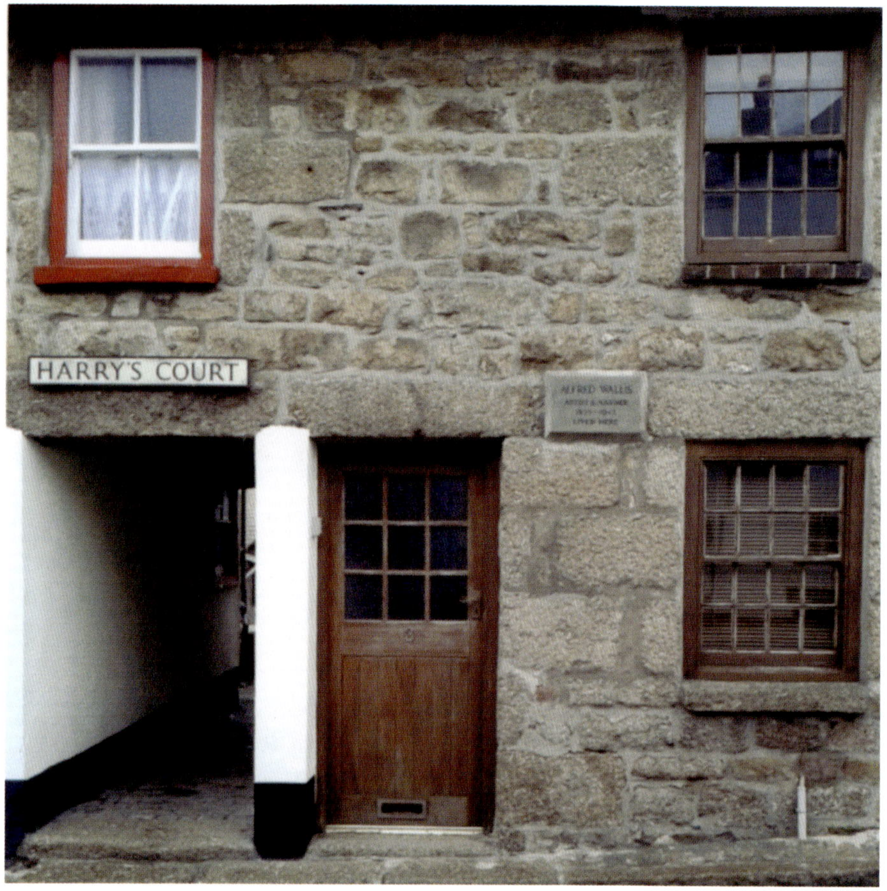

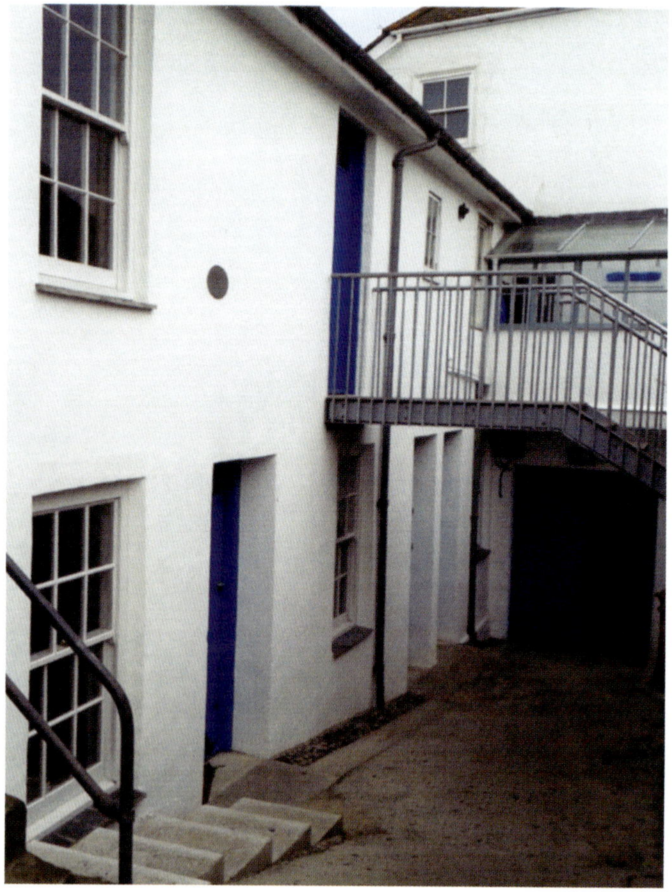

Above left: Alfred Wallis's Cottage

Above right: The Studios and Cellars

the sand at Porthmeor Beach. Stand there and watch the surfers and thrill to the giant waves surging towards you. Far left, looking out to sea is Man's Head. This is the coastal path that will take you to Zennor, and on to Land's End. To your immediate left is the Tate Gallery, dressed in elegant white. Turn your head to the right and you will see the Island, with the tiny chapel on top. Direct your gaze to the buildings fronting the beach and there, centrally situated, are the newly refurbished Porthmeor Studios. You will find the entrance to the studios by walking along Back Road West, past Alfred Wallis's cottage, and then down the slope a few metres on. It is in these buildings that the history of art was painted from the 1880s, and continuously, to the present day.

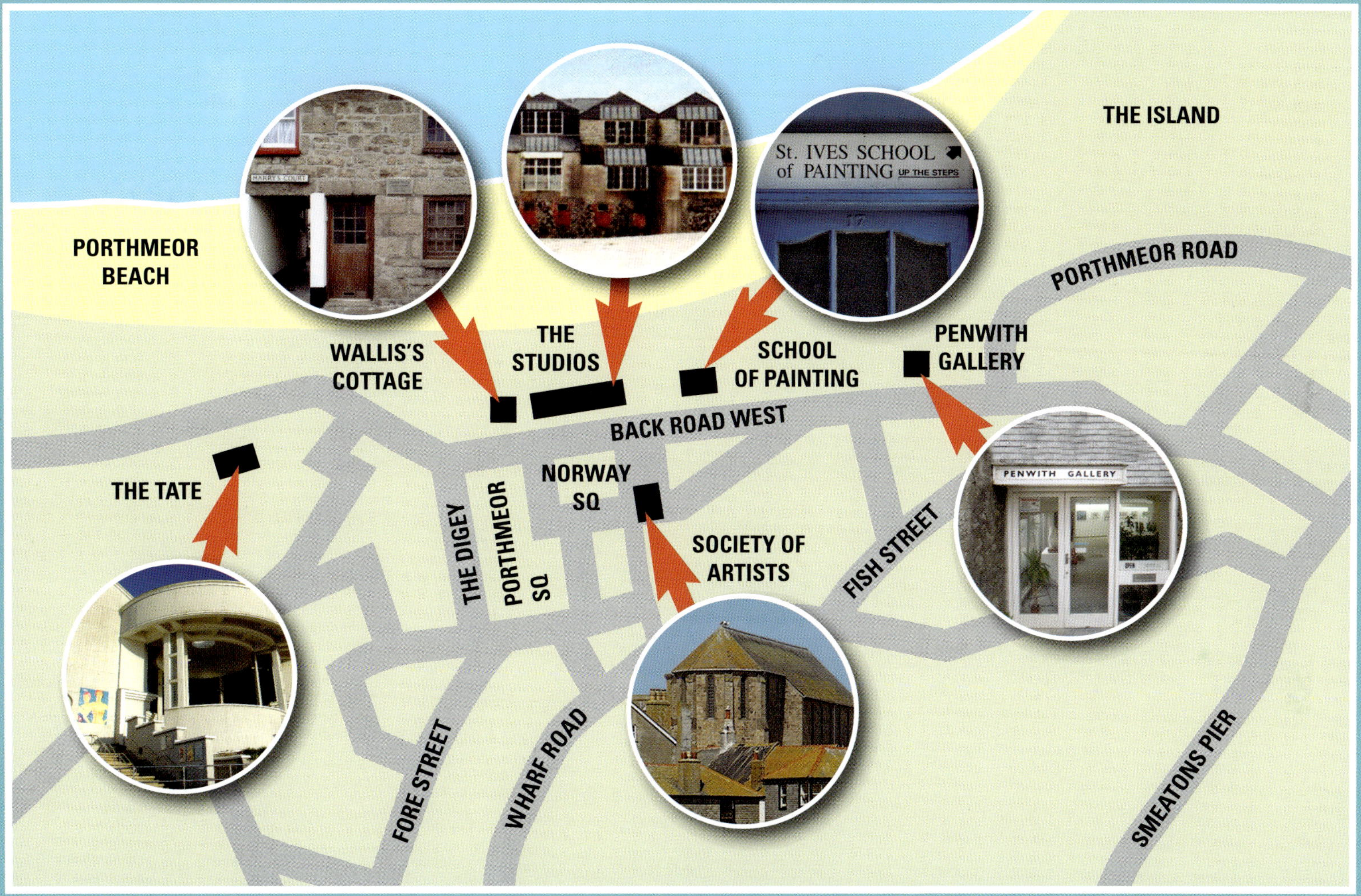

Back Road West

Earlier Times

Long before the turn of the nineteenth century, St Ives and its people were almost totally dependent on one industry; fishing. With the decline of this major source of income the townsfolk were happy to rent out rooms, houses and net lofts to visiting artists and students, who opened up spaces to light and colour. Their easels appeared on the cobbled streets and from America, Finland, France, Germany, Sweden, Australia and New Zealand, and all corners of the British Isles, the artists came flocking.

> *The fish-odoriferous town of St Ives is a veritable gem of beauty... Whistler, struck with its charms, is said to have sketched it, and certainly many have done it since. Now there are some 200 studios tucked away in many an odd corner of the place, forming a little colony of the artistic world.*[2]

The artists arriving in St Ives were of independent means and employed the local people as housekeepers, maids, nannies, gardeners, cooks and models. They rented houses and spent money freely in the town. They became at one with the local population, working alongside the fishermen and sharing accommodation. In the fishing port of Newlyn the same transformation was taking place.

The art colonies came together to cement and embrace the artistic heritage attached to each area. Newlyn, before and during the early part of the twentieth century, was the inspired centre for artists who recorded social realism. They portrayed the lives of fishermen and women. The harsh and tragic reality of their lives was captured in the paintings of catches of fish, boats, and people working on the sea shore; or a cottage showing a burnt down candle and a family hopelessly awaiting the return of the man of the house, lost at sea.

These paintings were frequently exhibited at the Royal Academy and told the story of the inhabitants of Newlyn. St Ives artists coasted alongside, showing less drama and more picturesque scenes of harbours, seascapes and the softer side of life, although living conditions were equally difficult.

A Change of Scene

However, change was about to take place with the arrival of artists with a broader pallet and a wider mind set. At the beginning of the Second World War, with the rise of Nazi Germany and its anti-progressive art movement; the closing down of the Bauhaus and the fleeing of avant garde artists to Britain and America, the Modernist process was underway.

Britain had its own born-and-bred stable of artists with radical ideas and a progressive approach to modern art. It was spearheaded by Barbara Hepworth and Ben Nicholson. They arrived in St Ives and developed their paintings and sculpture with a feeling for place and spirituality, and understood and interpreted the power that Cornwall exerts on creative people. They followed on from the traditional colony and introduced a new dimension to purely visual representations of beautiful scenery, hosting a whole new philosophy whose followers became leaders in the field of experimental art. They moved on from the art movements in France and America and introduced to this small town the abstract ideas in painting and sculpture which would go on to influence future generations.

Those artists who brought international fame and recognition to St Ives because of their contribution to abstract art have passed into history, as have their equally successful traditional predecessors. But the town continues to draw on its heritage, showing a fierce determination to perpetuate its standing as an art colony and the newly refurbished Porthmeor studios ensures the future for the artists now occupying the spaces of their forerunners.

Borlase Smart

In 1947 the artist, Borlase Smart, a stalwart of the art colony and the St Ives Society of Artists, died. In his memory and to honour the part he played in negotiating the sale of the Porthmeor studios in perpetuity for the artists, the Borlase Smart Trust was established. Moffat Lindner, artist, friend and owner of the studios had agreed a reasonable price of £6000 with Borlase and, together with an interest free loan from the Arts Council, the deal was sealed.

'St Ives Bay to Godrevy Lighthouse' by Borlase Smart

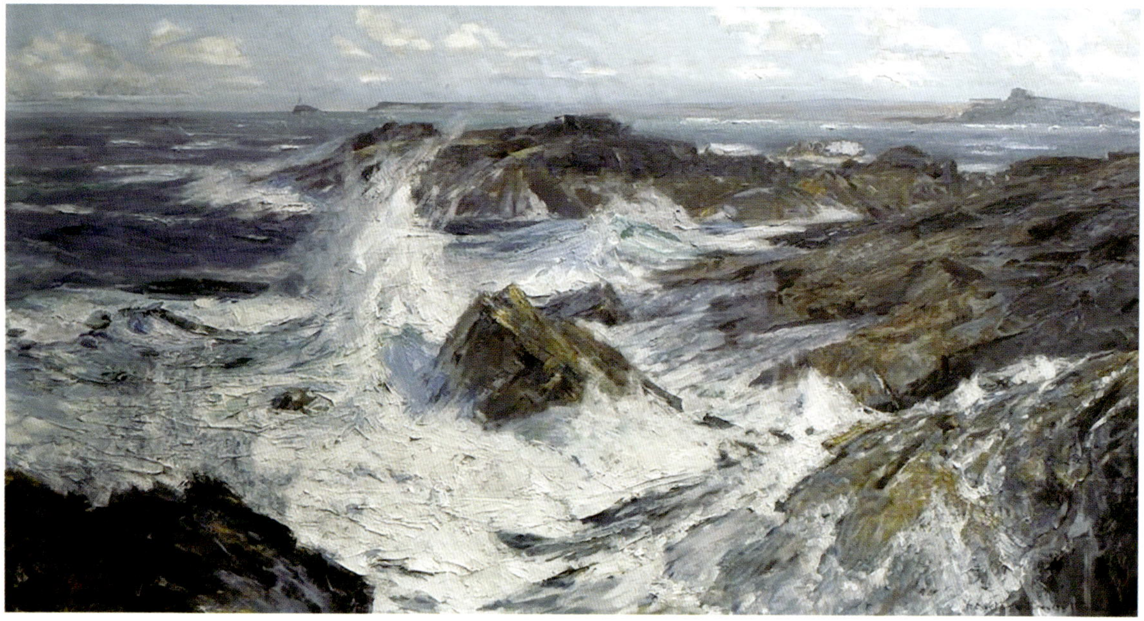

In the present day the renamed Borlase Smart John Wells Trust was able to raise funds to form a 'regeneration' programme to save the studios, and also the net lofts occupied by the fishermen, from a state of dilapidation to a joyful renaissance that will ensure the future for both artists and mariners.

Tate Gallery St Ives

In 2013 the Tate Gallery at St Ives celebrated twenty successful years of its history. The building, which opened in 1993, is a remarkable achievement for so small a town. The art community was responsible for raising a large amount of money by the auction of their paintings: 250 works of art were donated. This was altruistic generosity. Most of the artists at that time working in the town would not be asked to exhibit in the new edifice, but were quietly creating in their studios with outlets in local galleries and around the country.

The auctioneer, David Lay of Penzance, and his staff gave their services free and, together with a variety of other events, raised £150,000. The artists had shown their commitment in supporting the idea of a building to house the paintings, sculpture and pottery of the Modernist movement in St Ives. They had also shown that this great effort was successful in attracting other monies from charitable organisations and major investors.

The Tate Gallery has in its London collection a great number of works from such sculptors as Barbara Hepworth and Naum Gabo, and the painters Ben Nicholson, Patrick Heron, Wilhelmina Barns Graham, Terry Frost, Sandra Blow, Bryan Wynter, Peter Lanyon, Karl Weschke, and many others who came to St Ives from the 1940s onwards with fresh ways of seeing. They helped change the face of modern art. This collection will now be housed in its own new extension to the gallery, in Phase 2 of the Tate building programme. Not only will it showcase the St Ives Modernists, but will also feature changing exhibitions of international, modern, and contemporary art.

Tate St Ives has its own unique position. It stands on the edge of the wild Atlantic Ocean overlooking the beautiful, unspoilt, Porthmeor beach. It is the final accolade to a town that has created over a century of art and artists, attracting visitors from across the world.

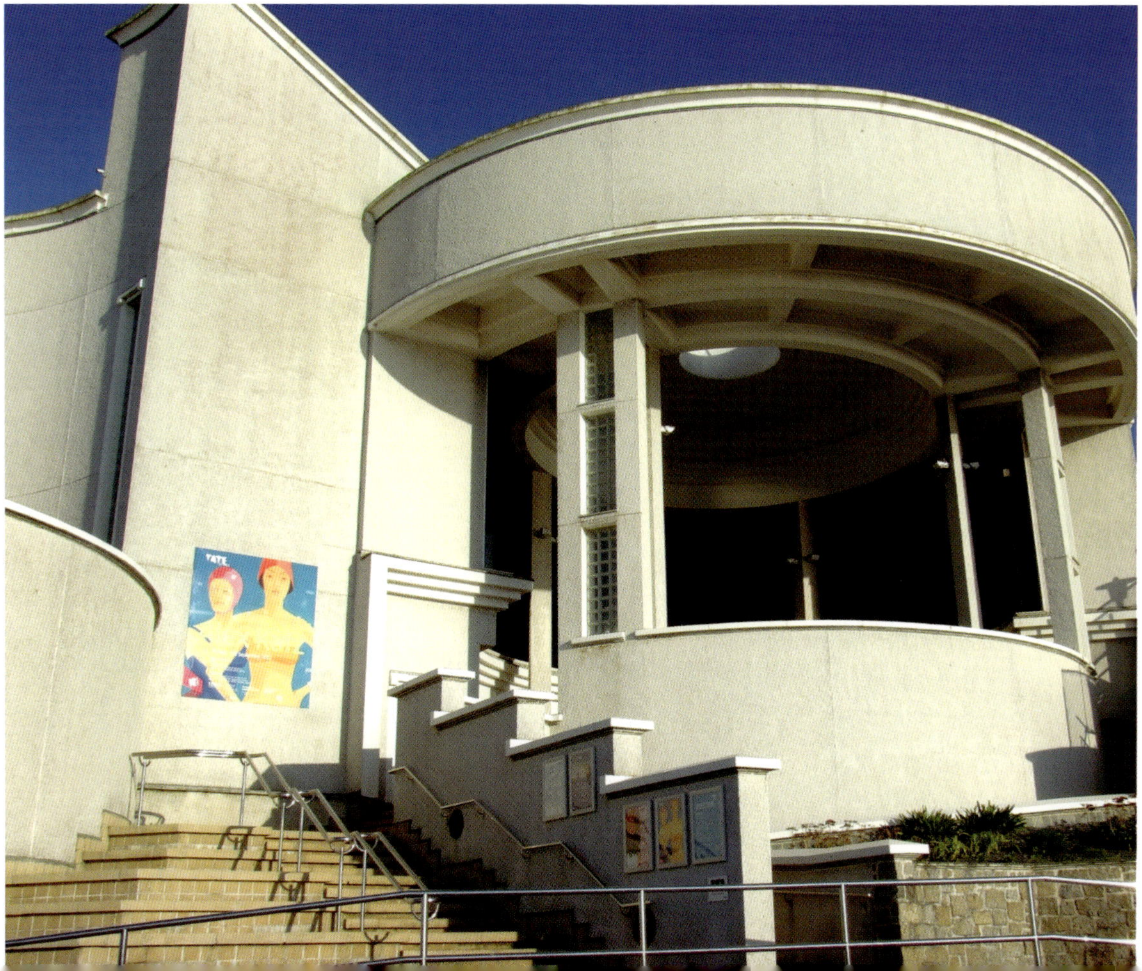

20th Anniversary.
Tate St Ives 2013

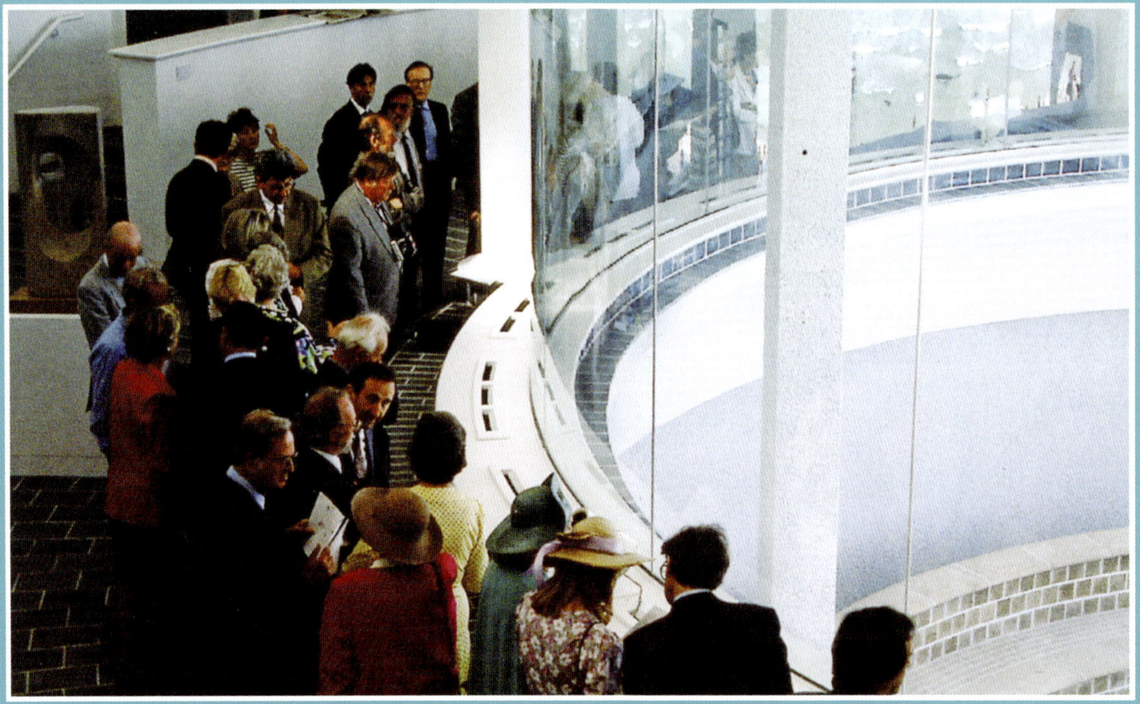

The Opening of Tate St Ives 1993

Watching the opening ceremony from inside the Tate Gallery

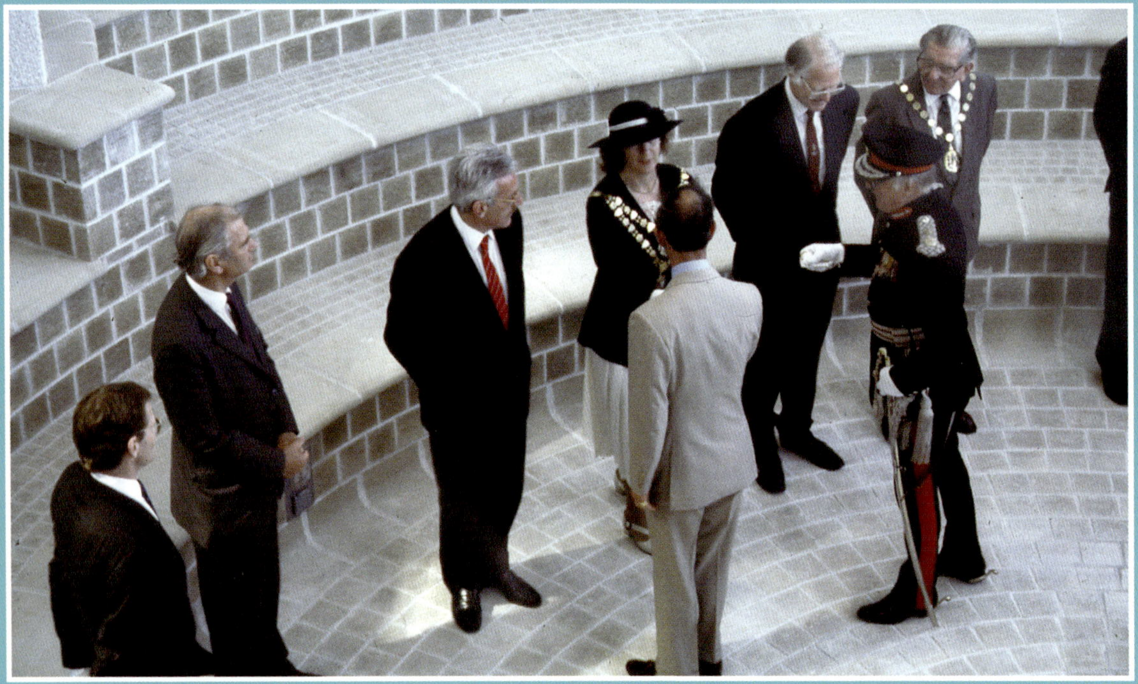

The Prince of Wales with Lord Falmouth. From the left: Sir Nicholas Serota, Sir Richard Carew Pole, Malcolm Veal, Shirley Beck (Mayor of St Ives), Malcolm Furneaux, Alan Harvey

Artists at the Tate Opening

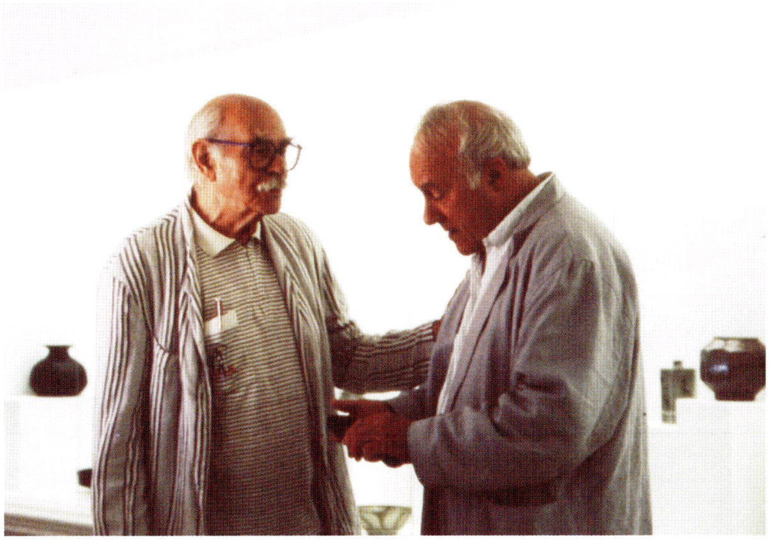
1

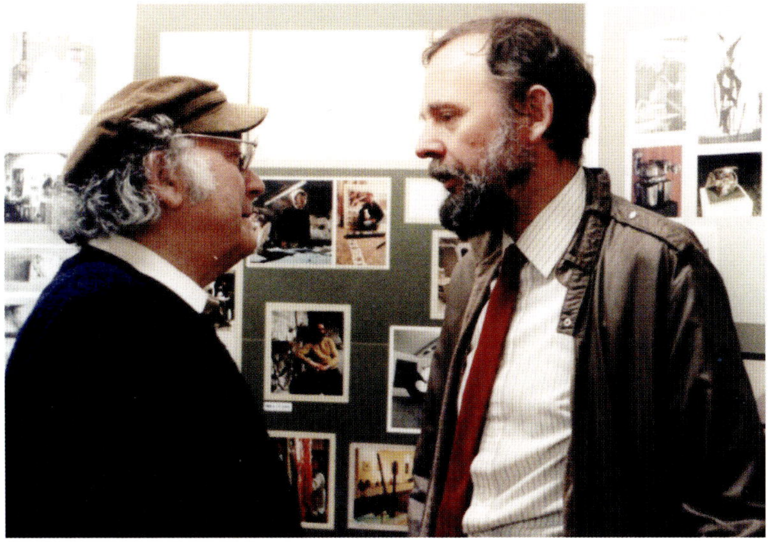
2

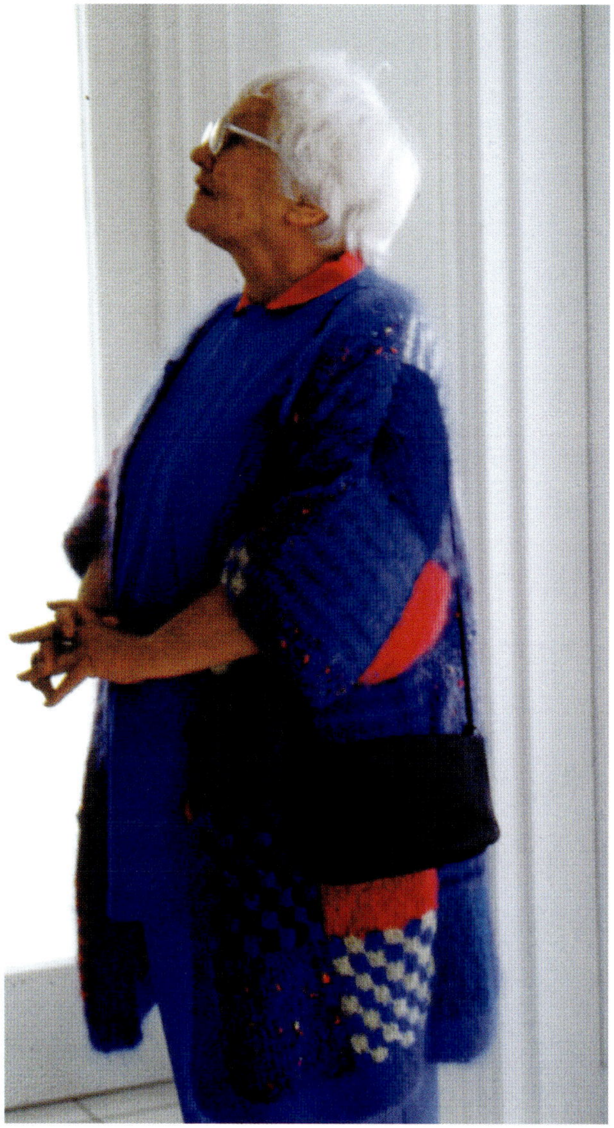
3

1. Artists Sir Terry Frost and Patrick Heron 2. Artists Roy Ray and Maurice Sumray 3. Artist Wilhelmina Barns Graham

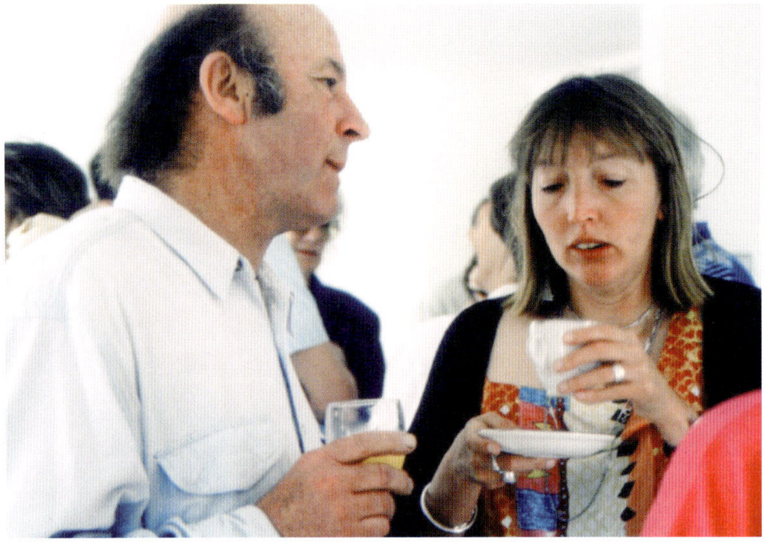
1

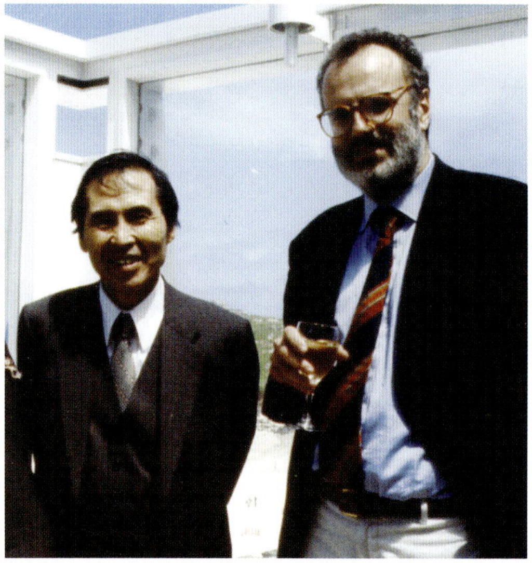
2

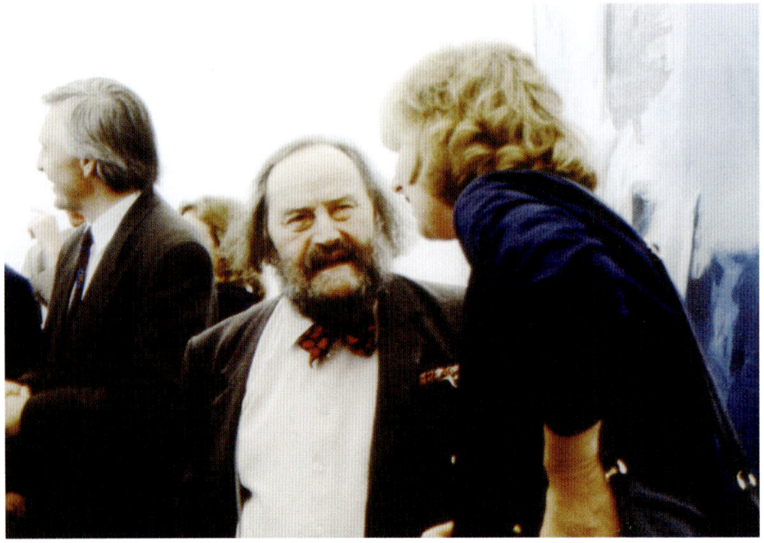
3

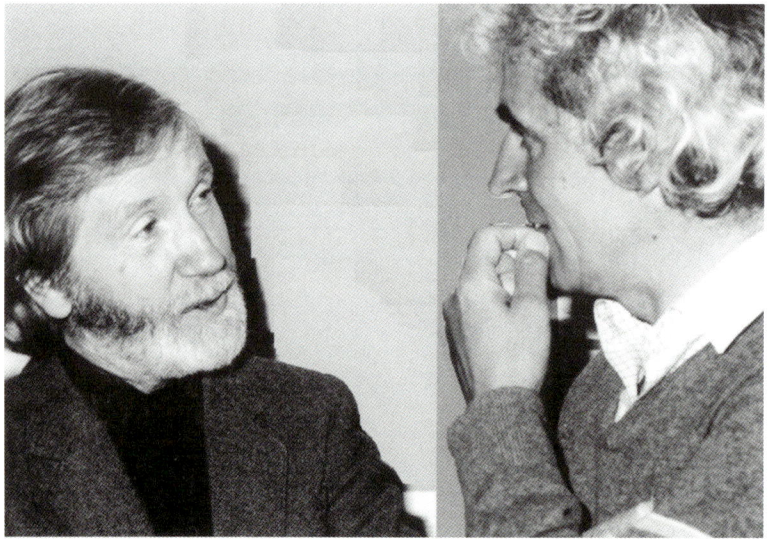
4

1. Artists Roy Walker and Louise McClary. 2. Professor Seiji Oshima, Setagaya Art Museum, Tokyo and author Michael Jacobs;
3. Professor Alan Livingston, Falmouth College of Art, Dr David Brown, Tate London and Isabella Livingston. 4. Artists Terry Whybrow and Colin Orchard

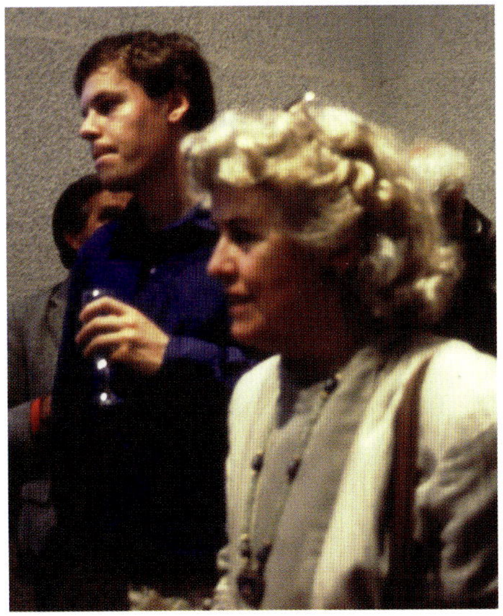
1

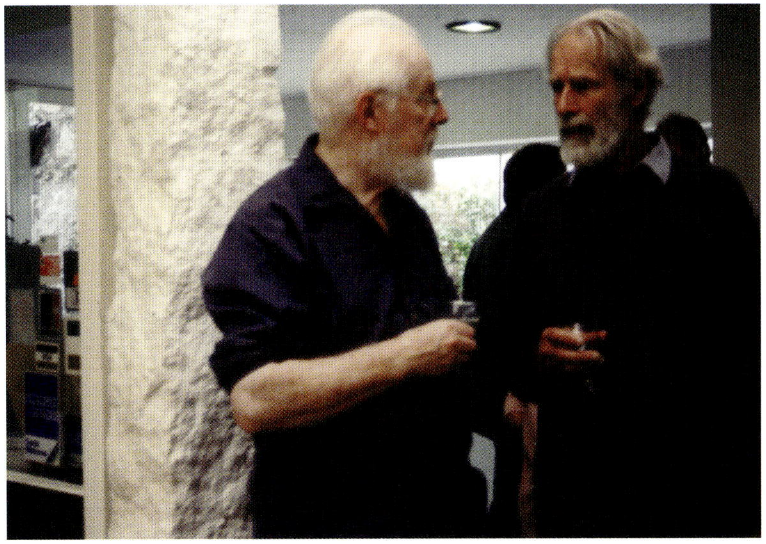
2

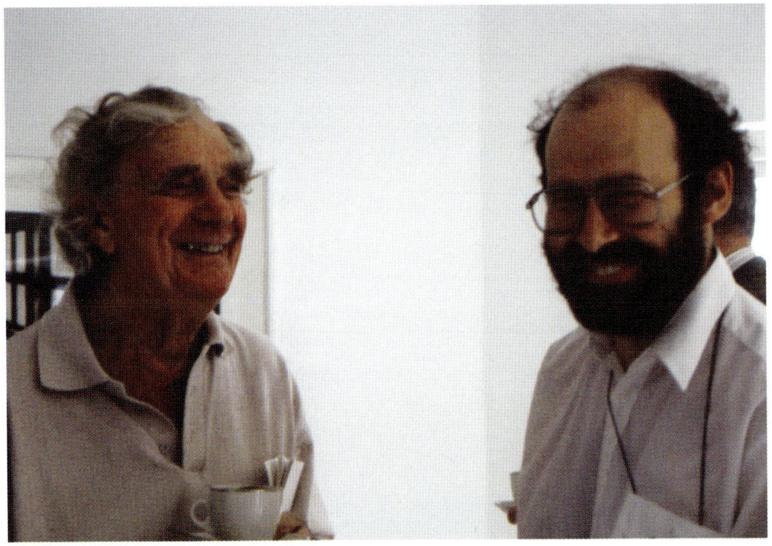
3

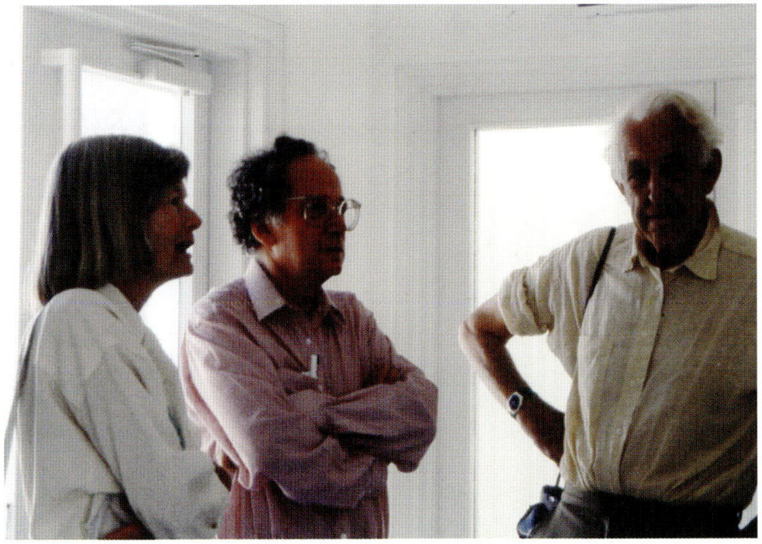
4

1. Matthew Rowe, Tate staff and Artist Margo Maeckelberghe. 2. Artists Paul Mount and Alexander Mackenzie, sculptor;
3. Cyril Gilbert, Wills Lane Gallery and Michael Tooby first curator Tate St Ives. 4. Janet Slack, David Shalev architect and Dr Roger Slack

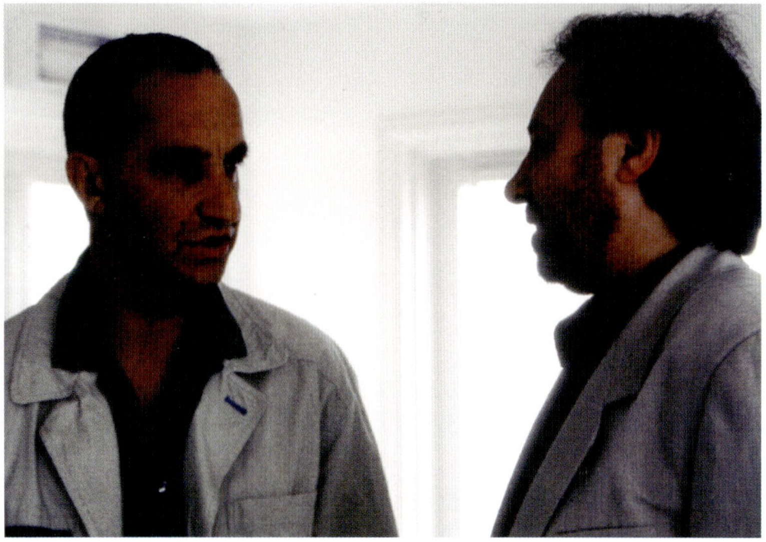
1

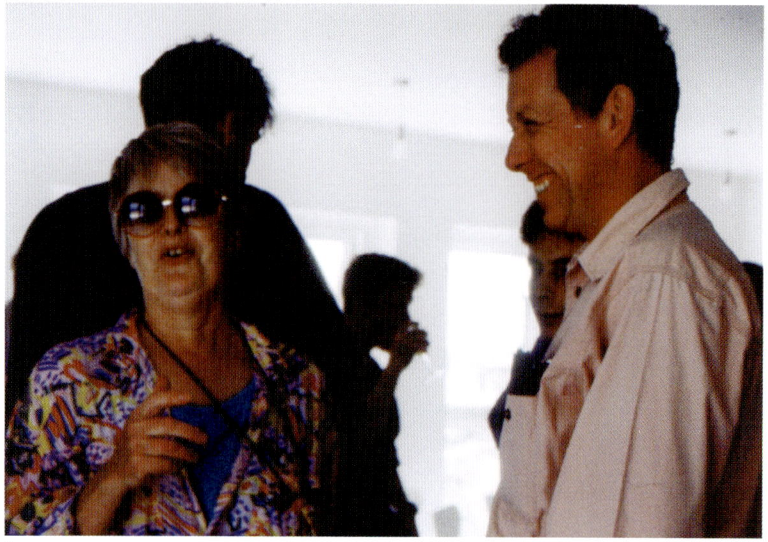
2

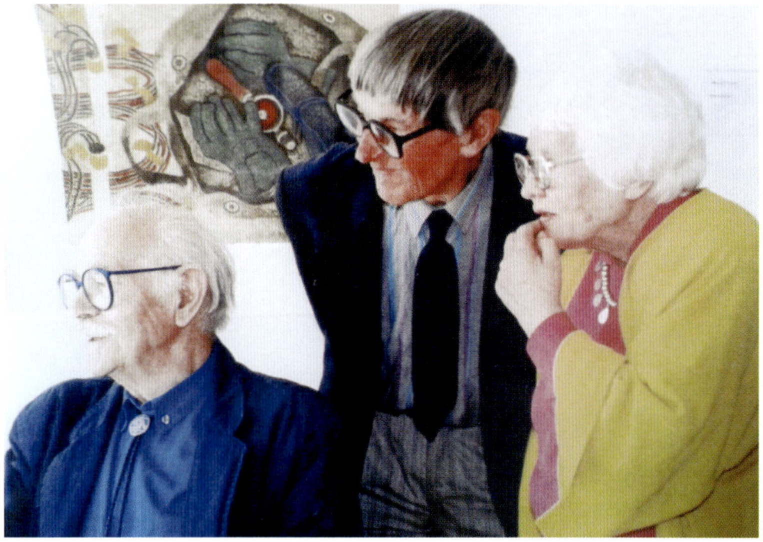
3

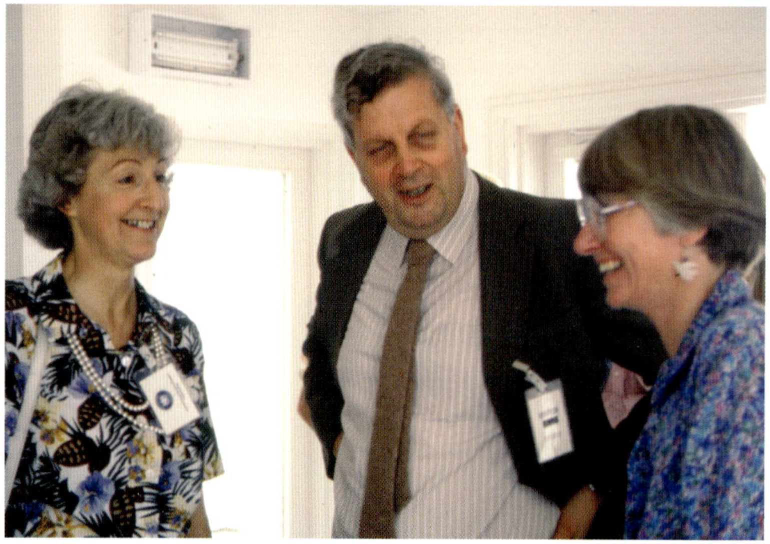
4

1. Artists Ralph Freeman and John Charles Clark. 2. Artists Sheila Oliner and Steve Dove. 3. Artists Sir Terry Frost, John Wells and Wilhelmina Barns Graham. 4. Lady Carol Holland, Sir Geoffrey Holland and Janet Axten.

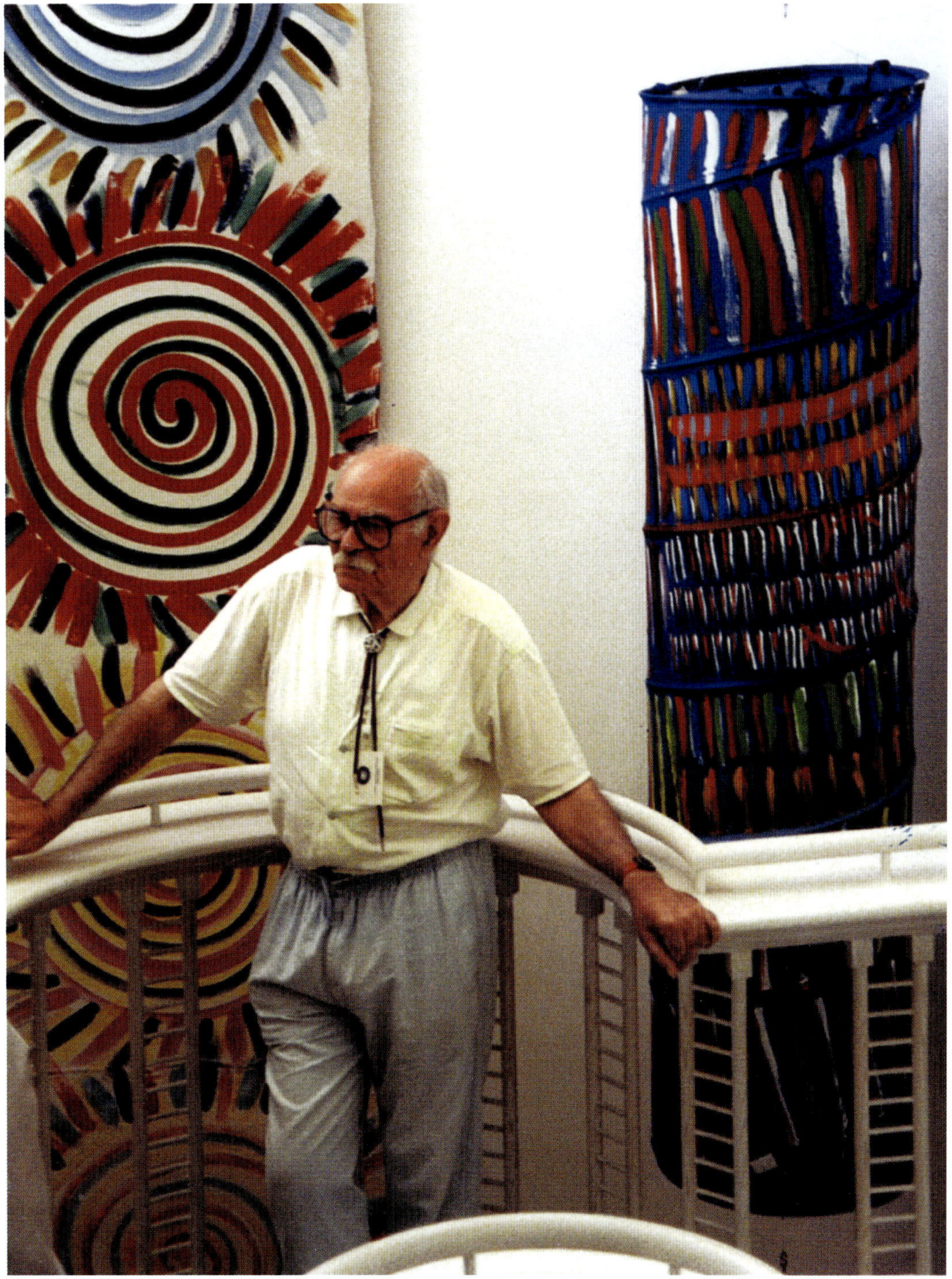

Sir Terry Frost with paintings made for the Tate stairwell painted on Newlyn sailcloth

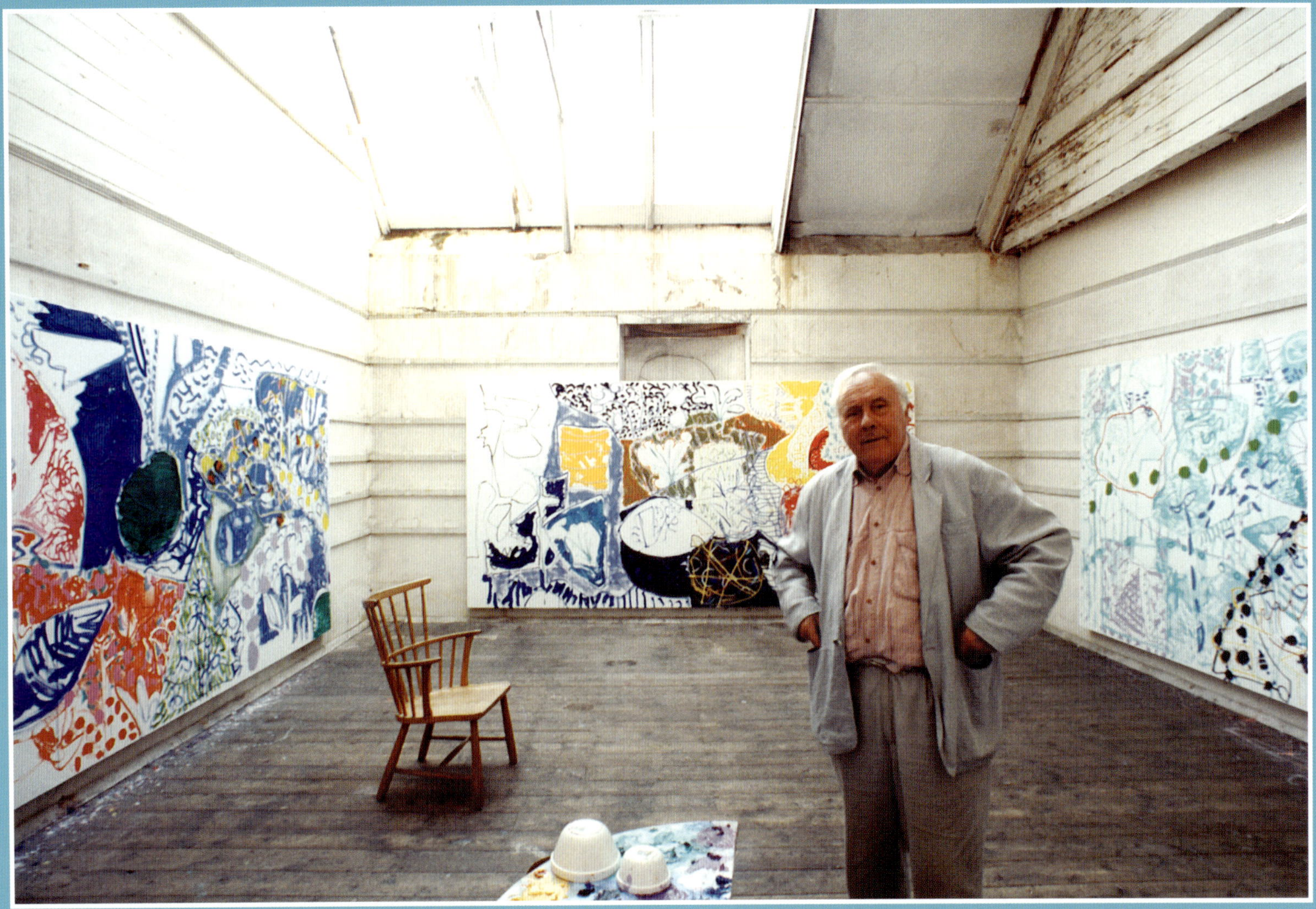

Patrick Heron in Porthmeor Studio 5.

PATRICK HERON
1920-1999

Colour is the subject and the means, the form and the content [3]

PATRICK HERON WAS a keen advocate of art schools and studios. He fought battles. He was an active campaigner to prevent the closure of art schools and the diminution of art education. He was a firm believer in the artists and artistic movement in St Ives. He appreciated his large Porthmeor studio with no view to the sea but with a huge, high skylight. Here he was able to enjoy his spacious surroundings and produce much larger paintings. When Ben Nicholson had moved into the studio in 1949 he said he was able to breathe deeply again, work on a large scale, walk about and paint at arm's length. Patrick acquired the studio after Ben in 1958 and treasured it until his death in 1999.

Childhood in St Ives

Patrick spent much of his childhood in St Ives. His parents' house, Ocean Breezes, backed on to Bowling Green and the home of the artist, John Park, who gave him a set of French oil pastels because he was interested in art. Patrick was a pupil at a private Dame School in St Ives with the Leach, Dow and Lanyon children. Also Mark Arnold Forster from Eagles Nest & Ellen Griggs from Tremedda farm. Patrick's father Tom was a partner and director in the unique textile company of Crysede, with the designer Alec Walker. Crysede produced silks hand printed from wood blocks and fashionable garments in silk, linen and crepe-de-chine from factories based in Newlyn. The St Ives branch was established in 1926. Tom Heron then moved to Welwyn Garden City and created his own textile business, Cresta, in 1929 and as a school boy of 14 Patrick made his first designs for his father's company.

For a brief time, about eighteen months, Heron studied at the Slade School of Art. 'I just went for two days a week, and then I walked out.' His fellow students were Bryan Wynter and Adrian Ryan; both came to live in Cornwall. Wynter lived in an isolated cottage, The Carn, on the lonely moors above Zennor. The footpath leading to the house was across the road from Eagles Nest. There was no access by car. Adrian Ryan lived for some time in Padstow and Mousehole.

Patrick Heron's 'Harbour Window with Two Figures', St Ives 1950

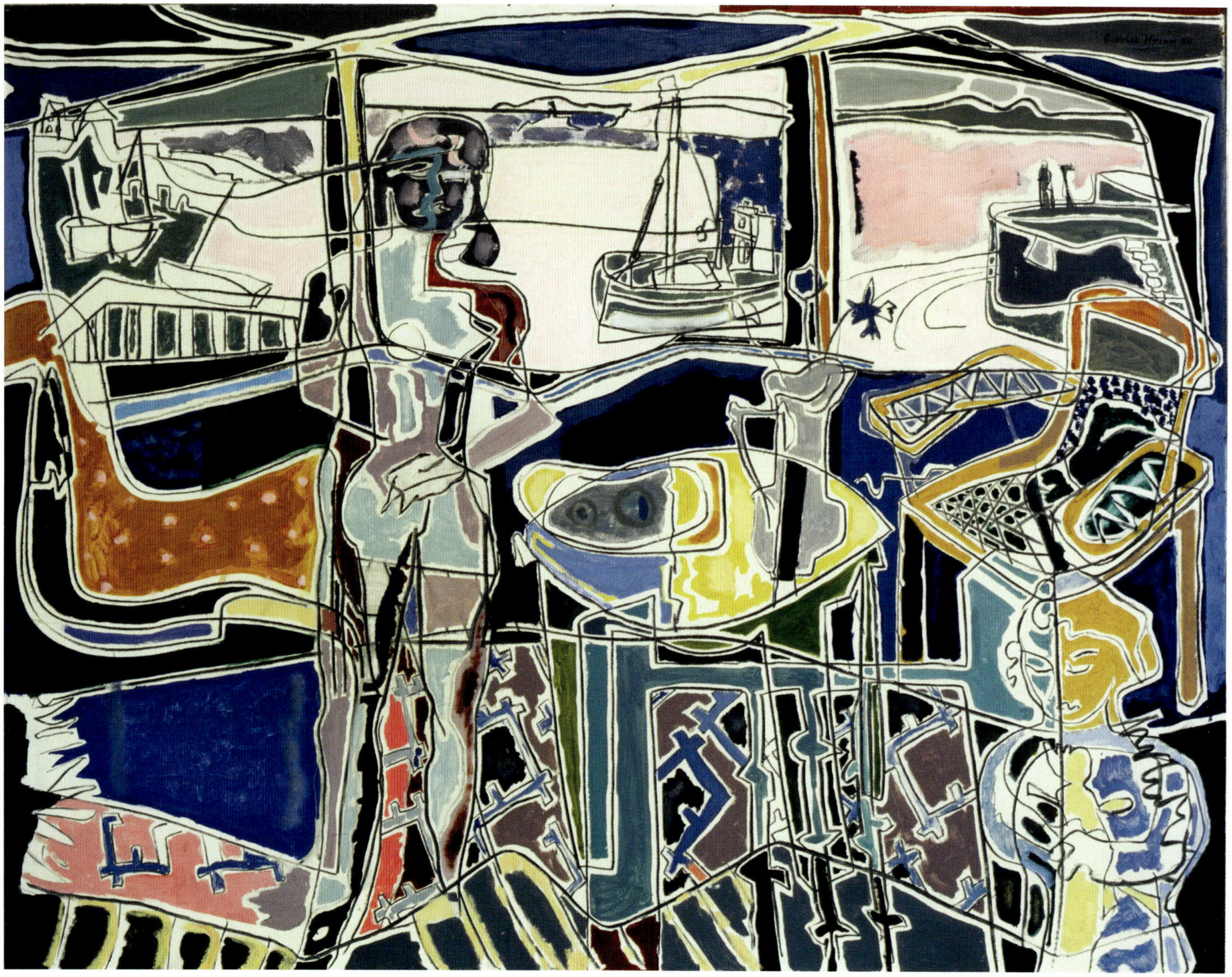

The Balcony Studio and the Redfern Gallery

In 1947 Patrick Heron achieved his first London exhibition at the Redfern Gallery, an association between artist and gallery which extended over the next few years. He rented a cottage at 3 St Andrew's Street where the family lived during the summer months. The living room had a balcony which overlooked the harbour and the two piers. From the windows he painted a series of pictures of objects and members of the family in the room and the scene without, of boats and the harbour, split up by the intersections of the window frames and the balcony balustrade. His sudden consciousness of the interior of the room intruding upon his contemplation of the bay would be registered upon the canvas. This series of paintings for his Redfern Gallery shows included still lifes, landscapes and interiors. They were figurative and much influenced by Braque.

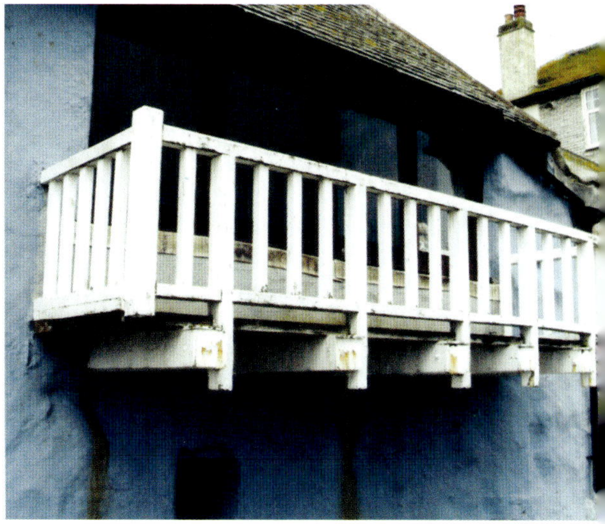

Balcony Studio,
3 St Andrew's Street, St Ives

Two years later, on a tour of Europe, Heron visited Braque in his studio and noted the objects as food for his paints and canvas. His pots, plants, artist materials were waiting their transformation into pictorial compositions of harmony. Picasso's studio ephemera too were elements to be used to express sensory experience – a mixture of the material and the thoughtful. Matisse had a profound influence on Heron through the early years of figuration to the later more abstract forms.

In 1947 George Downing opened his bookshop at 28 Fore Street, St Ives. He allowed space for the controversial artists to show their work; they included Heron, Lanyon, Hepworth, Mitchell, Nicholson, Wynter, Wilhelmina Barns Graham, David Leach and others. Posters were designed and printed by Guido Morris, who also exhibited.

In 1950 Heron reviewed a show at the new Penwith Society and claimed that the exhibition had been enhanced by the paintings of Ben Nicholson, the sculpture of Barbara Hepworth and the pottery of Bernard Leach and then prophetically stated, 'One might claim that this society numbers among its members the most distinguished painter, sculptor and potter working in England today.'

The Leach Pottery

For over a year during the war Patrick was detailed to work at the Leach Pottery. He was a Conscientious Objector. During this period Patrick was joined by Delia who also worked at the pottery.

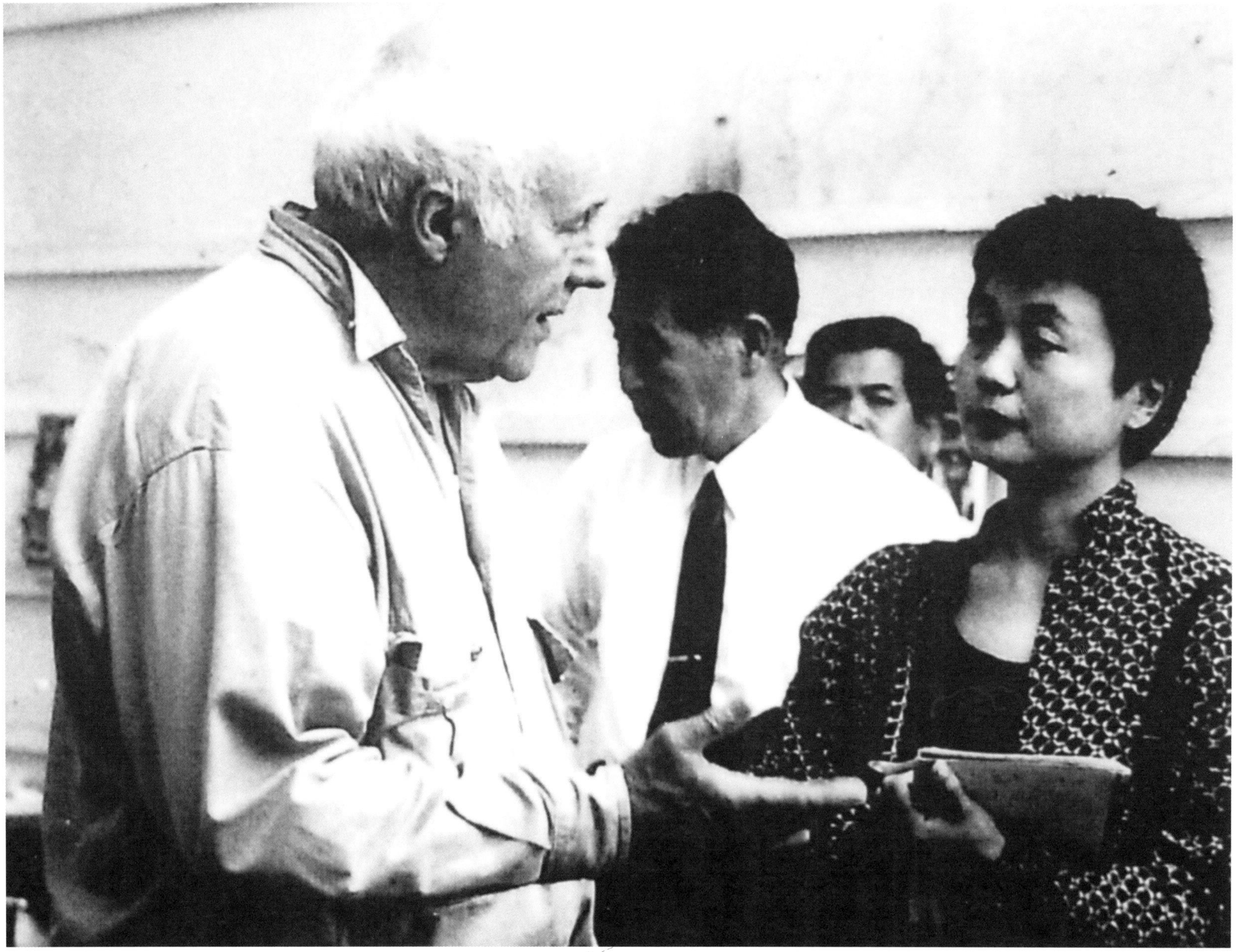

Patrick Heron welcomes Imi Arimoto and the Japanese delegation to his Porthmeor studio on their visit to the Bernard Leach Pottery in 1995

Leach had established his pottery in 1920 when he returned from Japan with his potter friend Shoji Hamada. Patrick worked happily with Bernard, making some of the standard ware, talking philosophy and art and establishing friendships. During this period Patrick had met with Ben Nicholson and Barbara Hepworth, Naum Gabo and Adrian Stokes and Margaret Mellis at Little Parc Owles, the home of Stokes and Mellis.

Eagles Nest

In 1955 Patrick and his wife Delia bought Eagles Nest, the house he had visited as a child, and had coveted since. Virginia and Leonard Woolf had stayed there many times when it was owned by their friends Will Arnold Forster and his wife Katherine Cox. In 1957 Sandra Blow stayed with the Herons before renting a cottage at Tregerthen in the lane below.

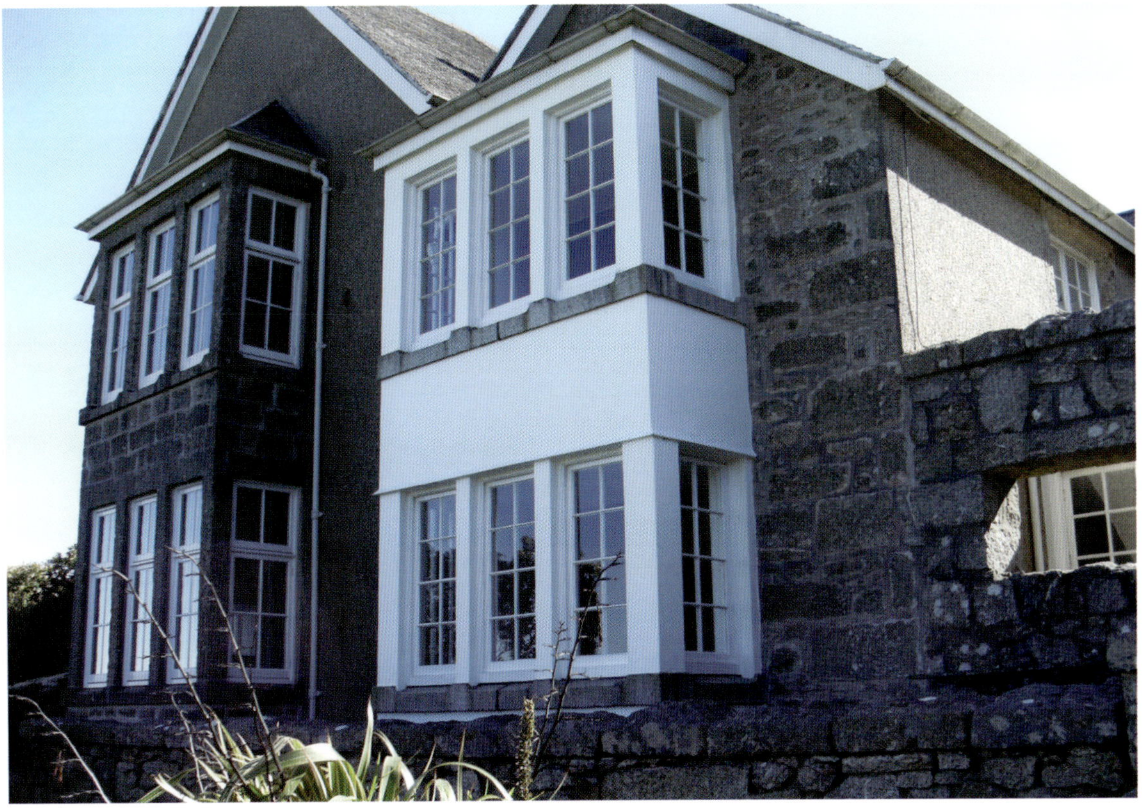

Eagles Nest

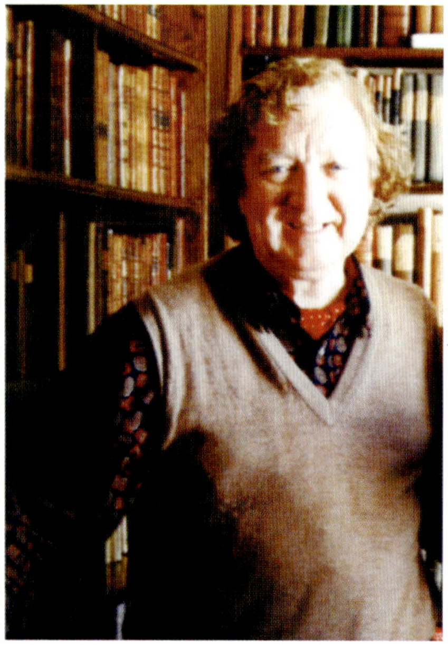

Eric Quayle at Carn Cobba

The house sits astride a rocky hillside, taking the full force of winds blowing in from the Atlantic. It overlooks small farms and moorland with Bronze Age stone walls and fields, and a spectacular view of the sea 600 feet below. In the hamlet of farm and cottages beneath the hill is Tregerthen, once the home of D H Lawrence, his German wife Frieda and writer friends Katherine Mansfield and John Middleton Murry, who lived next door. The painters Wilhelmina Barns Graham with her husband David Lewis; Karl Weschke and Trevor Bell lived there decades later.

The village of Zennor, a mile away, is famous for its attraction to writers and painters many of whom stayed at the local Tinners Arms or with Mrs Griggs in her comfortable cottage next door. Little has changed or been built in the village. It is much the same as when Virginia Woolf saw it as a child. Eric Quayle, friend of Patrick, writer and bibliophile, housed his 10,000 books in his house, Carn Cobba, leading down to Zennor Cove. Eric had his last conversation with his friend on the telephone the evening before Patrick died.

At Eagles Nest Patrick and his wife Delia further developed the gardens created by Will Arnold Forster in 1920 and about which Forster wrote his book *Shrubs for the Milder Counties*:

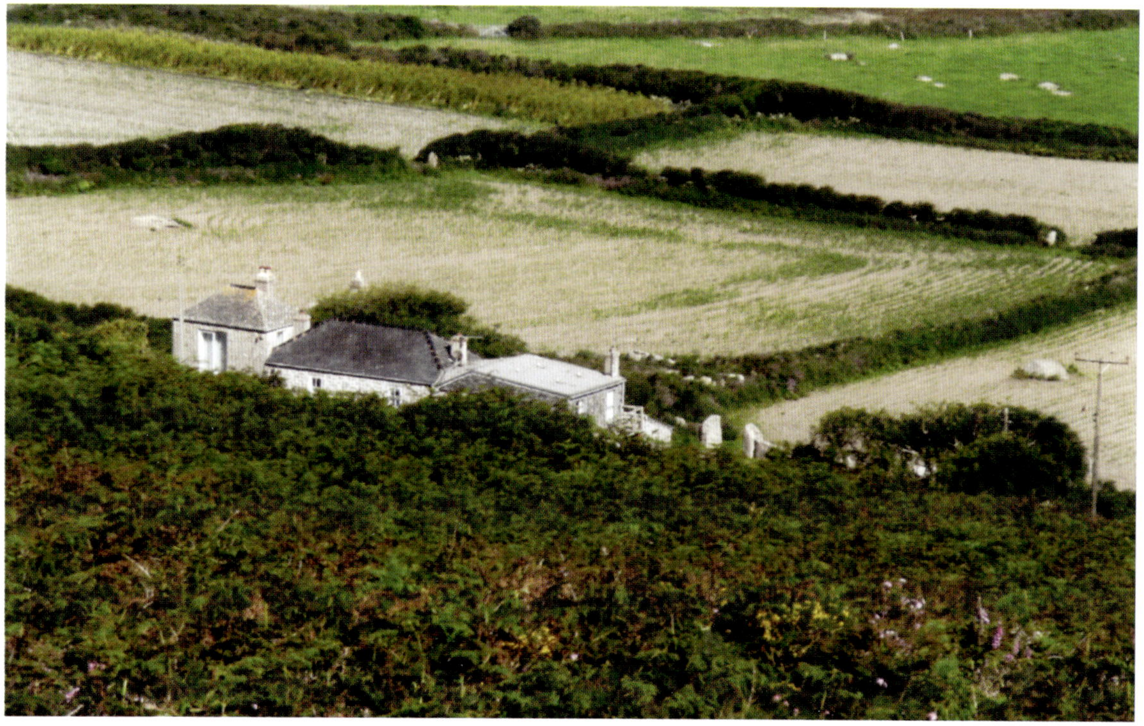

Looking from the garden of Eagles Nest to Tregerthen where D H Lawrence lived in 1916–17 and Katherine Mansfield in the Tower House next door on the left

As the garden was on top of a hill topped by a rocky outcrop, there were large slabs of granite and big boulders everywhere. The real forte of this garden were the camellias, rhododendrons and azaleas … Pink, purple and white heaths of all sizes… grew round the rocks. Brilliant flame trees, Embothrium, flowered in the cave garden below a rocky precipice, to which one descended by a long flight of stone steps or climbed precariously down by a wooden ladder.[4]

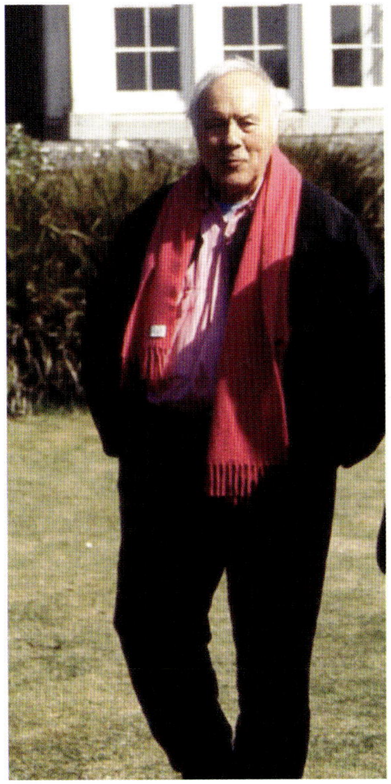

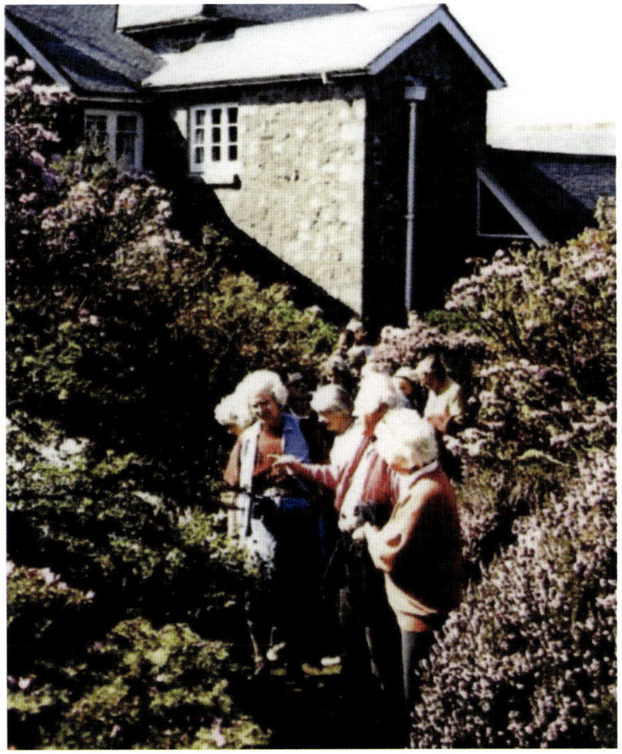

Far left: Patrick Heron

Left: Patrick Heron showing visitors around the garden

Below: A tour of Eagles Nest gardens

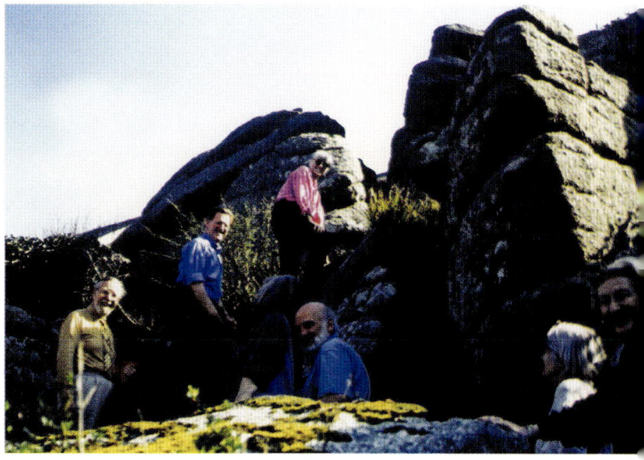

The Garden Influence

Patrick Heron's garden had a direct effect upon the series of paintings he was engaged with, but it wasn't until he saw his house and land from the air, that he realized that these paintings with their stripes and bright daubs of colour were his garden paintings. He realised that those colours, shapes and forms of plants and nature had moved him and etched themselves into his subconscious.

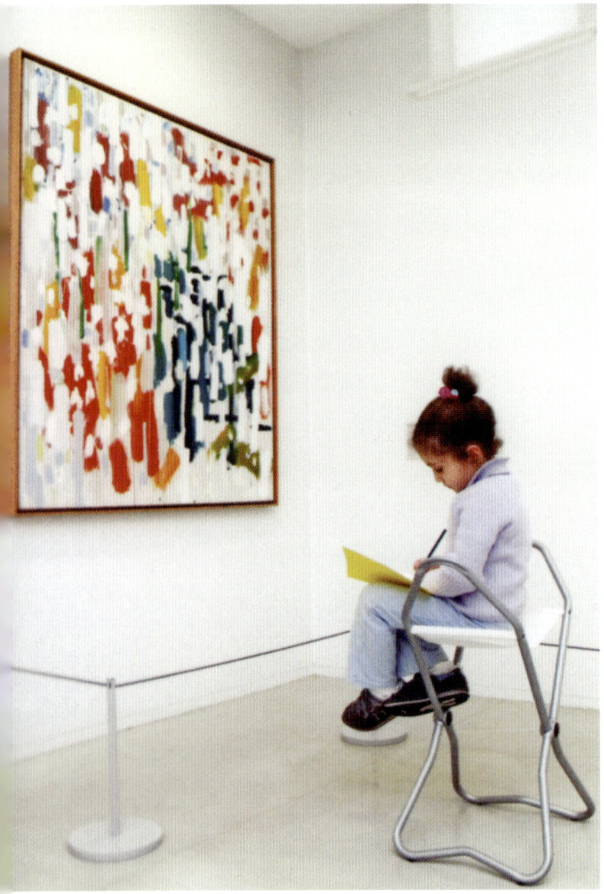

Alan Bowness wrote 'On Patrick Heron's Striped Paintings' in the catalogue for Heron's 1968 exhibition at the Museum of Modern Art in Oxford, 'One should remember that these striped paintings were the first ever seen anywhere.' Eagles Nest had released the garden paintings and laid a new foundation for Patrick's painting life with its plethora of colour, the boulder strewn landscape, the moors and the blustering wind and sea. It was as though the environment flowed through his paintings.

No. 5 Porthmeor studios, vacated after Ben Nicholson moved to live in Switzerland in 1958, was a completely different environment, with no view to the sea but with a large high skylight. It gave Patrick the opportunity to make larger paintings and stimulated a change to soft rounded abstract shapes and rectangles, with colour still the dominating force. These paintings were shown in his first exhibition in New York in 1960.

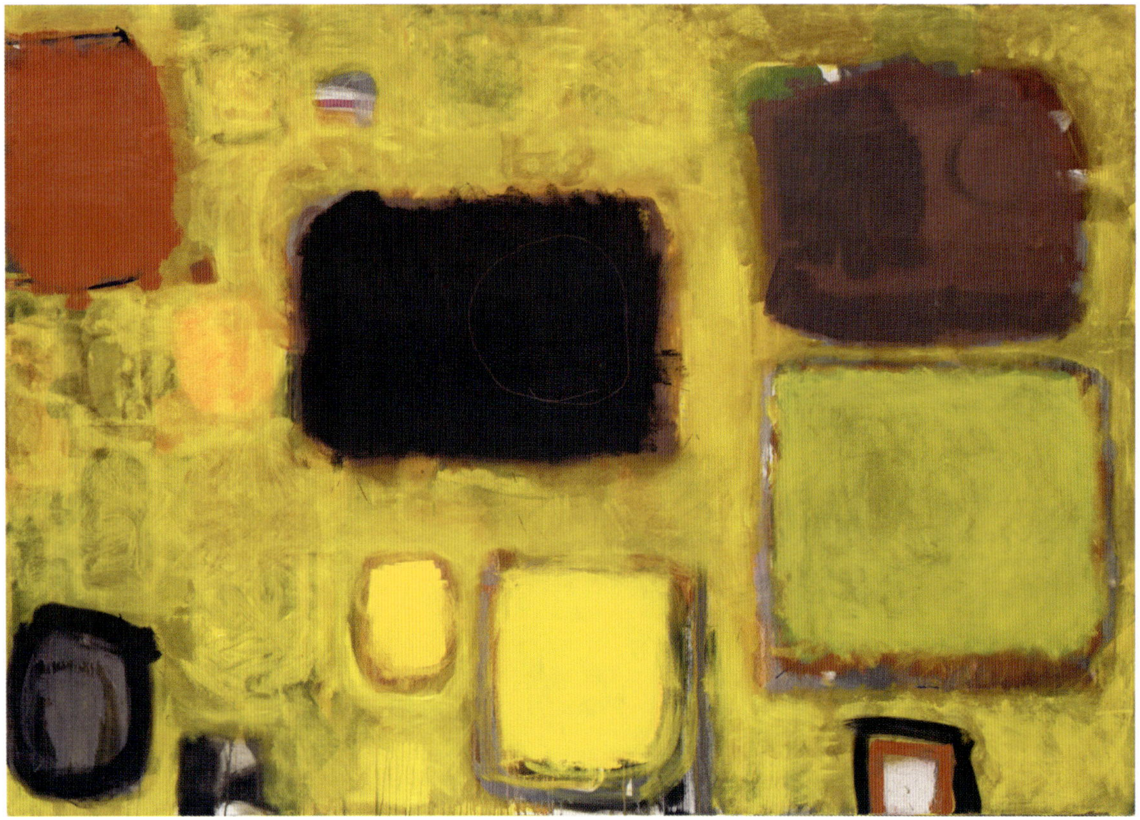

Above: Tate St Ives Super Sunday 2006 with a girl copying Patrick Heron's 'Azalia Garden', May 1956

Right: Yellow Painting
October 1958 May/June 1959

In 1958 both Heron and Hepworth took part in films made by the BBC *Tonight* programme and *Monitor* in an attempt to answer the question, 'Why do artists come to St Ives?' Whether they went away satisfied with the answers given by the many artists interviewed for the programmes is debatable, but those working here know how powerful is the pull of Cornwall.

In the second John Moore's exhibition at the Walker Art Gallery, Liverpool, 1959, Heron won the Grand Prize for his abstract work 'Black Painting, Red, Brown and Olive'. Peter Lanyon gained Second Prize for his painting 'Offshore'.

The Threat to the Moors

In 1963 the military planned to use the moorland, between St Ives and Zennor, in an area of outstanding historic and natural beauty, for troop-landing exercises by helicopter. Heron said, 'When you've got a landscape like this, you can't possibly just sit by and let it go.' He was always on guard to make sure the wild moors and countryside were protected from the intrusion of developers and entrepreneurs whose projects would destroy this unique environment. The troop landings were successfully stopped; so too was the building of a holiday village in an area of open downs near the farming hamlet of Towednack. This action was supported by Barbara Hepworth, Ben Nicholson (now living in Hampstead), Friends of the Earth, John Betjeman, and many significant others, and through their efforts planning permission was revoked.

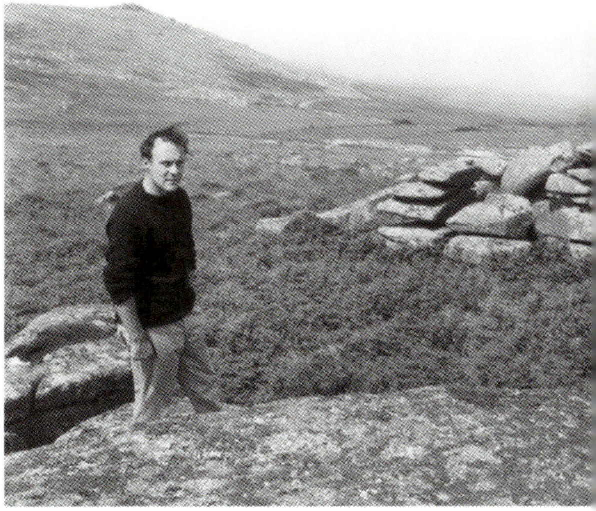

Patrick Heron on the moors overlooking Eagles Nest 1963

Heron's Critical Writings

Much of Heron's creative output included writing critical articles on painting and painters. He also lectured on these subjects from time to time. Now that Heron was a permanent resident in Cornwall his collection of essays, reviews and articles on art and artists were published in book form in 1955 under the title *The Changing Forms of Art*. He wrote regularly for *The New English Weekly, The New Statesman and Nation, The Guardian, Studio International* and *Arts New York*. In 1967 he lectured and travelled extensively in Australia, but always returned to his more physical activity of painting, expressing his distinctive exuberance and sensitivity for painting colour on canvas. On a return trip in 1989 Heron became Artist in Residence at a gallery in New South Wales, where he produced both large paintings and smaller gouaches relating to the Botanical Gardens in Sydney, reminding him of his own fabulous gardens in Cornwall.

A Tribute to Alfred Wallis

In 1974 Patrick Heron unveiled a plaque on the wall of a cottage in Back Road West to the memory of the artist Alfred Wallis. This naïve painter was much admired by the artists in St Ives, especially Ben Nicholson and Christopher Wood who came across the old man on their first visit to St Ives in 1928. On seeing the paintings in the cottage they recognised the pure uneducated, but instinctive, work of a man who knew the life of boats and the sea, who understood his subject matter but did not understand the power of his images and the influence he exerted on these two artists. They were looking to simplify their approach to their own paintings and, in this respect, their education stood in the way. Patrick Heron declared his belief in Wallis's originality by unveiling the plaque.

Patrick Heron unveiling the plaque to Alfred Wallis in 1974

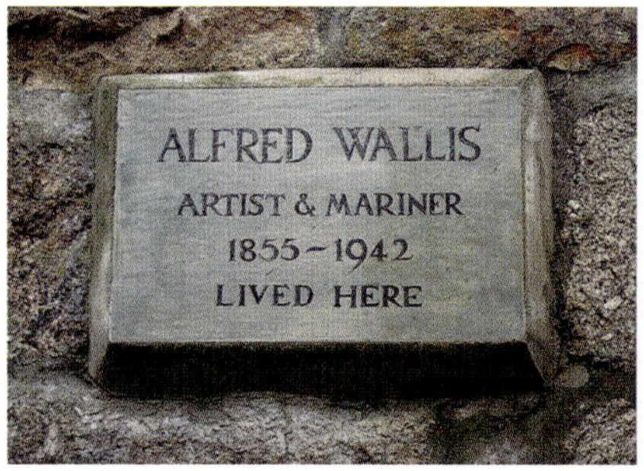

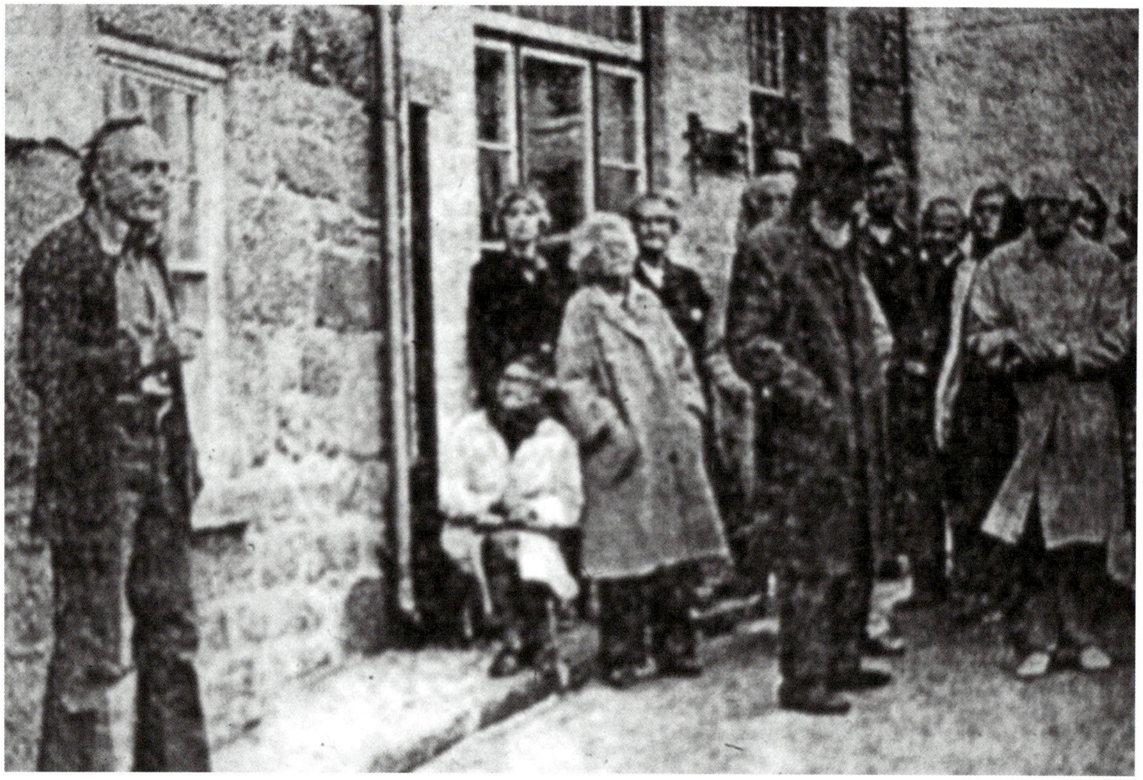

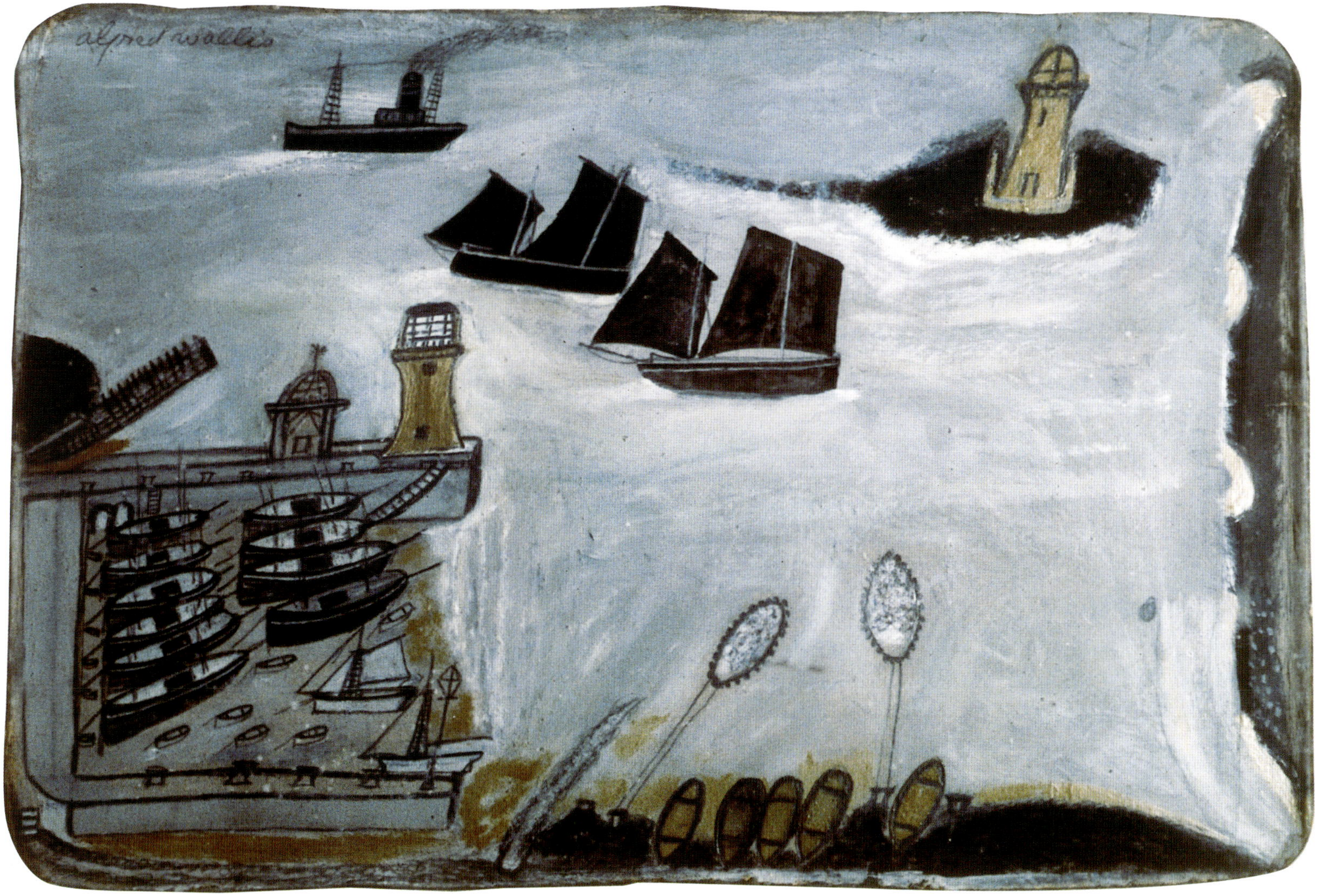

'St Ives Harbour and Godrevy Lighthouse.' Alfred Wallis

Honours

In the New Year's Honours List of 1977, under a Labour Government Patrick was created a CBE. Unfortunately, and tragically, in 1979 his wife Delia died suddenly and this disabled his ability to paint for some considerable time. But in spite of suffering this great loss, tributes continued to accrue. In 1982 he was granted Honorary D. Litt of the University of Exeter and in 1986 the same tribute was conferred on him by the University of Kent. The following year he was made Hon. Doctorate, of the Royal College of Art, London. In 1989 he received an Hon. Ph.D. CNAA from Winchester School of Art. In 1993 he was Honorary Fellow of Bretton Hall College, University of Leeds. He gladly accepted honorary doctorates and tributes from many universities and colleges for his support of art schools and art education.

Newlyn Gallery, Penzance

In 1985, coinciding with a major exhibition at the Barbican centre, Heron displayed 49 of his paintings at the Newlyn Gallery, Penzance. Named 'From Eagles Nest Paintings and Drawings 1925-1985.' the exhibition included drawings from his childhood and pre-war early works. Heron said his earlier drawings overlapped with the work he was doing now. *'One can almost fit them one over another… works which span a number of years; but there are these moments in life when you break the mould.'* [5] Even in this diverse and wide-ranging exhibition the main theme of the show was his devotion to colour.

The opening evening at the Newlyn Gallery was a very personal and local occasion when Patrick Heron talked to those people who knew him, and his paintings, and who wanted to listen to a man they admired for himself and his work. People sat and stood in every available space in the gallery and it remains a memorable event in many lives.

A Visit to Patrick

I was at the Newlyn Gallery talk making copious notes in shorthand. Some years later I visited Patrick to ask his permission to produce some of these notes and other mentions of him in my book *St Ives 1883-1993: Portrait of an Art Colony.* He asked me to read aloud any references to him. He approved them all.

I hastened to leave, having overstayed the twenty minutes he had allocated for my visit. 'Ring Terry' [my husband] Patrick said, 'and tell him you're having coffee.' A couple of hours later, he said, 'Ring Terry and tell him you're having lunch.' I believe we had tomato soup. After a tour of the house; the studio and a look at some of his paintings; a walk around the gardens, Patrick said, 'Ring Terry and tell him you're having tea.' I had arrived early morning and Patrick drove me home about seven in the evening. It was a wonderful day.

Colour in Space

Throughout the 1990s Patrick Heron was commissioned to work on several projects in public places. Three of those were in London. He had already designed a stained glass window for the new Tate St Ives in 1993 for the entrance foyer. It is the largest single coloured glass window in the world, measuring 4 metres by 4.5 metres, with no connecting lead strips to hold pieces together. This would have spoilt the overall unique design, which is about large areas of colour meeting each other. The cut coloured glass is laminated on to clear plate glass for strength. His original design for the window was a small gouache on paper and was developed and realised by his son-in-law, architect Julian Feary working with the German specialist Derisc Glass Studios. It amused Patrick to remember how this small sketch developed into such an enormous structure.

In 1994 Camden Arts Centre in London hosted an exhibition for Heron's large-scale canvases which he had been working on at the beginning of the year for a September opening. They were conceived with the Camden Arts Centre in mind and at six foot six inches high and eleven to seventeen foot long, they made an impressive appearance in a gallery suitable for such a display of colour.

Patrick Heron was a Trustee of the Tate Gallery in London for a number of years, and in 1998, a year before he died, a major retrospective show was organised at Tate Britain. Many people from the town and members and friends from Tate St Ives travelled to London to see the exhibition.

Lifting Patrick Heron's glass window over the rooftops and into the Tate

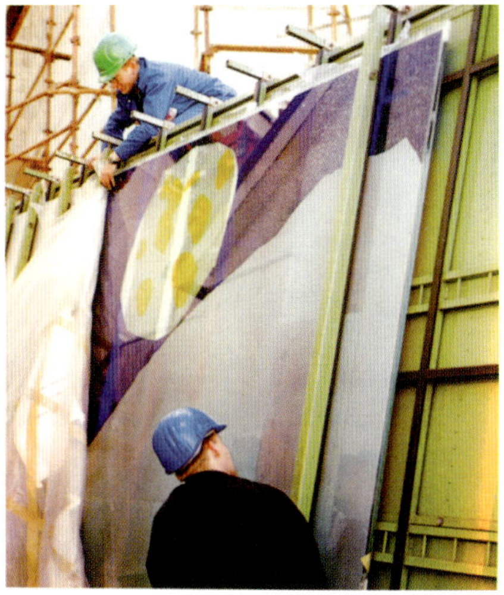

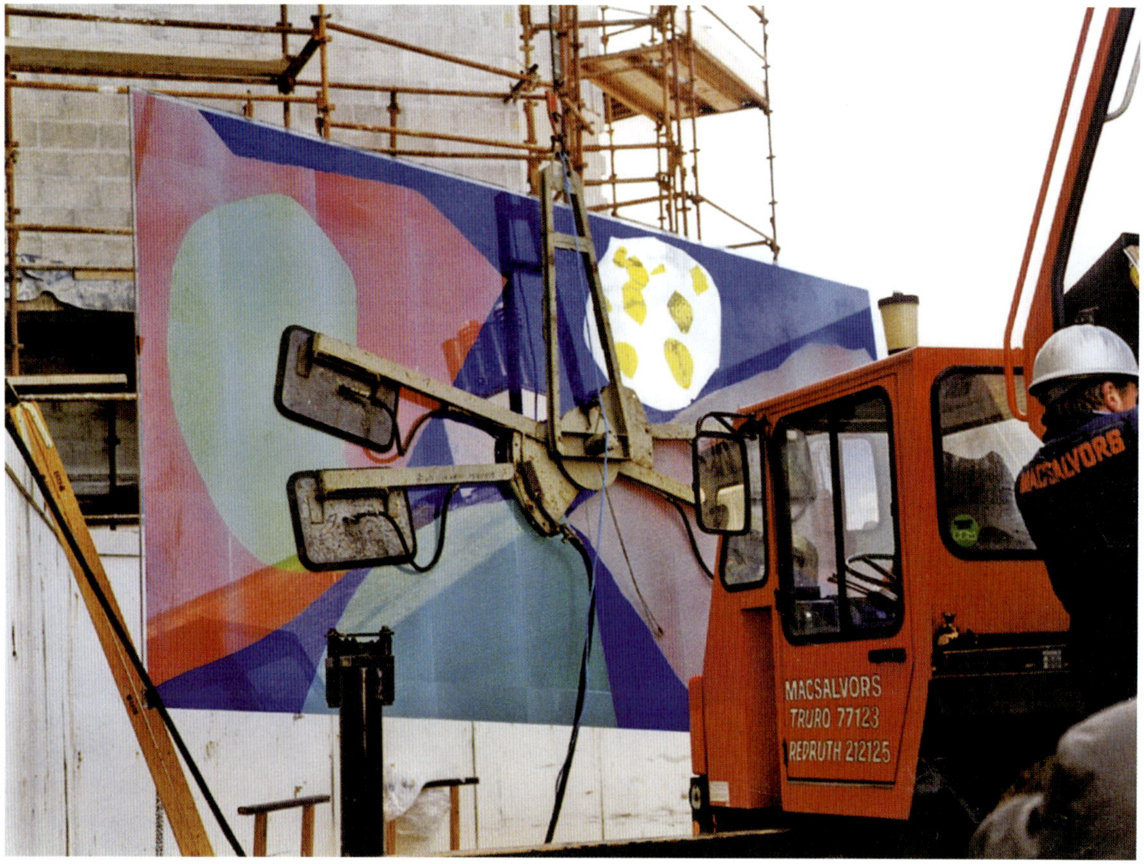

Patrick died in 1999 and is buried in Zennor churchyard with his wife Delia. After the funeral service at Zennor church it was a poignant reminder of Patrick to see his pink scarf in his room at Eagles Nest. Patrick Heron was a man true to himself and his ideals. He turned down a knighthood, which would have been conferred by a Conservative government. This would have been against his Socialist values. He also refused the title of Royal Academician as he did not wish to be part of the 'establishment.' Patrick Heron was a man true to his principles.

Occupiers of Porthmeor Studios – A Short List

STUDIO 1
Borlase Smart
Wilhelmina Barns Graham
Roy Conn
Phillip Medley

STUDIO 2
John Milne
Peter Blake (temporary)
John Emanuel

STUDIO 3
Commander George Fagin Bradshaw
Francis Bacon (temporary)
Breon O'Casey
Patrick Hughes
Roy Walker
Naomi Frears

STUDIO 4
Terry Frost
Tony & Jane O'Malley
Steve Dove
Felicity Mara

STUDIO 5
Julius Olsson
Borlase Smart
David Cox
Ben Nicholson
Patrick Heron
Rachael Kantaris

STUDIO 6
Louise McClary
Ralph Freeman
Richard Nott

STUDIO 7
Frances Hodgkins
Bob Crossley
Clare Wardman
and
Iain Robertson

STUDIO 8
Moffat Lindner
Lucy Walsh
Trevor Bell
Douglas Portway
Robert Floyd
Sax Impey

STUDIO 9
A J Shearer Armstrong
Robert Floyd
Karl Weschke
Sandra Blow
Faye Dobinson

STUDIO 10
John Park
Hyman Segal
Community Studio

STUDIO 11
Leonard Fuller
Marjorie Mostyn
Roy Ray
James Barber

STUDIO 12
William Redgrave
Bryan Pearce
School of Painting

STUDIO 13
School of Painting

STUDIO 14
School of Painting

STUDIO 15 new
Marion Taylor

STUDIO 16 new
Gareth Edwards

STUDIO 17 new
Andy Harper

STUDIO 18 new
Sam Bassett

STUDIO 19 new
Lucie Bray

The Studios

No. 5 Porthmeor Studios is probably the best known for housing the traditional painters, Borlase Smart and Julius Olsson, and for the modernists, Ben Nicholson and Patrick Heron. It is impossible to overstate the important role the Porthmeor studios played in the painting lives of the artists who occupied them. Here are some of the tributes recorded in my book *Studios – Artists in their Workplace* 1994.

Roy Conn – Studio 1. 1963 to 2012
'After over thirty years in the same studio it has of course now become my atmosphere with my paintings as well as books and personal effects collected over the years. It is a place for quiet relaxation as well as work.'

Bob Crossley – Studio 7. 1973 to 2010
'Gales from the West are a reminder of place when the windows rattle; they caved in once under a mountain of sand blown by winds and heaped up by high tides. My studio is a workshop where completed paintings fight for space amongst paints, framing and other materials.'

Steve Dove – Studio 4. 1991 to 2012
'I am fortunate in having a large studio and although principally a painter, it does allow other activities to take place, such as drawing, printmaking, framing, administration, without the need for clearances and movement of effects.'

John Emanuel – Studio 2. 1983 to present
'I think the studio comes alive during gales. There is always a feeling of apprehension. I never know what will happen next, either with the gales or with the work. The light is very special. It is at its best on late summer evenings.'

Ralph Freeman – Studio 6. 1995 to 2012
'My studio is my laboratory. It is the place where I "go to work" and which demands of me a certain daily discipline which I must respect regardless of feelings or moods. It is the place where a piece of work either succeeds or fails.'

Louise McClary – Studio 6. 1991 to 1995
'The sound of the sea as I work is somehow humbling. It reminds you of its power, but at the same time it washes and cleanses you inside. The beach, in a sense, is a "clean slate" to walk and take a painting break, then come back to the painting re-charged.'

Bryan Pearce – Studio 12. 1973 to 2007
'I have a little walk and go to my studio about 9 o'clock. I put on my apron and get my paints ready and do the outlining before I do the main painting. I choose the colour and put paint on my palette. I mix the colours and do the painting.'

Roy Ray – Studio 11. 1979 to 2010
'To be able to work, study, think, take risks and make mistakes in this well-lit, uncluttered space without interruption, is something I value highly. The time I spend alone in this studio enables me to maintain a balance between my painting and my more public activities in this busy art community.'

Roy Walker – Studio 3. 1982 to 2000
'Because my work stems from an internal process of distillation, the studio has become the centre of my creative gravity, and just to be there I am somehow working. The elements of my artistic journey surround me in the form of etchings, scribbles, drawings and paintings provide the dynamic in my continuing output.'

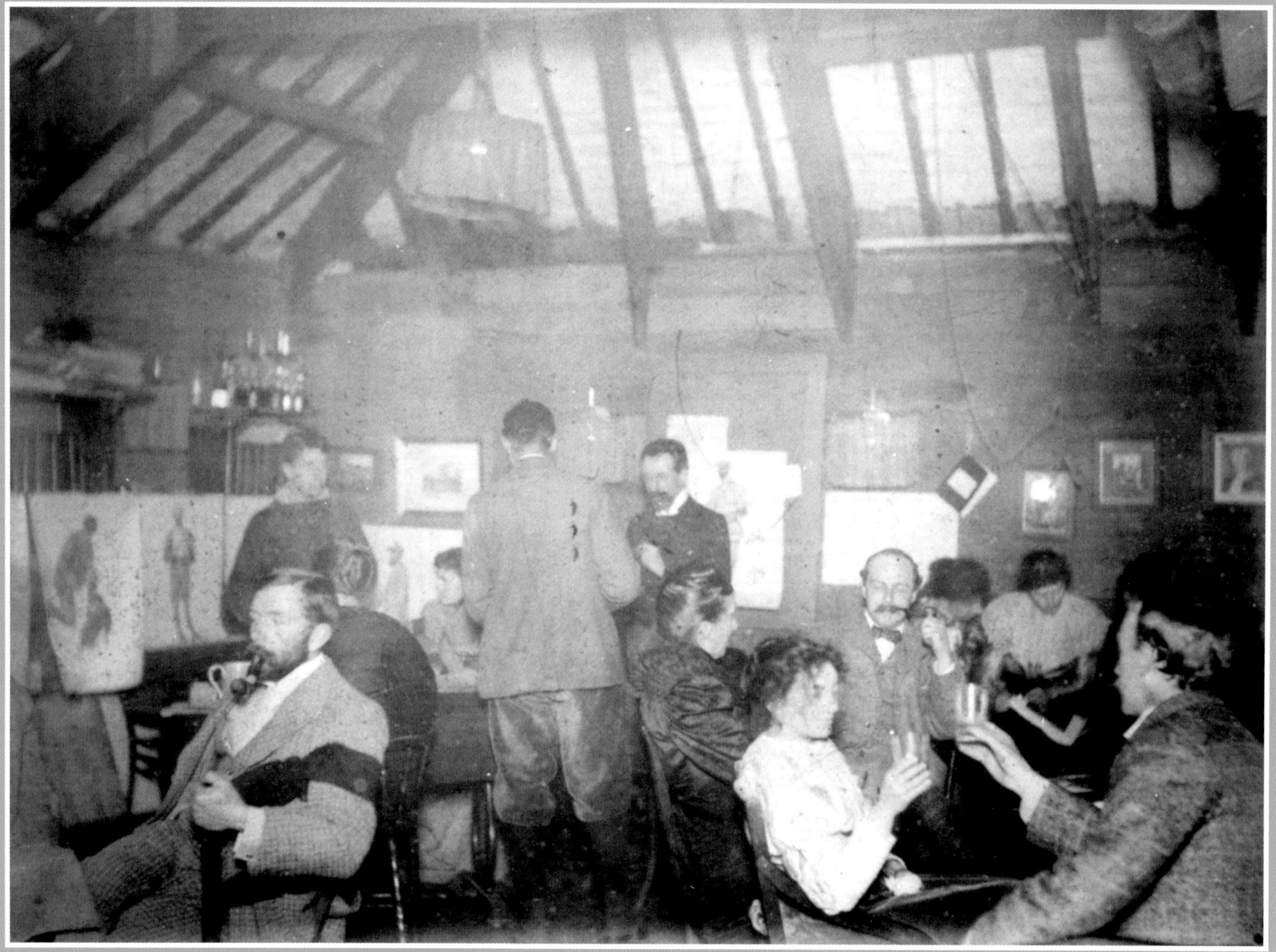

St Ives Arts Club 1895. Louis Grier, founder member seated left. Standing Alexander, John Bromley, Harewood Robinson. Seated centre Maria Robinson, Helen C Ludby, unknown man, Lily Kirkpatrick, Daisy and Sarah Whitehouse, Lowell Dyer

PORTHMEOR STUDIOS

The Middle Generation

THIS IS AN EVEN more formidable group of artists who made waves and who occupied the Porthmeor studios. They are well-known faces in the art world and named the 'middle generation.' Those predecessors, such as Patrick Heron, Ben Nicholson, Wilhelmina Barns Graham, Terry Frost, Bryan Pearce, and others of that era like Peter Lanyon who did not have a Porthmeor studio, but together their paintings and sculpture are the subject of discussion, criticism and interpretation. They are recorded in art catalogues and dictionaries of artists. Their works are sold in auction houses throughout the country and displayed on the walls of National Galleries. They have illustrated books written about them and are researched and studied in art colleges and universities.

The New Group

Following the 'regeneration' and the saving of the artists' studios, a new group of enthusiastic and fearless, mostly younger artists, are now occupying these spaces. These newcomers have pedigrees of their own. They have studied, developed, created and are producing their work in their individual styles. Each artist has a distinct voice and all are exhibiting and selling their paintings through art galleries to a growing public of admirers and buyers.

They are confident in their approach to their art and bold in their discussion of its meaning. They have tenacity and are secure in their sense of purpose but must throw off the shadow of previous ghosts, as one artist wrote, 'It is thrilling to walk in here each day and to know that painting has

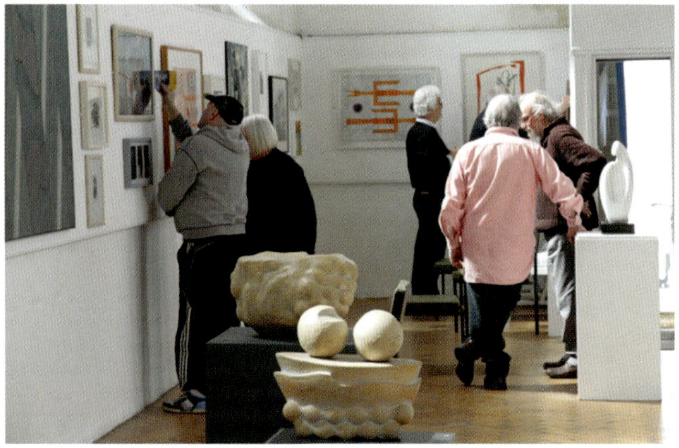

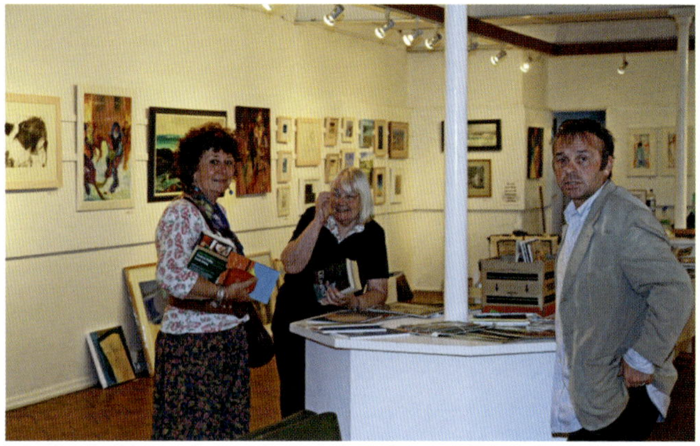

Top: St Ives Society of Artists Upper Gallery.
Hanging the Spring Opening with, sculptor Mark Stoddart, and artists Adrienne Peveral, Brian Busselle, Ray Denton and guest curator, Gary Long

Above: St Ives Society of Artists Crypt Gallery.
Hanging the Square Deal Show.
Artists Sue Dove, Adrienne Peveral and
Society Chairman John Watson

Portraits by Ken Symonds. Left. John Wells, Terry Frost, Denis Mitchell, Paul Feiler, Alexander MacKenzie, Wilhelmina Barns Graham, Tony O'Malley, Maurice Sumray, Jack Pender, Roy Conn, Roy Walker, Breon O'Casey

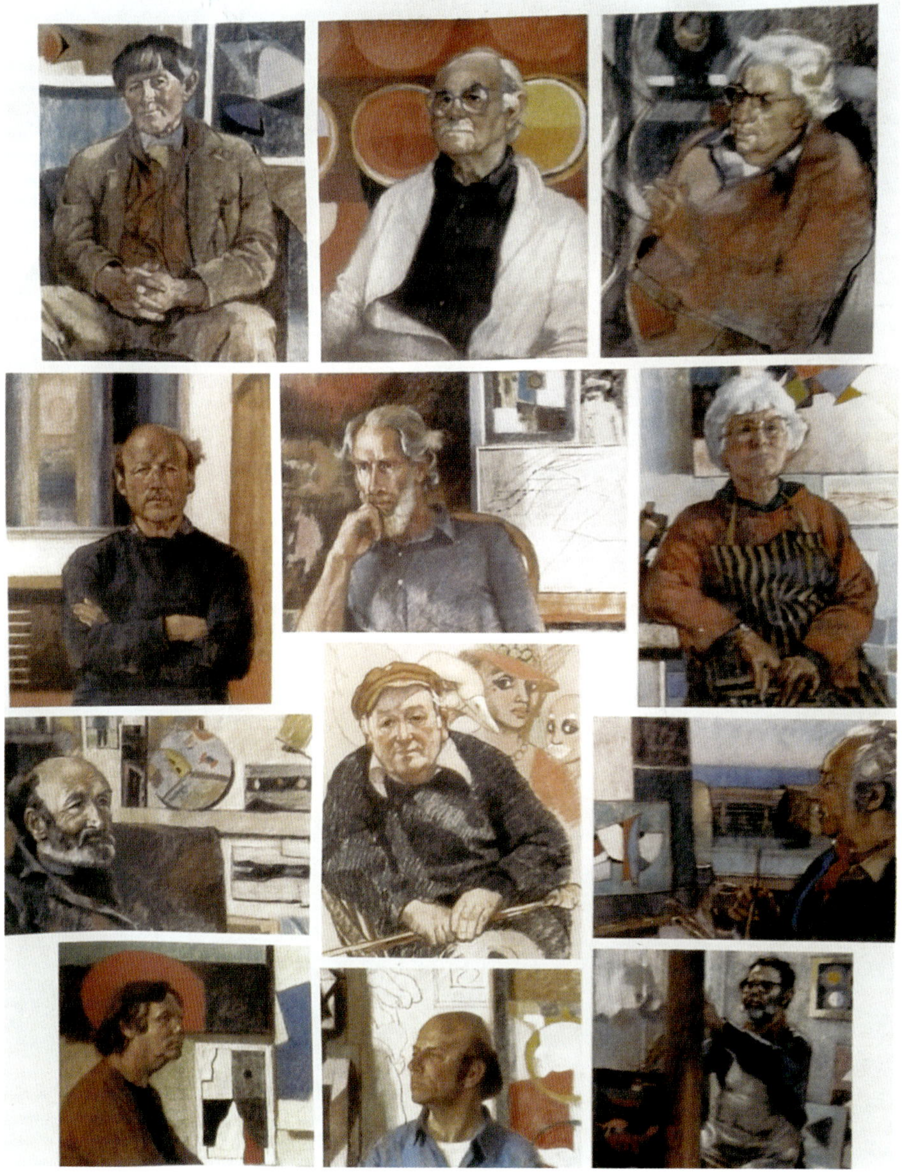

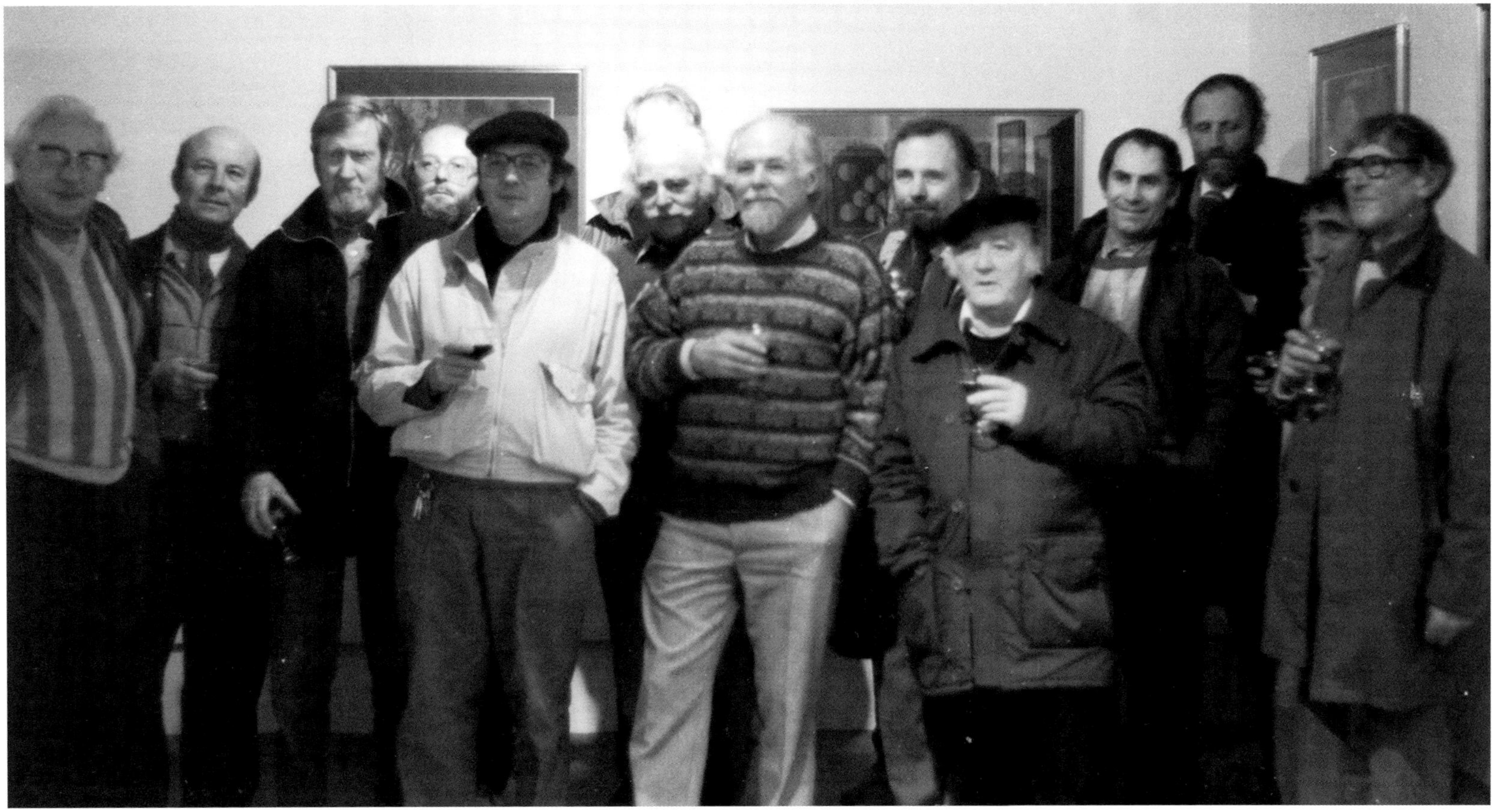

Members of the Penwith Society, 1980s
Denis Mitchell, Roy Walker, Bob Crossley, Paul Mount, Roy Conn, Jack Pender, Alexander MacKenzie, Ken Symonds, Roy Ray, Maurice Sumray, Mike Praed, Bob Bourne, Max Barrett, John Wells

been the purpose of this space for so many years – but one also has to sidestep and not be afraid of this in order to do something new.' It is a challenge to live as a practising artist but this is their time and place.

These are exciting times for the younger, and the older occupants, in the rebirth of the studios. These contenders are willing to accept the challenge to carry the St Ives Art Colony into the future. That is not their aim, but in merely occupying these studios, with the history of their former occupants, they are continuing the long line of art history. They are a diverse group of personalities with a Modernist approach to different ways of seeing, feeling, and interpreting their world. It would see their predecessors applaud their progress into the future. It will be interesting to see what the future holds.

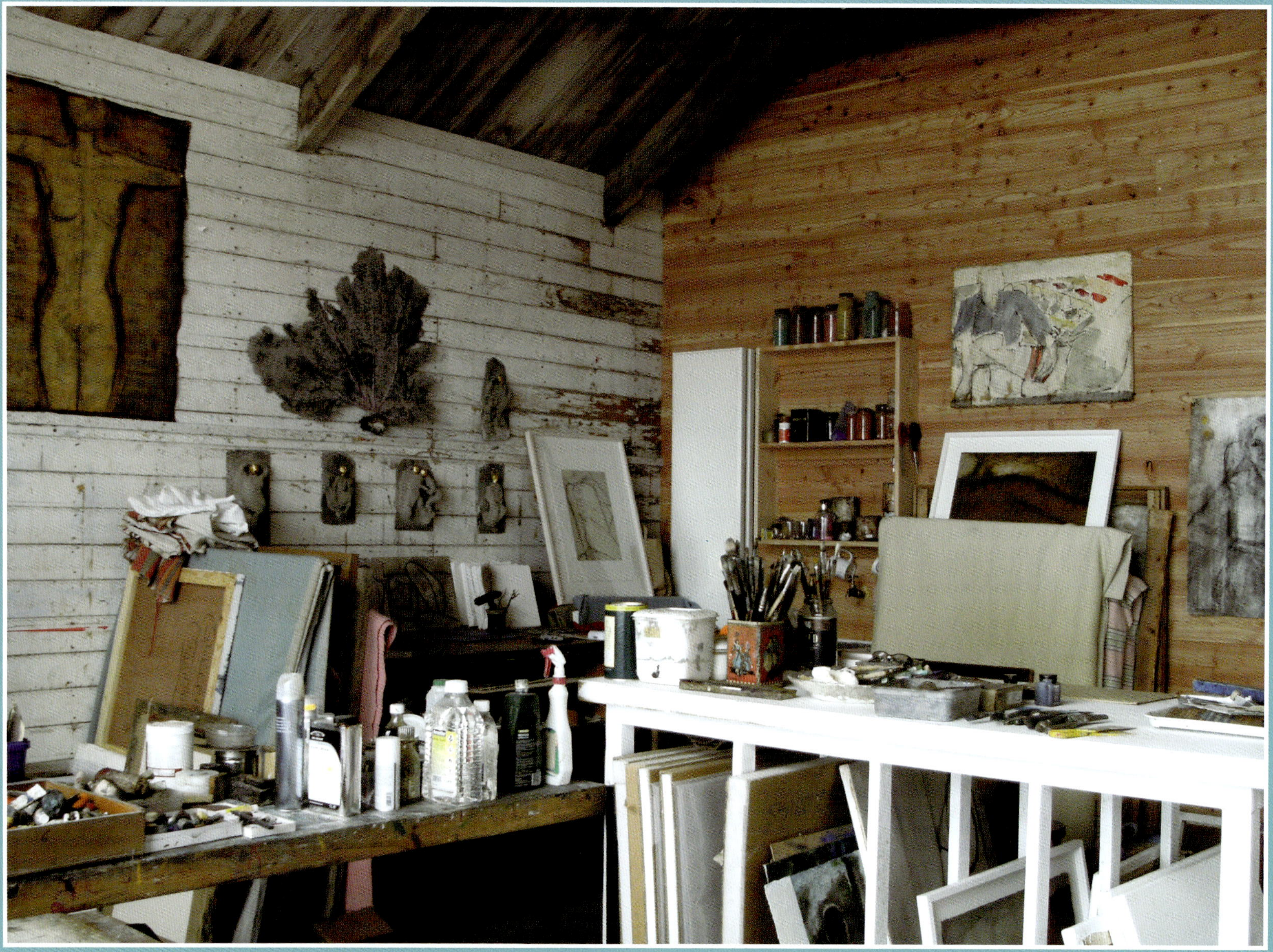

John Emanuel's studio interior

THE PORTHMEOR ARTISTS

St Ives is inexhaustible in its attractions to artists [6]

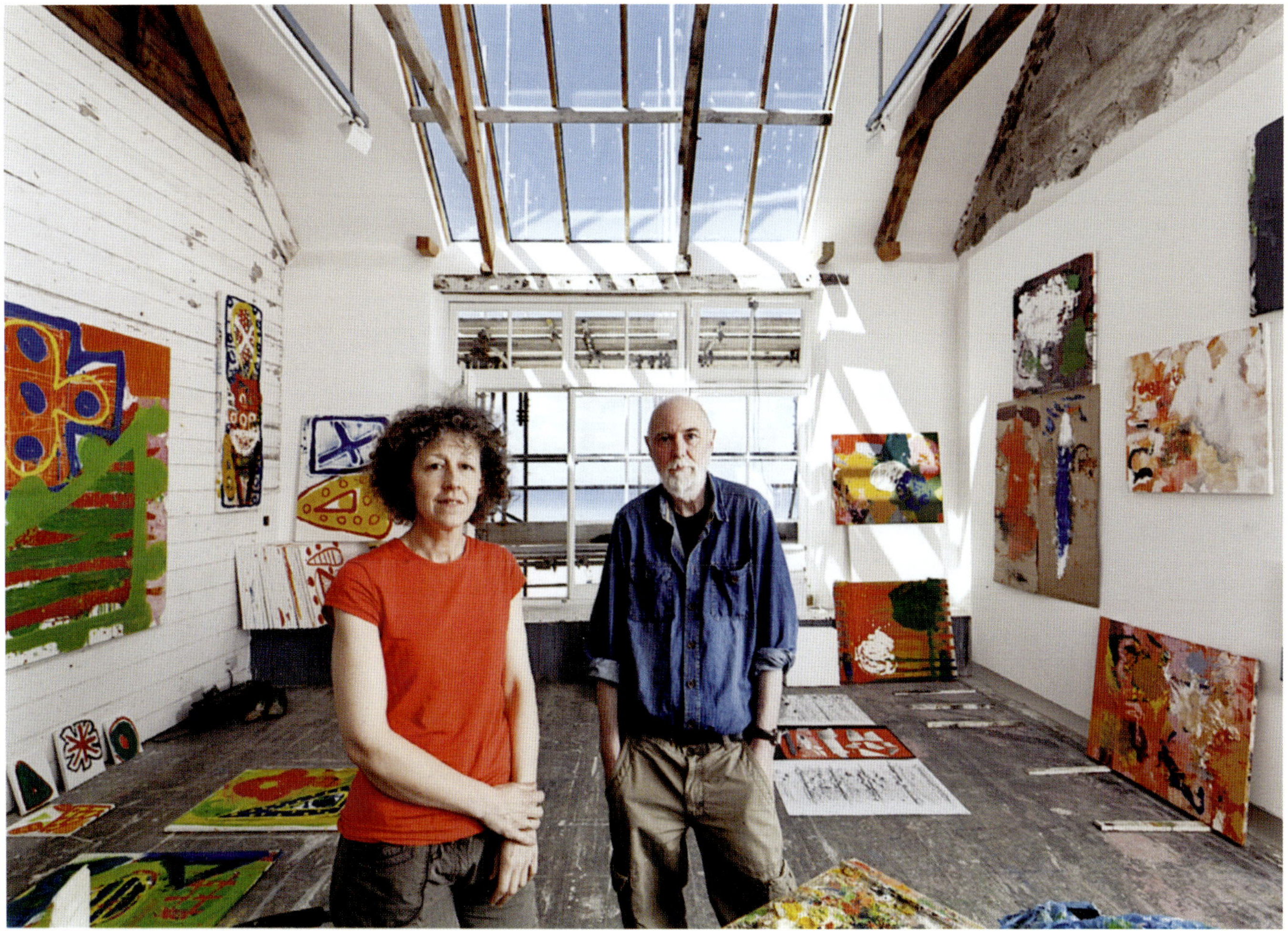

Clare Wardman and Iain Robertson in No.7 Porthmeor Studios

Iain Robertson

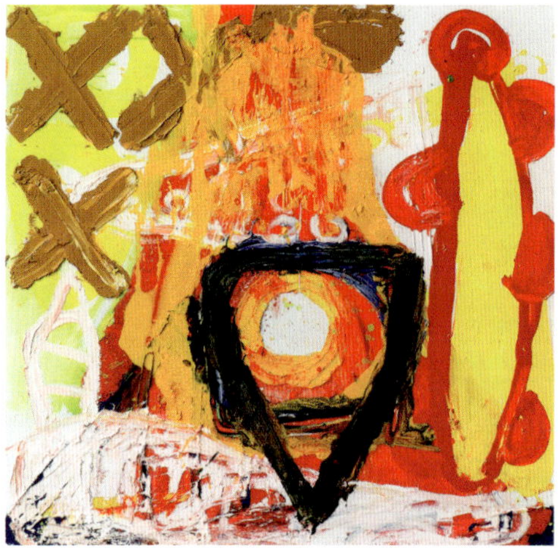

'Hard Bop' 2007

My paintings start in random application of colour and shape working with a language of developed forms archetypal symbols recalling primitivistic signs and referencing contemporary culture, expressing a direct approach to image making, communication and execution.

Pouring, gravity, mark making and a tension implicit through the co-existence of considered action and chance, help me to get closer to dealing with a multiplicity of information and the influence of visual and audible stimulus on the process.

Listening to music and personal musical memory encourage emergent chance imagery also informing style, look and attitude.

Born: Cyprus. Studied Exeter College of Art and Design. Lives in Carbis Bay

Clare Wardman

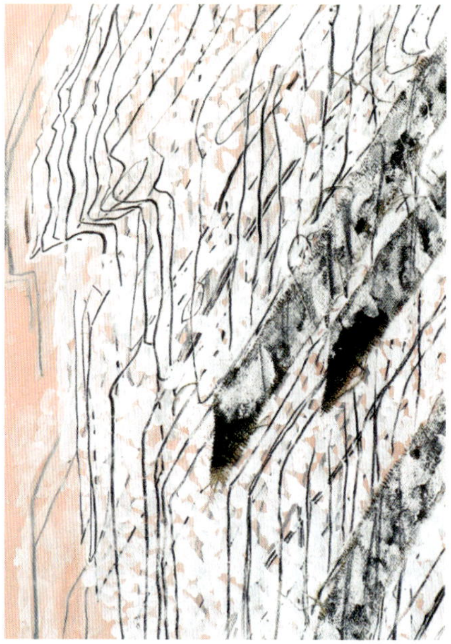

'Experimental Pink' 2008

'Weathering,' a pervasive element in this studio, is where, through the making and doing of art practice, I inquire into the notion of the fragment's generative phenomena. The abstract image emerging from this material interplay between loci and experiential studio practice exists both in my phenomenological drawings and the paintings on canvas. Studio context is a modality I enjoy with echoes of previous activity and events, including the marks and paint patinas on the walls and floors. Working with the series as an unfinished object creates a space for time and for these processes to unfold; by deciding to leave the physical and conceptual parameters open, the residual material becomes a continuum of the 'weathering.'

Born: Yorkshire. Studied Exeter College of Art and Design. Lives in Carbis Bay.

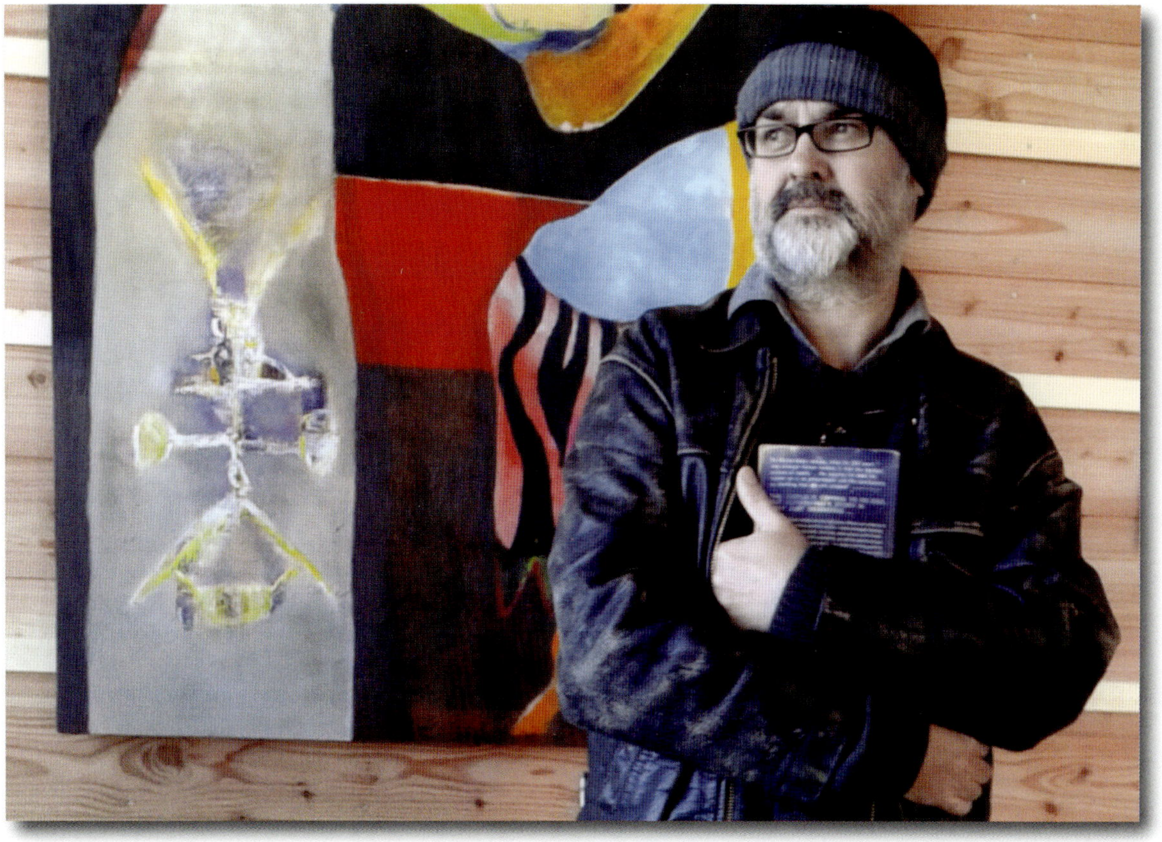

Philip Medley (studio 1)

When I come into the studio, I don't know what is going to happen. I want to surprise myself. Painting is a series of contradictions, a synthesis of paraphrased elements, hiding and revealing images to achieve an evocative presence, the culmination of transformations which produce feelings outside that of language and explanation, allowing the painting through receptivity, chance and enquiry to stand somewhere between alchemy and personal enlightenment. Subjectively, my work is fed by many sources, primary amongst those are the writings of Franz Kafka, and the often extraordinary theories of Physics.

You can pick me up and put me down anywhere and as long as I have materials I am able to work.

Born: Chester. Studied North Staffordshire Polytechnic.
Lives in St Ives

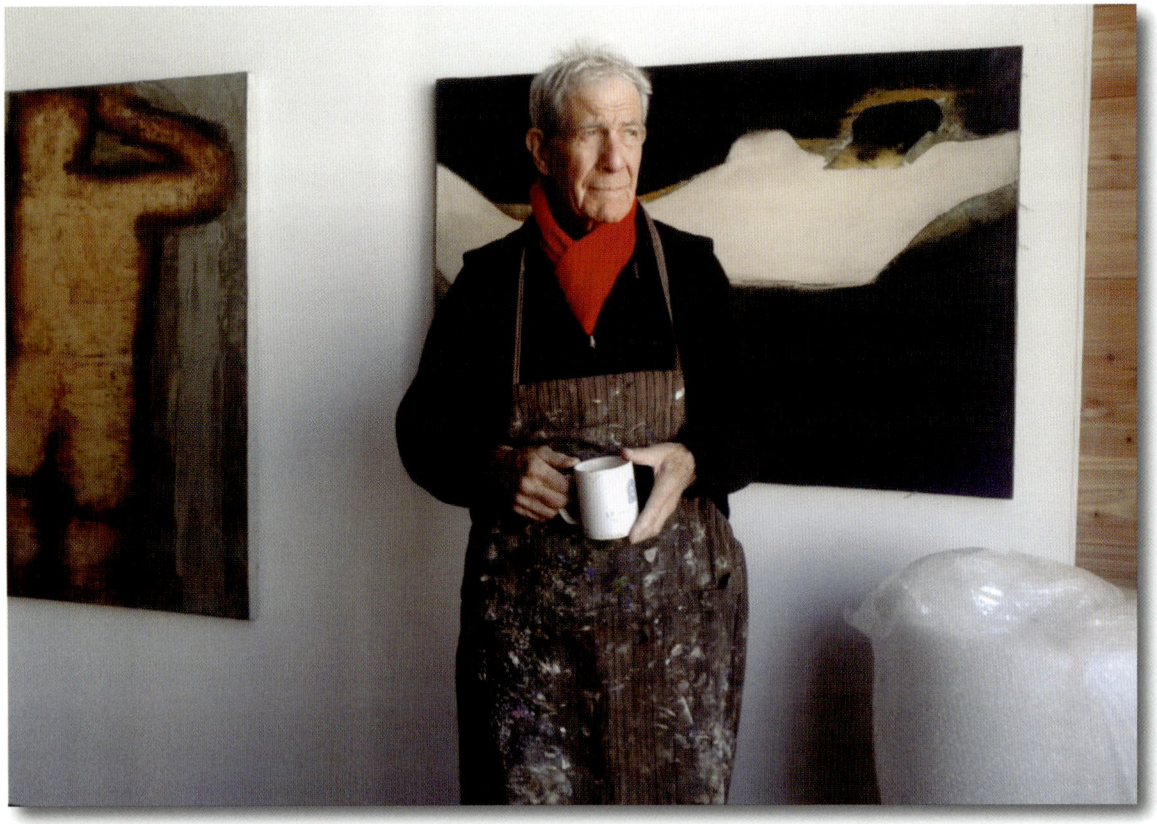

John Emanuel (studio 2)

My work revolves around the figure and the figure in landscape. The paintings are in oils, on board, paper and canvas. I draw from life regularly using a variety of papers including a heavy hand-made one, which I have used for many years.

Sketchbooks are an essential part of my work. I always have one with me and they consist of drawings of Cornwall, Scilly and Cumbria, etc. They bring the landscape into the studio.

As well as the drawings from life I also work on a series of small monoprints. They bridge the gap between the life drawings and the etchings I produce.

I have been in No.2 Porthmeor Studios since 1983. The recent renovations will preserve the building and its studios.

Born: Lancashire. Started painting in 1962. Lives in St Ives

Naomi Frears (studio 3)

I love beginning paintings. I don't plan what I am going to do, I just start and almost always in paint. The drawing comes later so it's all a bit back to front.

Although I start confidently, I change my mind again and again about what I want until the right thing happens. My work feels to me like the last frame of a film – only I know the rest of the story.

I think my paintings might be about love, loss, intimacy, distance. They are a way for me to communicate with and about people I love.

My studio space is very important to me. The work can't happen without it. If I had to move, I know I would keep working but it would be quite different I think.

I am influenced by artists from the distant past as well as by many contemporary artists using film and photography.

Born: Leicester. Studied Loughborough and Sunderland Schools of Art. Lives in St Ives

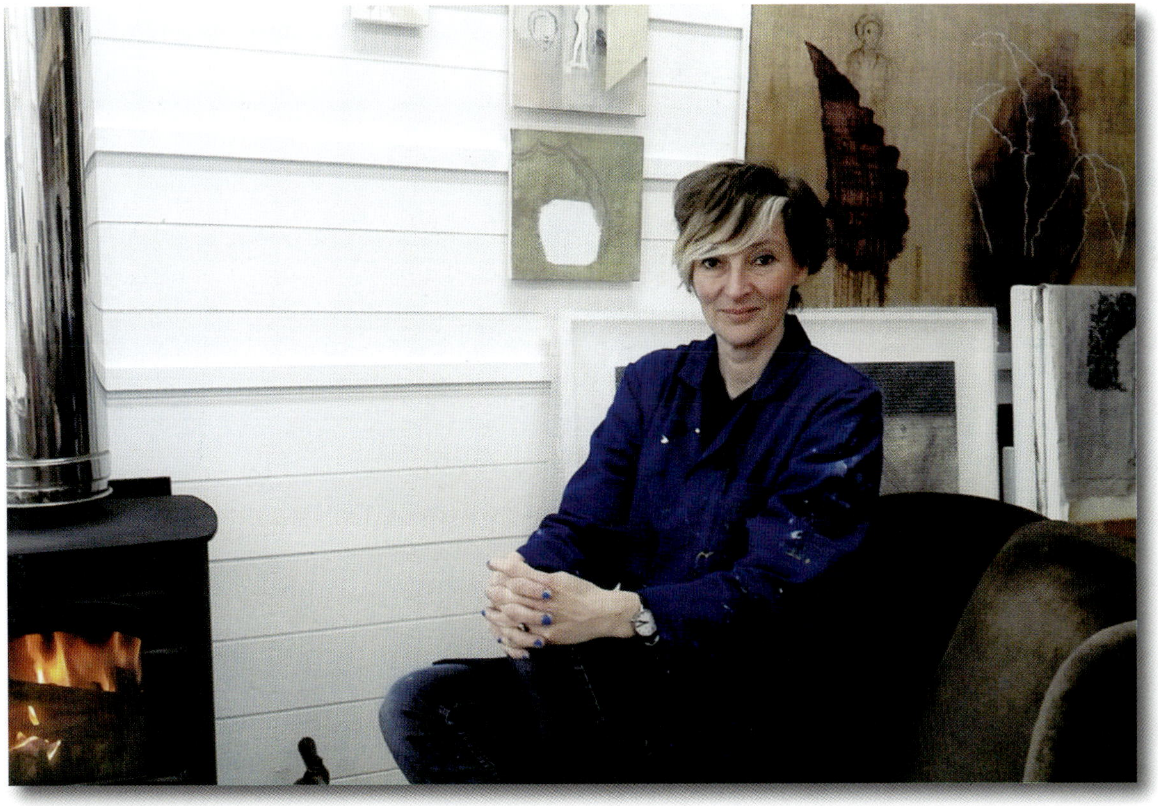

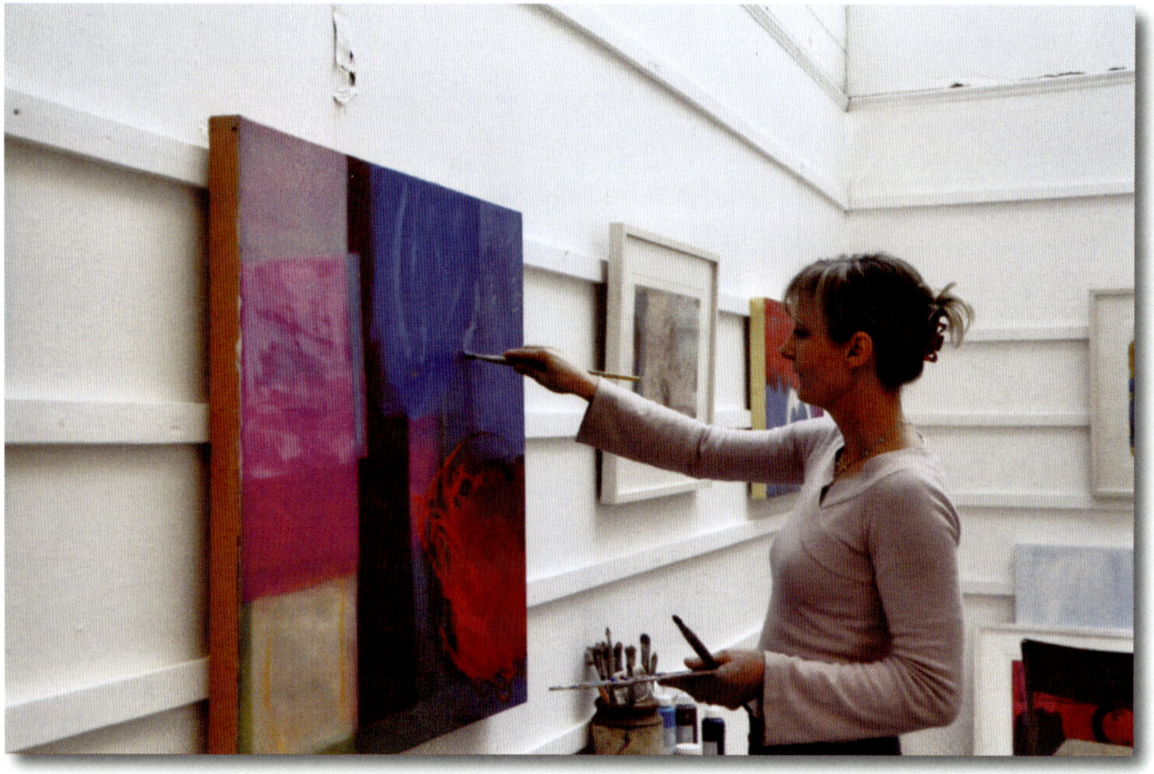

Rachael Kantaris (studio 5)

The process of unearthing an image is like a journey and I am not sure where I'm going until I get there. The language of colour fascinates me and I try to achieve a sense of glow within the work. When I manage this, the piece seems to resonate and come alive. When I start working on a painting or etching it will be related to something I have felt or seen, a colour, sense of space, a place or experience. I am there to nudge it, persuade it, shape it. It's a visual, sensory experience rather than a rational one, a dialogue between colour, light, weight and form. I usually understand most clearly what I was trying to do after it is finished. The title comes at the very end. Etching is my main medium, and I work on multi-plate colour etching in the Print Workshop. This studio is for my painting although the two are inevitably linked and elements of print-making sometimes appear in the paintings.

Born: Australia. Studied Brighton School of Art.
Lives in St Ives

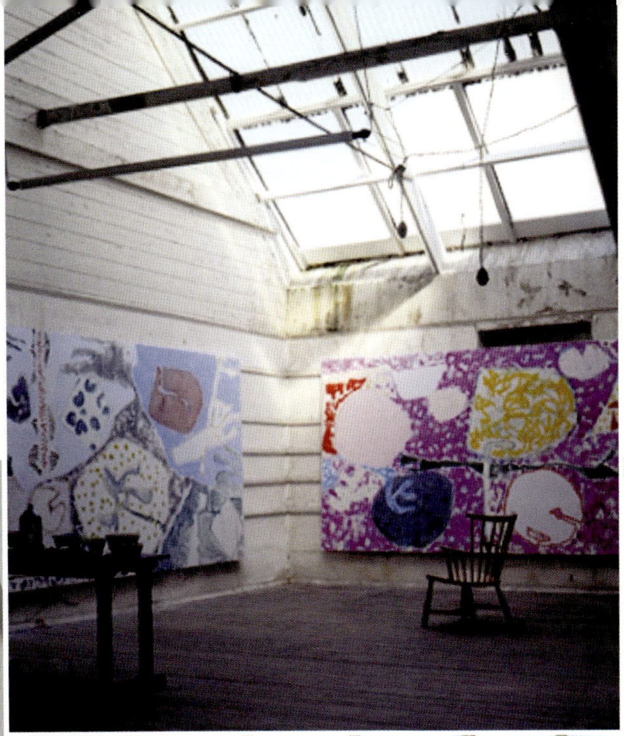

Left: Studio Five in Patrick Heron's time with structures for supporting walls and skylight. 'Pale Garden Painting'. 'Big Purple Painting' 1984

Below: Studio Five with Rachael Kantaris. Previous occupants were Julius Olsson, Borlase Smart, Ben Nicholson and Patrick Heron

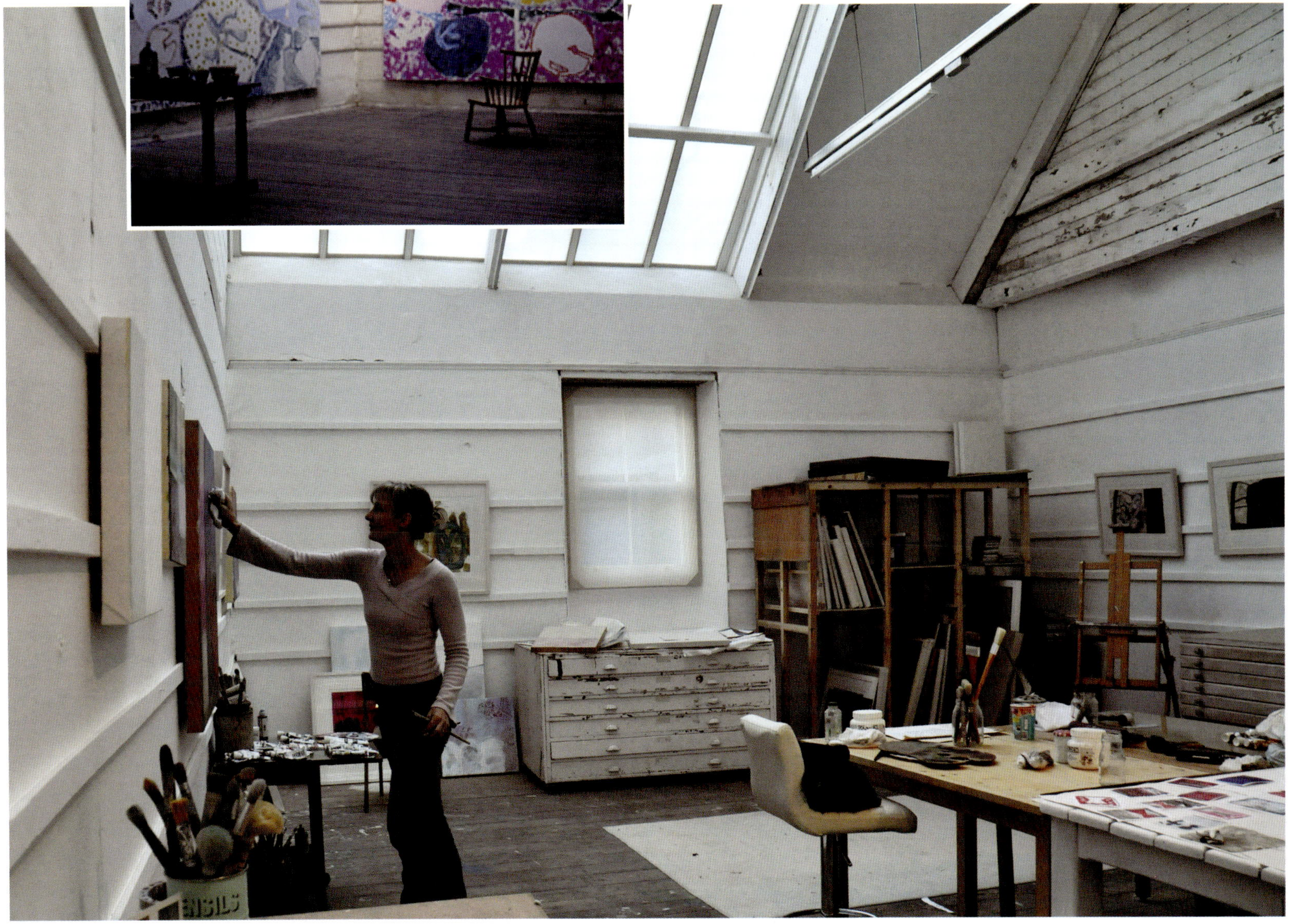

Picnic on Porthmeor Beach, 1904

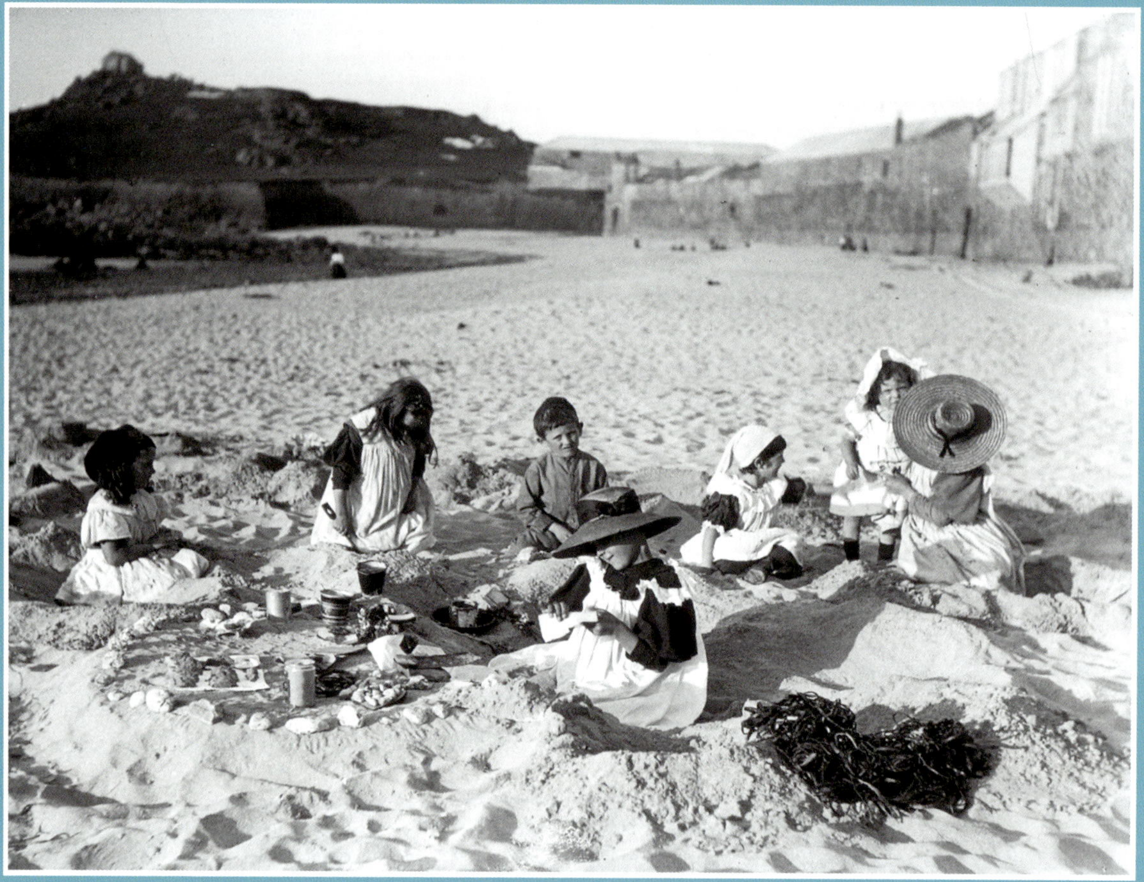

Below left: Porthmeor Beach, 1956
Below right: Porthmeor Beach, 2013

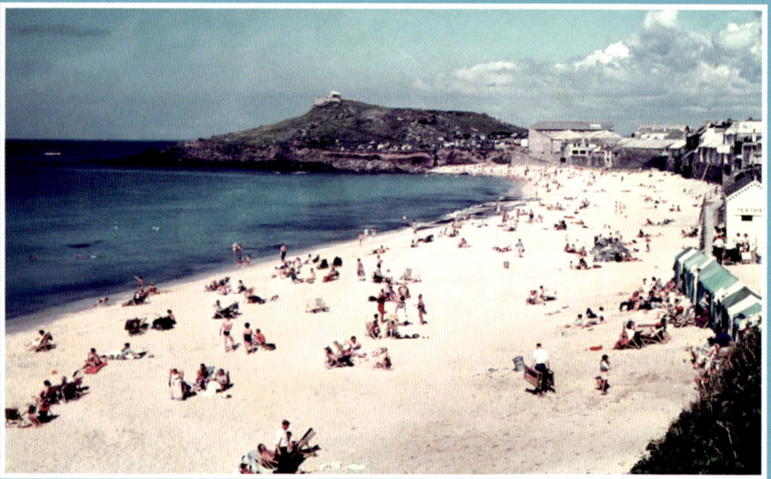

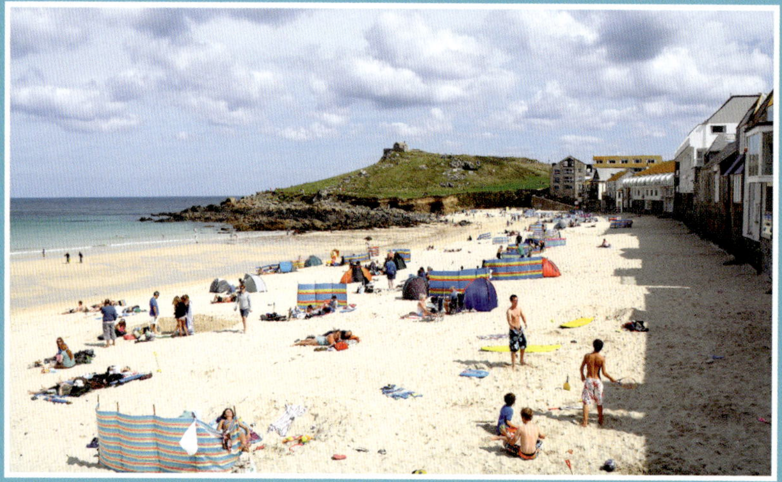

Richard Nott (studio 6)

I start with a basic white emulsion paint. I build up the layers with lots of PVA, could be cement, varnishes; build up the texture with cement powder and bitumen. White spirit brings the bitumen through. During the process I take the work outside.

I drench the painting in white spirit and burn the surface. It blisters the painting. It is quite a big flame but the bitumen comes through clearly. Things develop. They have a quality, to do with geology, granite, nature and walking around St Ives and filtering these experiences; absorbing the spirit of the area and realising an understanding of how you fit into the world. Eventually something interesting happens. The paintings become quite meditative. Sometimes they are quite angry pieces and then they get toned down. The smaller pieces of work take longer to resolve than the bigger pieces. They are more tightly constructed. The larger ones are slightly more chaotic. Titles are done at the last minute.

Everything seems to happen in the studio. I work on a lot of ideas at once and in a series of ten or twelve. When I came here I started painting but now I avoid oils and acrylics and attack the surface with sanders, blow torches, chemicals and industrial materials, which can create havoc and involves a fight to bring something to the surface which I know to be there. A painting is finished when I recognise myself in it. I trained as a sculptor, and this underpins my whole process of working. I still think about working in three dimension.

Born: St Eval, Cornwall. Studied Lancashire Polytechnic. Lives in St Ives

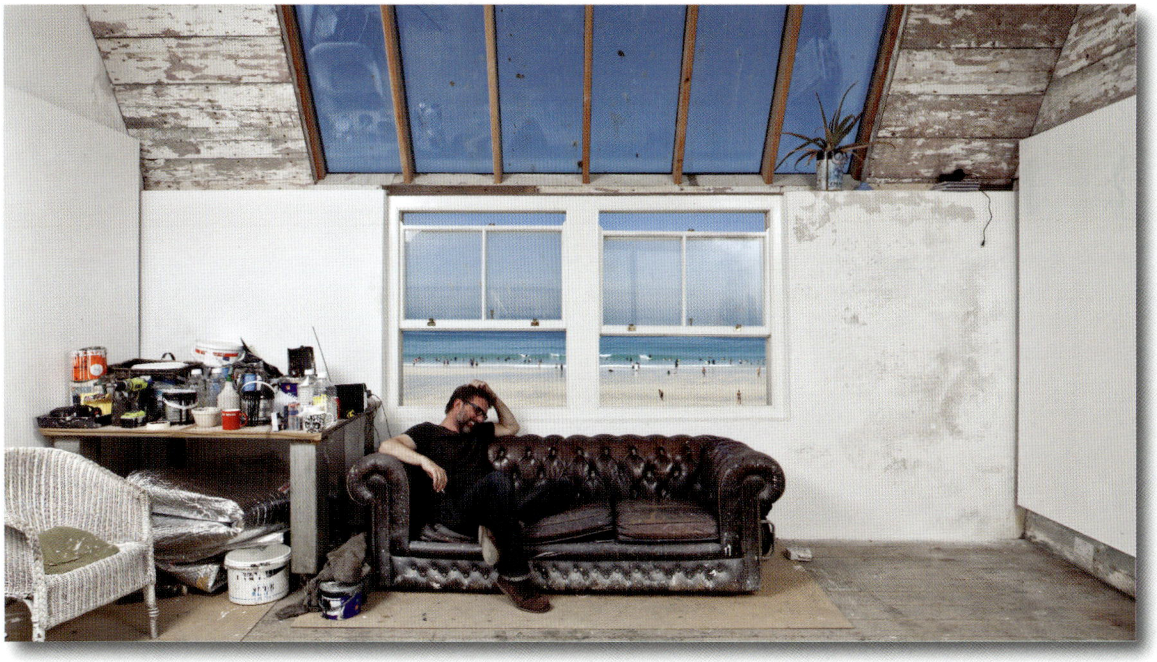

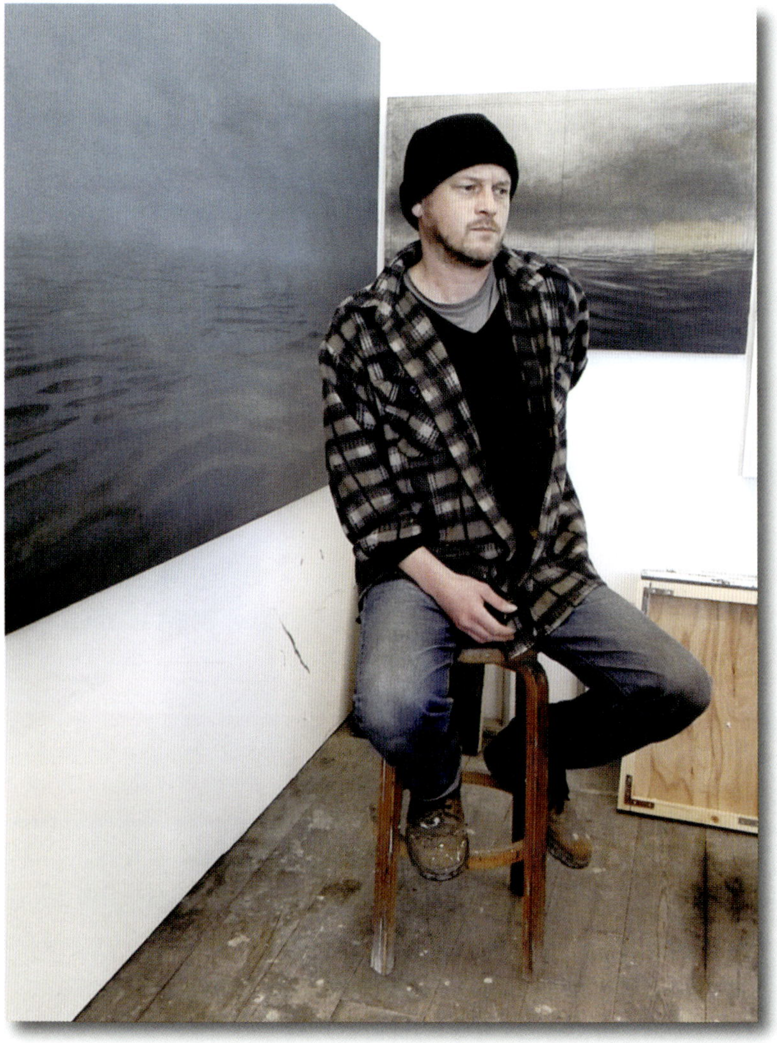

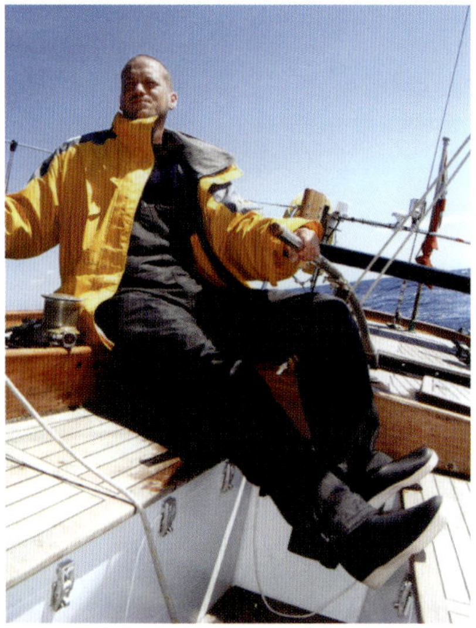

Sax Impey (studio 8)

In recent years my work has derived almost wholly from experiences at sea, working on long-distance yacht deliveries. These journeys become the basis for the paintings, which are related to the experience of a specific time and place at sea. This autobiographical narrative, whether begun in a storm in the Irish Sea, the night skies of a transatlantic passage, or still Indonesian waters, is completed in the studio utilizing the charts, log, drawings, photographs and memories. Some works will be simple pencil or charcoal drawings – many will be composed of a mixture of materials as I seek to get close to the nature of that original experience.

Born: Penzance. Studied Newport College of Art.
Lives in St Ives

Faye Dobinson (Studio 9)

Much of my work starts with drawing – it helps me to really look at things. Every day I am faced with a blank canvas which is both exhilarating and daunting. I apply paint and then the dance between me and the work begins. I factor in chance happenings with the paint; that is when the magic happens and the work often takes itself in a new direction. The landscape I am inhabiting is a huge influence on my work and I am interested to see how my current studio's location on the beach will affect what I produce. Different sized works have their own qualities to play with. I worked very large when studying at Falmouth and the thinking process with a 5′x4′ canvas is very different to a smaller piece. A larger surface has me tracking my way around it, getting to know it, whereas smaller pieces often become more immediate, more concerned with ideas and concepts. Having a studio at Porthmeor has come at a time of great activity for me – working large and small, with both the figure and landscape, it's a really interesting journey. The sea and sky give me freedom.

Born: London. Studied Falmouth College of Arts.
Lives in Perranuthnoe

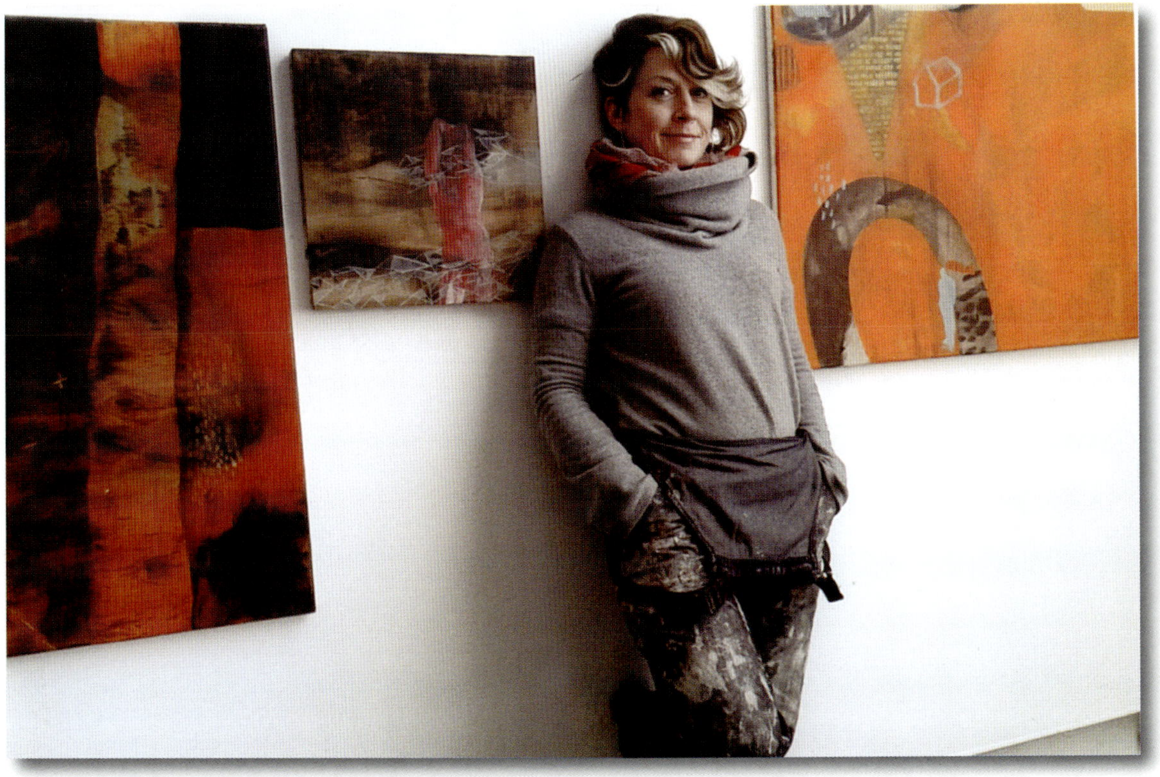

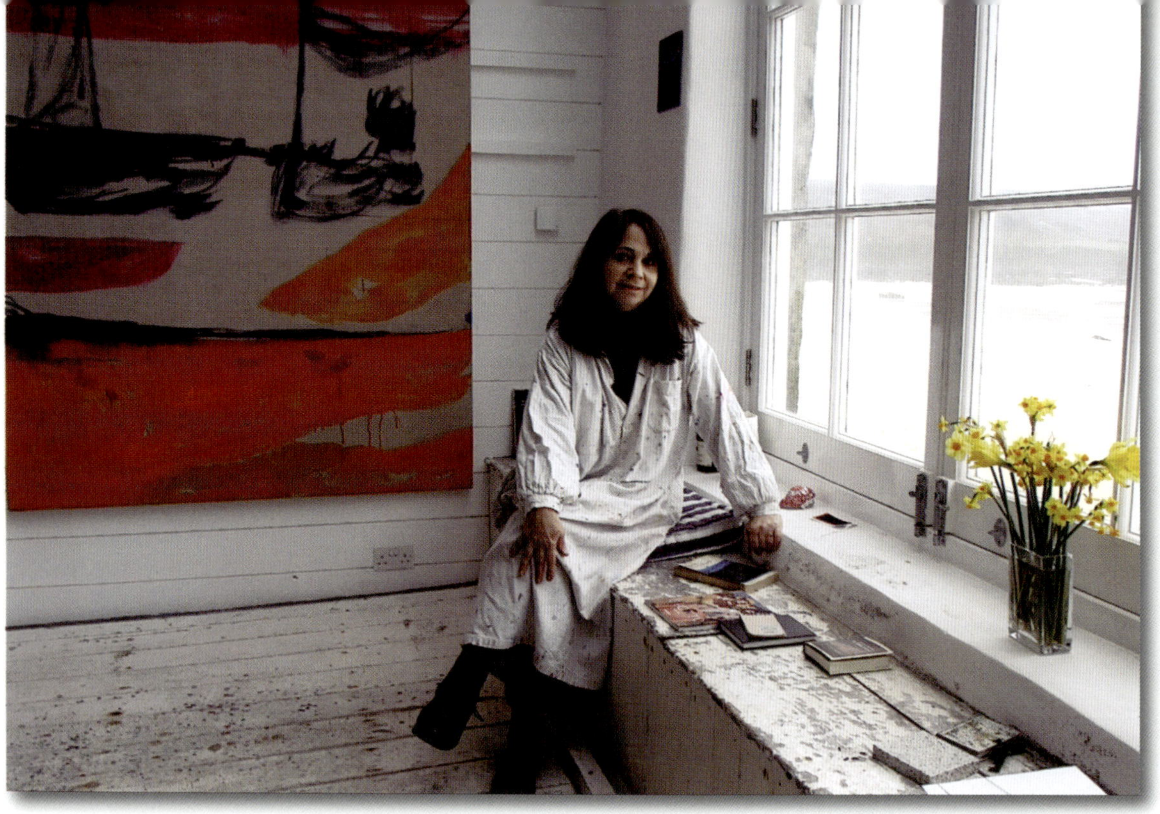

Felicity Mara (Studio 4)

I like to have a large canvas to work on. There's something about the human scale which allows one to become part of the painting – to enter the imaginative space where everything starts. I do small drawings and notes, but I have no real ideas until I begin painting. Visual references are important, in the images, books and objects I have around me in the studio. Some phrases have recurred on my studio walls over the years – 'the imaginative space' and 'silent poetry – visual music'. For me, these are analogies for the process of painting. What excites me is that dreamlike state, a kind of *reverie*.

I draw every day, and I hope that notation and calligraphy are also present in my painting, in the balancing of line and weight of colour. I am usually working on more than one painting.

I often work on unprimed canvas and linen, sprayed with water to create a more fluid ground. But I also work in oil on paintings which may develop over a longer time. I draw from poetry and literature, but I do not want to depict the literal. Landscape is always present – and probably now the sea, as I am so close to it – but it is the atmosphere of these things that I want to evoke rather than a formal likeness. It is thrilling to walk in here each day and to know that painting has been the purpose of this space for so many years – but one also has to sidestep and not be afraid of this in order to do something new.

Born in Kensington. Studied at Camberwell School of Art.
Lives in St Ives

Marion Taylor (studio 15)

The new paintings are a reinvention that occurred when I attacked a developing series, that in the light of a new studio felt too tame and moderate for both my painterly language and for the subject. The results hark back to a former body of work where layers of figurative painting appear through passages of more expressive paint handling. Hong Kong harbour is a hub of worldwide import and export, a massive commercial enterprise on a scale that seriously threatens nature. The toxic assault was the overriding theme to my interpretation.

This series that began with urban environments; painted from a source but with an abstract sensibility, has grown to include other genres as a starting point.

Landscape, still life and occasional figures are the basic subject but the sheer enjoyment of the paint has led the way to a more complex content.

Born: Manchester. Studied Falmouth College of Arts.
Lives in St Ives

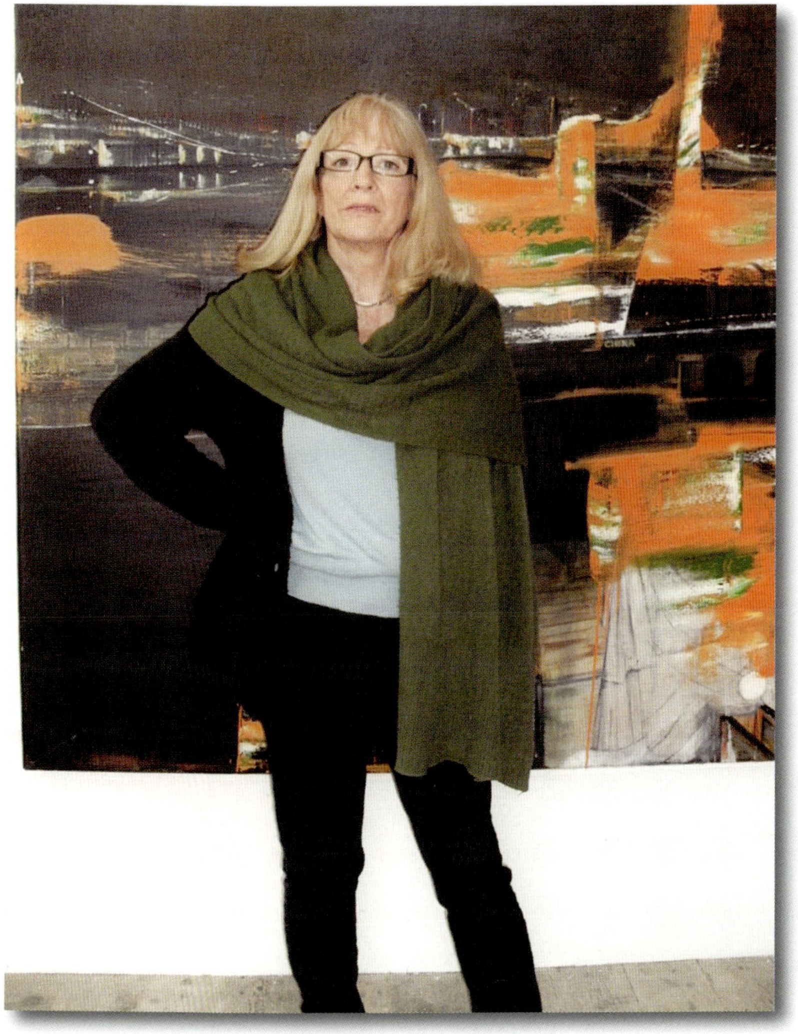

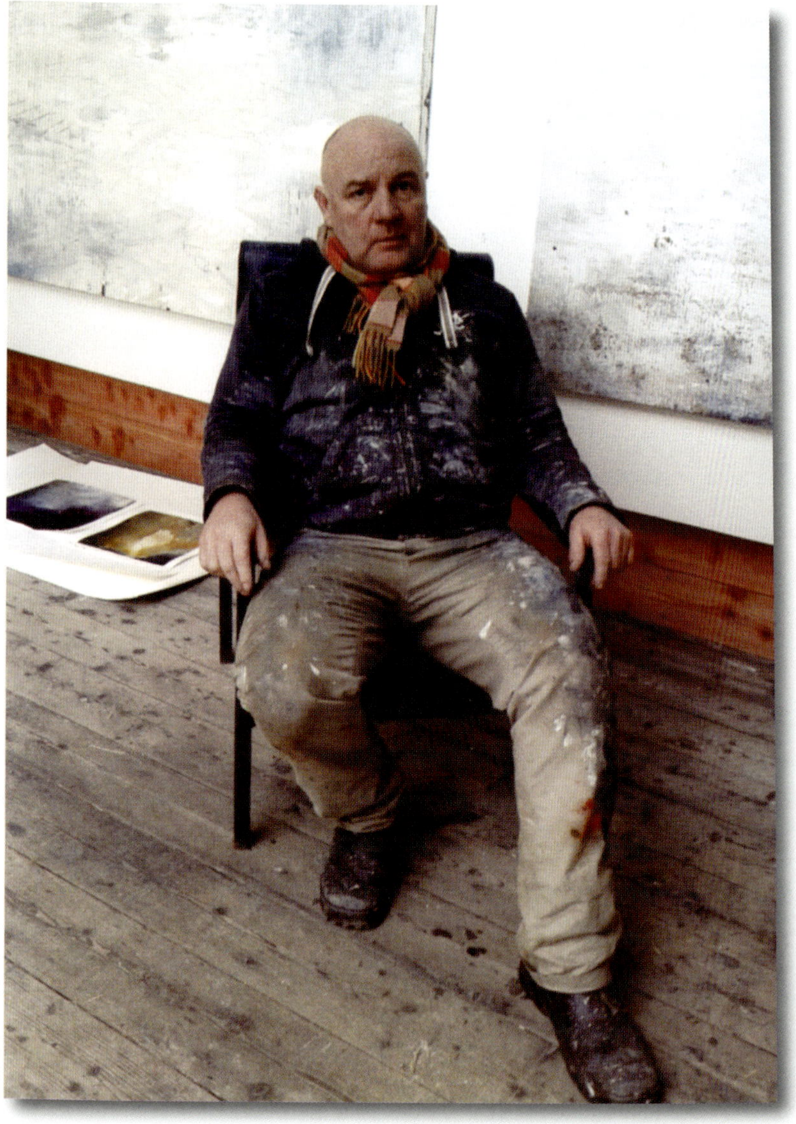

Gareth Edwards (studio 16)

Living in Lamorna and now working in the studios in St Ives it is interesting to travel back and forth. I am aware of the histories of the two places. These Porthmeor studios are architectural expressions of art history but they are also contemporary, new and forward looking.

My paintings are elemental fictive spaces. They have a kind of landscape, seascape, fields and tracks, spaces, air, rain. I like the idea of an atmosphere where people can experience space in an emotional way. They can penetrate and occupy the area and contemplate in an abstract way. I use a wide variety of materials, varnish, plaster, polyfilla; months of layering and working. Once the surface is settled I start creating atmosphere, feeling, poetry. I work in a series. I move between painting and sculpture. I have had a studio in Lamorna for many years; that is where my sculpture is made.

Born: East London. Studied Art History London Institute.
Lives in Lamorna

Sam Bassett (studio 18)

Landscape is important. I don't go out and record it, but it is always in my work, although my subject is more human based. I make it personal by painting the figure. There is no particular person. There is focus on the character and visual expressions. I like to put my figures in an ambiguous space. Some are quite sad or sombre. In the last few years I have formed a language of colour, and it is becoming important. My images have hues of blue. I was using deep and dark colours, but when I am in St Ives colour becomes acceptable. I like contrast. Mark making and texture are in parallel with my thought process. I try to find a reason for existence. Much of my work starts off big. Working big releases me and then it gets rejected and worked on again. There is a free approach to finalise the painting; the work becomes intuitive and organic in the way it grows. I work with watercolour and oils, photographs and the computer.

Born: St Ives. Studied Falmouth & Bournemouth Schools of Art. Lives in Newlyn

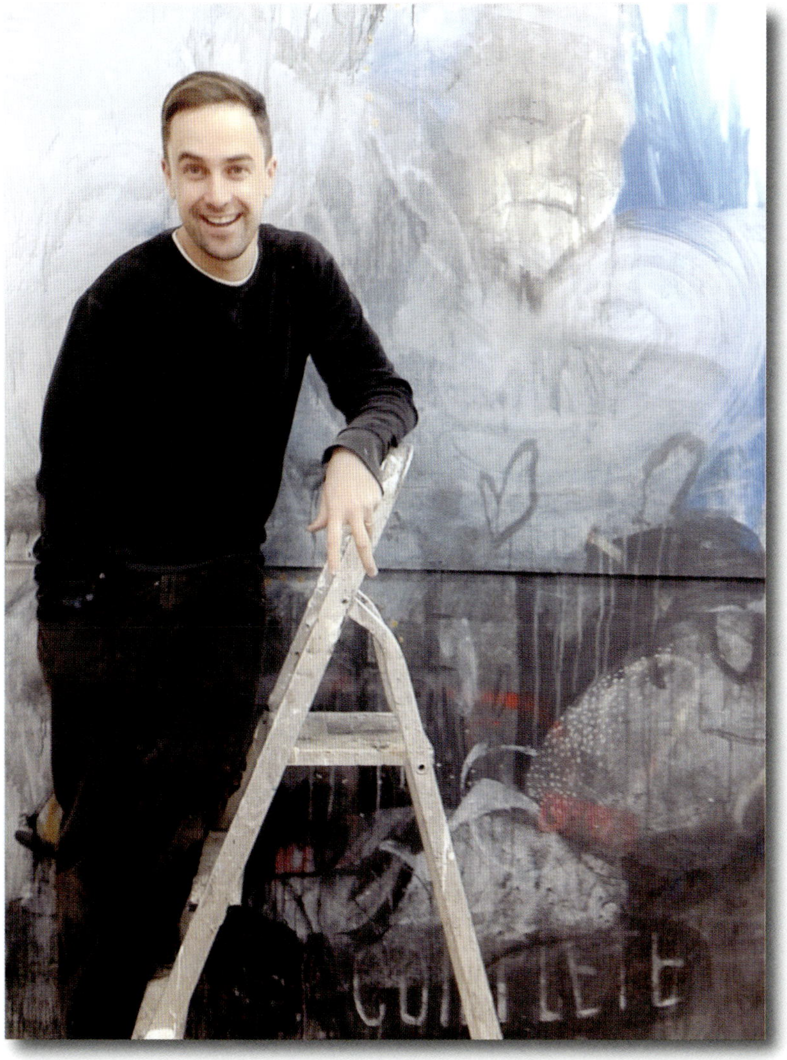

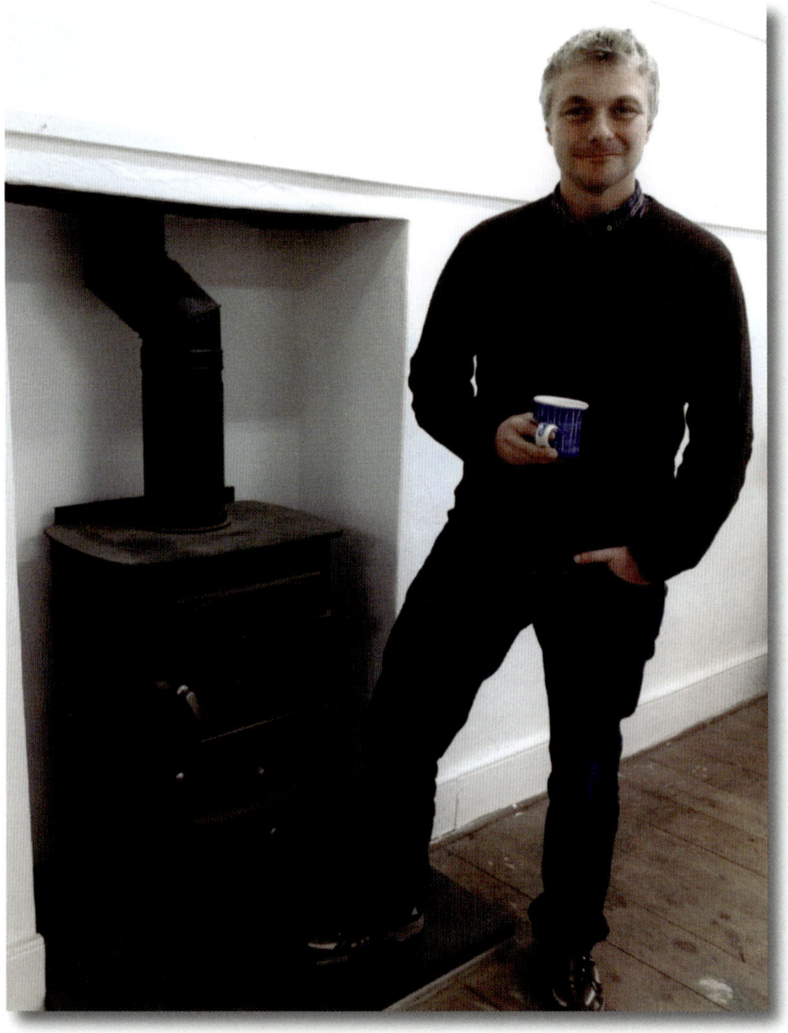

James Barber (studio 11)

Installation by definition is temporary. It is about fragments, the physical and conceptual. It can be understood as a democratic relationship with an array of material objects, sounds and other stimuli working collectively to immerse the viewer within an environment. My reference books are important. I create interplay with the fragments of history and am interested in the way we categorize knowledge.

I was invited to exhibit with the Tate in 2000 and saw the first installation of 'Dead Reckonings' on the Island. My work is site sensitive. It was connected to the Pedn Olva mine in St Ives and was nominated for the Paul Hamlyn Award and short listed. I am involved in a research post in partnership with Tate St Ives and the universities of Falmouth and Plymouth. Having this Porthmeor studio I intend to develop a site-stimulated practice incorporating this historic location.

I worked as an artist assistant to Sandra Blow RA, Roy Walker and Roy Ray. This apprenticeship grounded my practice at a critical stage.

Born: St Ives. Studied: Falmouth and Exeter Colleges of Art. Lives in Hayle

Lucie Bray (studio 19)

I am known for my sea and landscapes completed on site. Very often I can be found on Porthmeor beach itself where I can directly observe subtleties of colour in a scene. The paints I use are oil on board when painting outside. The studio paintings are acrylic on board. Works in progress are often several at the same time. I like to see how the paint settles before I put more on.

Studio life represents a new chapter for me. Here I can focus more on mark making. I'm interested in the way a mark feels and sounds as it is being made. I have started to make my own brushes out of Cornish palm leaves. I may use them more in splashing. It is a mechanical thing to do while getting used to my new studio. A brush becomes an extension of myself.

I am looking forward to painting on a larger board a subject which I have just been experiencing outside. Alternatively I may start with just a colour which I have in mind, like the red of bracken in autumn, and see where that takes me, linking in a painting from outdoors later on. In the studio I will be able to work on several large paintings at a time in order to build images slowly. Keeping them fresh and alive.

Born: Helston. Studied Wimbledon School of Art.
Lives in St Ives

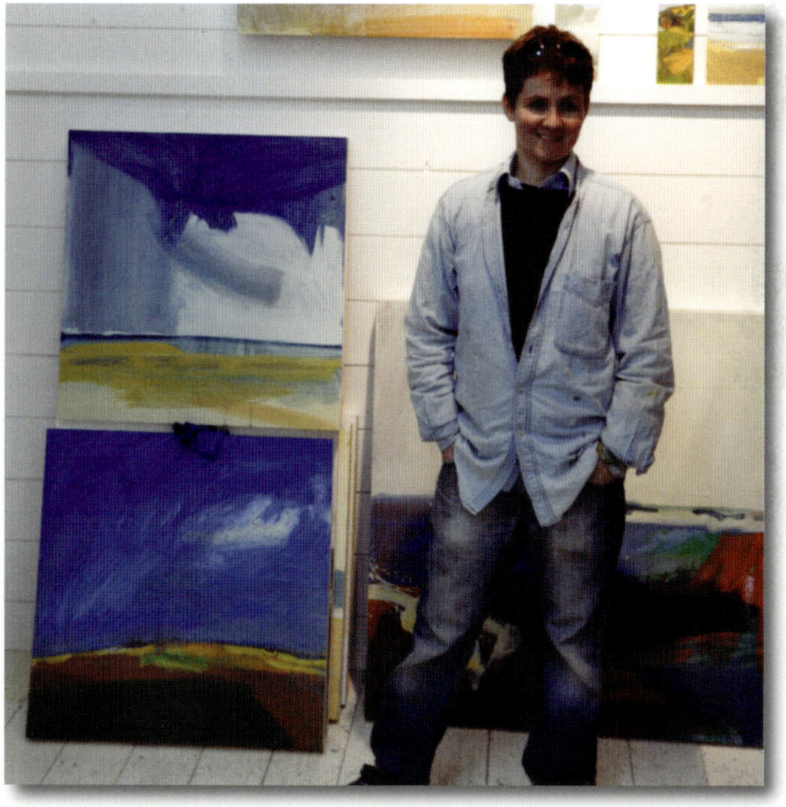

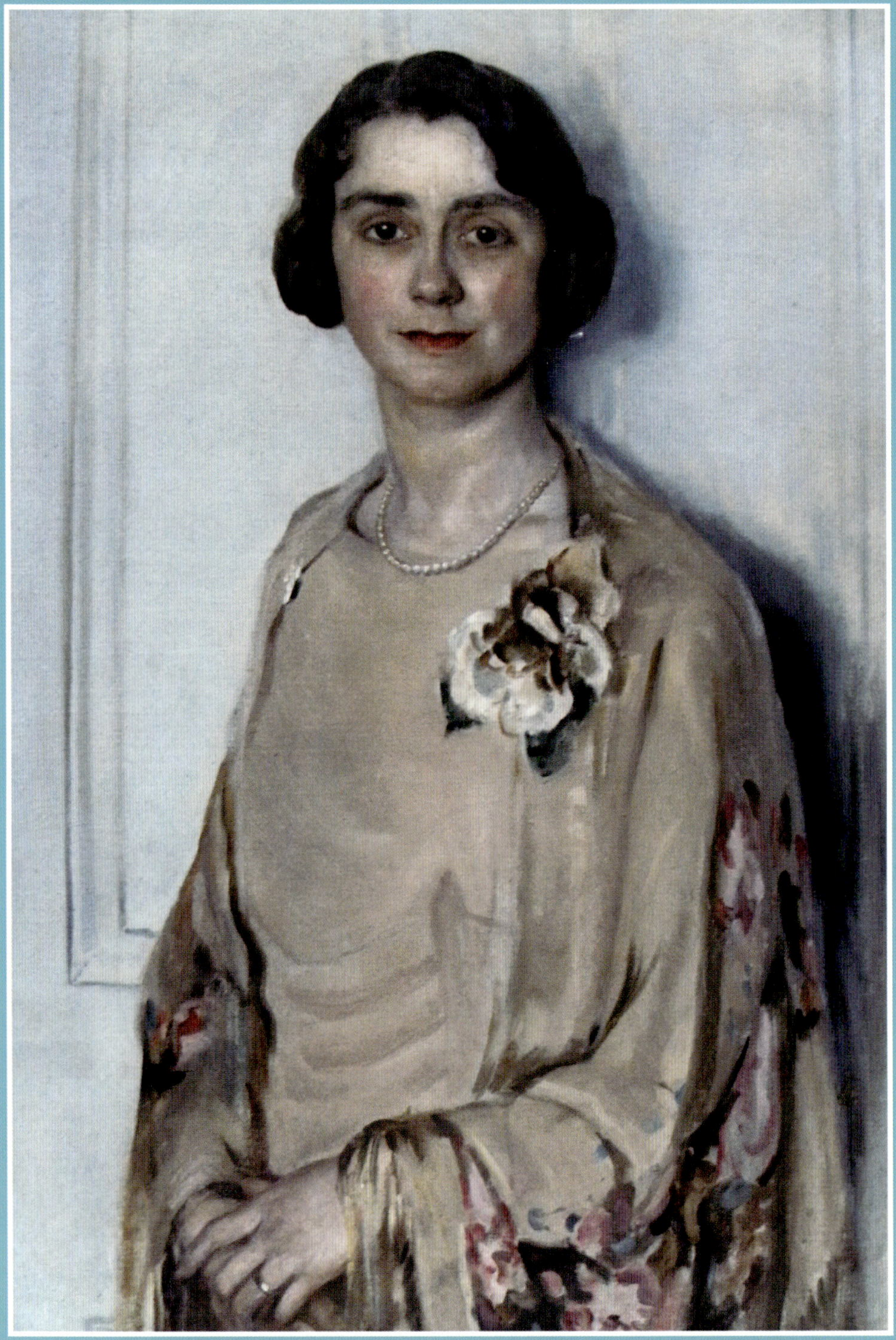

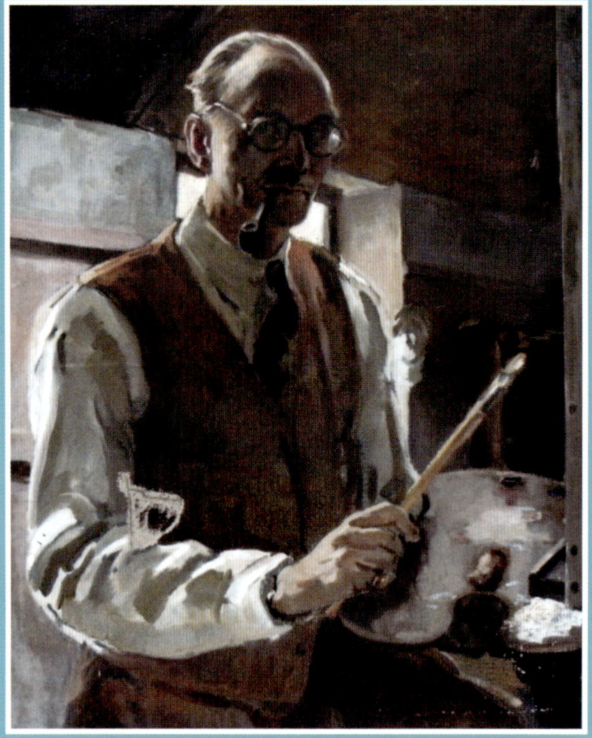

Leonard Fuller by Marjorie Mostyn

Marjorie Mostyn by Leonard Fuller

ST IVES SCHOOL OF PAINTING

IN 1938 THE artists Leonard Fuller and his wife Marjorie Mostyn opened the St Ives School of Painting at Back Road West. This was a promise fulfilled. The idea was first discussed with Borlase Smart, when he and Leonard Fuller were serving in the Artists Rifles in the First World War. They both had ambitions of living in St Ives, opening a school, and pursuing a life of painting.

Borlase Smart took no time in deciding to come to St Ives, with his wife Irene in 1919, and begin the life of a professional painter. The two men remained good friends after the war but it wasn't until 1938 that Leonard Fuller was able to realise his dream of coming to St Ives and setting up the St Ives School of Painting. The aim of the school was to meet the needs of the artists' community in St Ives and to cater for the many visiting students.

Leonard was a dedicated painter and teacher. He was a portrait, figure and still life painter. He provided a scholarly and broad style of training at the school, using his experience of teaching at St John's Wood School and at Dulwich College. Marjorie Mostyn studied at the Royal Academy under John Singer Sargent and was an accomplished painter of portraits, interiors and still life, winning medals for life drawing and composition.

In 1977 Roy Ray took over the school after the death of Leonard and at the request of Marjorie. He knew the Fullers well from his annual visits to the school in the sixties and when he moved permanently to St Ives in 1974 Marjorie relied on his support in teaching and helping the school to survive, so he was the natural successor as principal. It was Roy who brought in many artists with their particular expertise to expand the teaching facilities. These were John Charles Clark, Bob Devereux, Stephen Dove, Malcolm Haylett, Kathy McNally, Sheila Oliner, Ken Symonds, Roy Walker and Peter Ward.

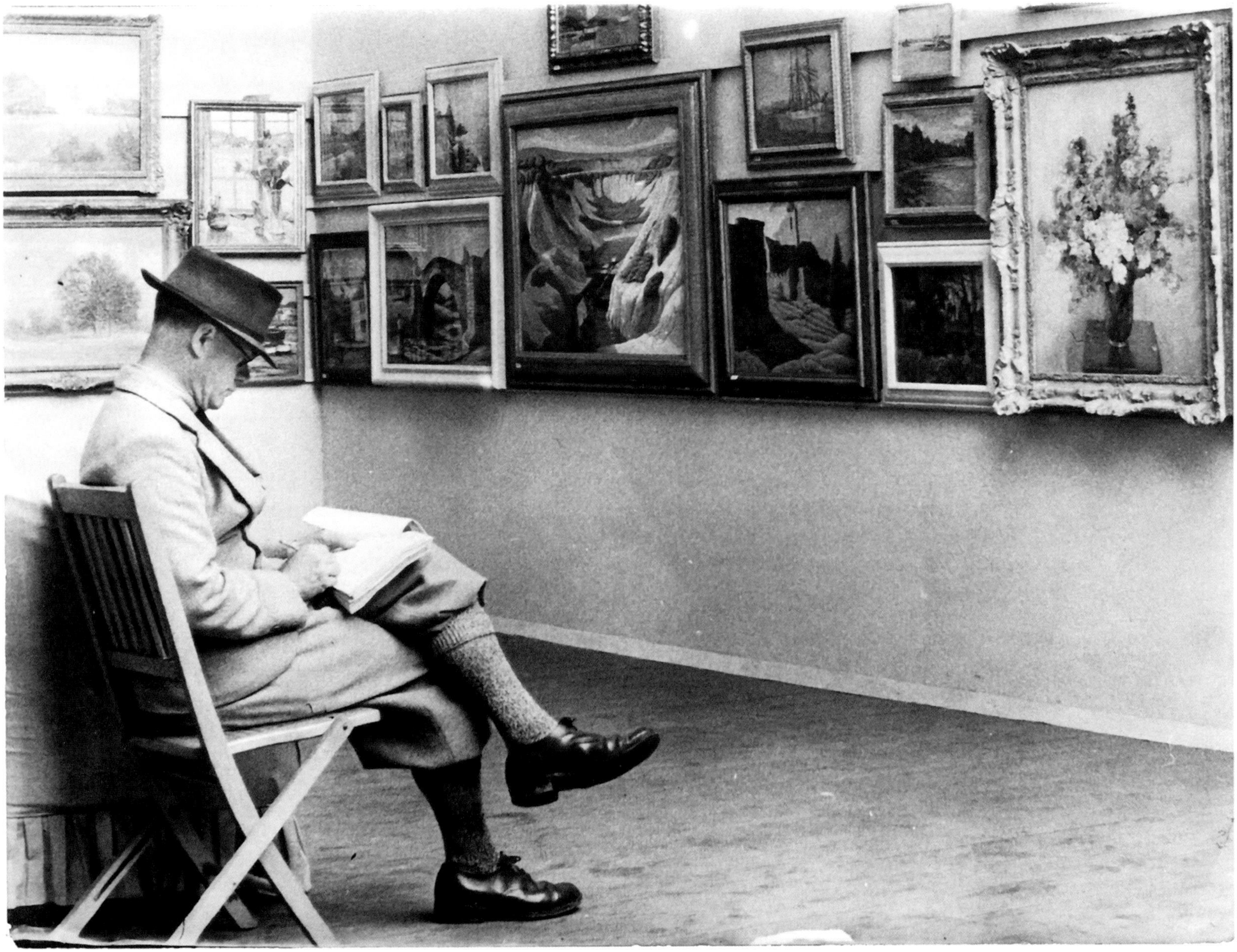

Borlase Smart writing a review for the St Ives Society exhibition c.1940s

When Roy Ray retired to concentrate on his own work, to ensure the School of Painting would survive, he applied to the Charity Commission. The school became a Registered Charity in 2000.

Present Day

The school is now in the hands of artist Alison Sharkey, Acting Director, who studied fine art at University College Falmouth. The school will continue to run its variety of classes and workshops with artists who are specialists in their fields.

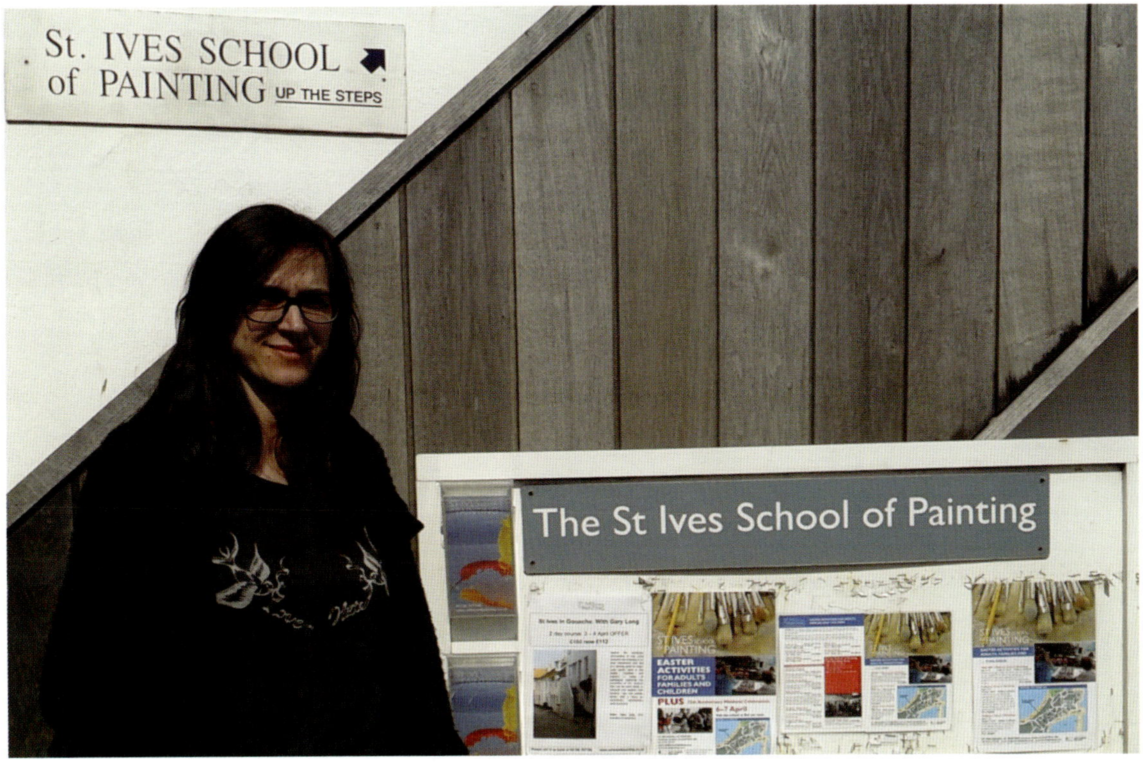

Alison Sharkey – Acting Director of St Ives School of Painting

'One of the things we are now focusing on is expanding the work we do with schools and young people, opening up the School as a creative community for anyone interested in being creative'. So the legacy of Fuller and Mostyn continues more than seventy five years on. People of all ages and experience are connected to the rewards of making and enjoying art in the inspirational setting of Porthmeor Studios.

The St Ives School of Painting links with being part of the traditional and yet contemporary establishments in St Ives, with its history, but with its updated studios and charity status it is in the unique position of giving people a chance to work in the environment and being taught by practising artists. This is on-going into the future.

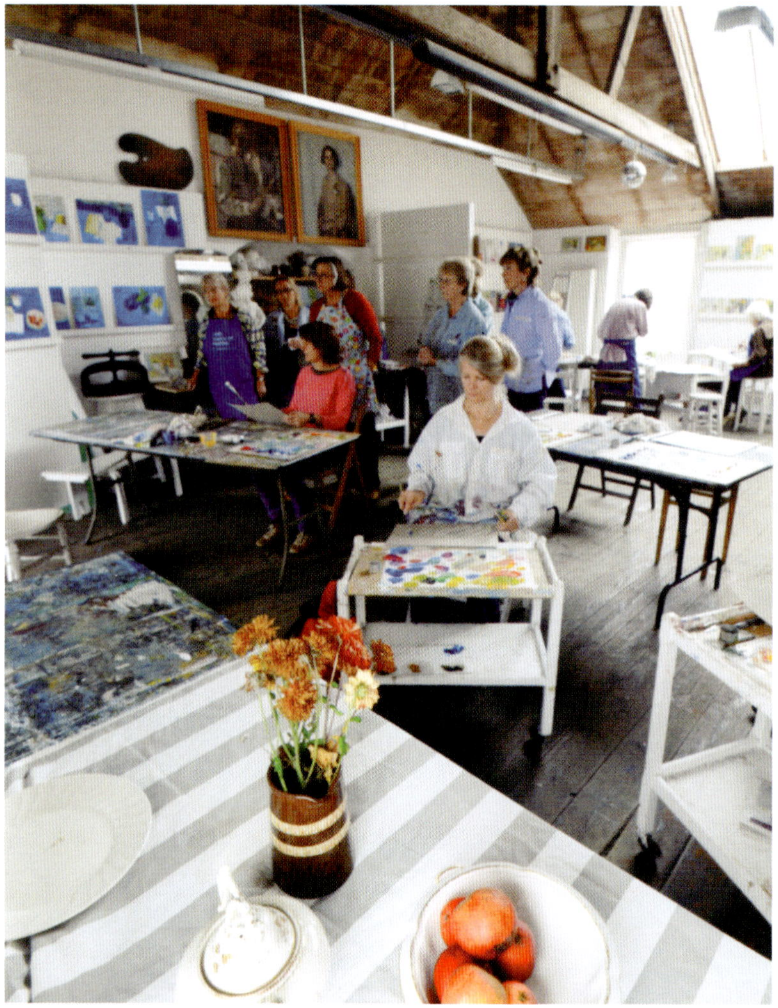

The newly refurbished studio of the School of Painting

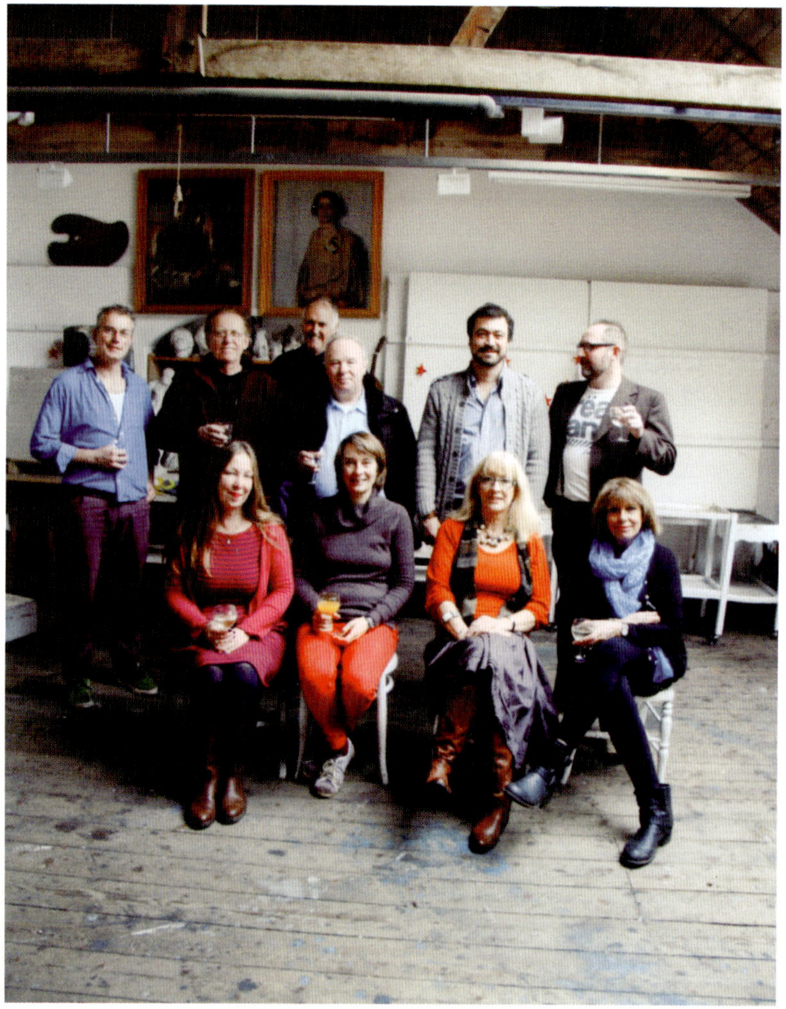

Artist Tutors at the School of Painting
Left: John Keys, Steve Dove, Eric Ward, Gary Long, Ilker Cinarel, Daniel Barnard. Hilary Jean Gibson, Alice Mumford, Marion Taylor, Liz Luckwell

BARBARA HEPWORTH 1903-1975

Perhaps what one wants to say is formed in childhood and the rest of one's life is spent in trying to say it.[7]

ONE REALISES WHEN considering the life of Barbara Hepworth, her ideals and her commitment to the traditions and history of St Ives that she would have supported wholeheartedly the saving of the Porthmeor studios. In her Pictorial Autobiography (new and extended edition 1978) she states, *Naturally after 150 years or more, roofs sink and timbers rot. But with the help of many devoted people, old fish cellars and other ancient structures have been saved and rebuilt to make a reconstitution of all that people so much love in this small town. After some 120 years, my own studio is getting very shaky indeed. It is on a famous corner of old St Ives, and, though repairs are essential, I want above all to keep its character and preserve its quality.*[8]

That is precisely the philosophy of the architects M J Long and Rolfe Kentish. Barbara would have approved of their desire to preserve the history and character of the Porthmeor buildings and improve, without spoiling, the quality of the studios.

Dame Barbara Hepworth is a sculptor who made St Ives uniquely her own. Her work, as with so many other sculptors, painters, writers and creative people is a reflection of her love for her chosen art and for this exceptional town.

Barbara Hepworth arrived in Cornwall in 1939 from London with her triplets, Simon, Rachel and Sarah and painter husband Ben Nicholson. Their friends, the artists Adrian Stokes and Margaret Mellis had invited them to stay at Little Parc Owles - later to become the home of Cornish artist

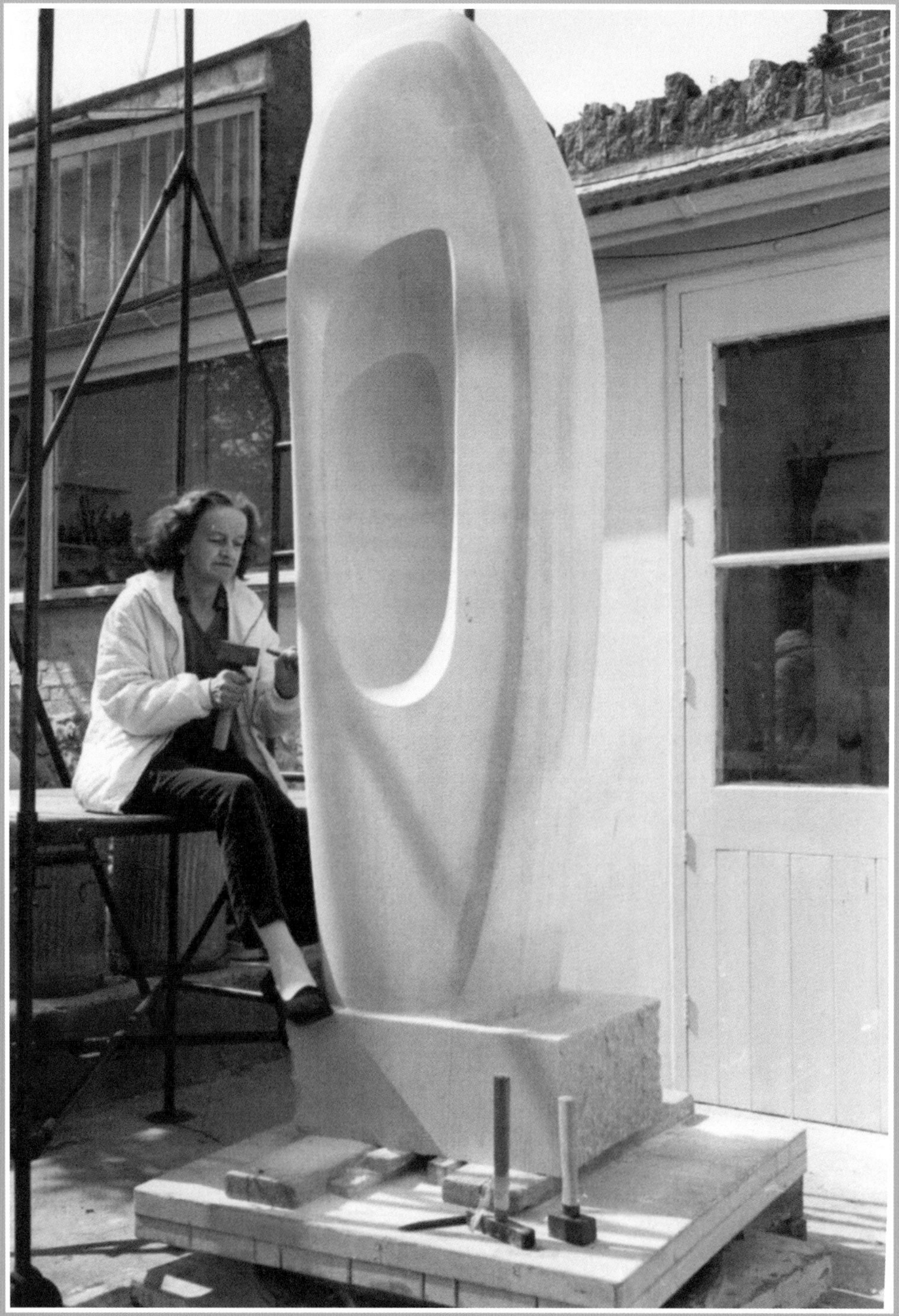
Barbara Hepworth at work

Peter Lanyon and his family - until they found their own accommodation at Dunluce and then Chy an Kerris, close by in Carbis Bay.

Hepworth and Nicholson were putting down roots that would have far reaching effects. They worked together in St Ives for many years and achieved international reputations and success. However, each artist eventually followed their own path. Barbara moved into Trewyn Gardens and studio in 1950 and it immediately became her permanent home, refuge and studio for the rest of her life. They divorced in 1951. Ben moved from Chy-an-Kerris in 1955 to live at Trezion, with a view to Smeaton's Pier, and out in the bay, Godrevy lighthouse. He left the town in 1958 to live in Switzerland.

Barbara Hepworth in her garden

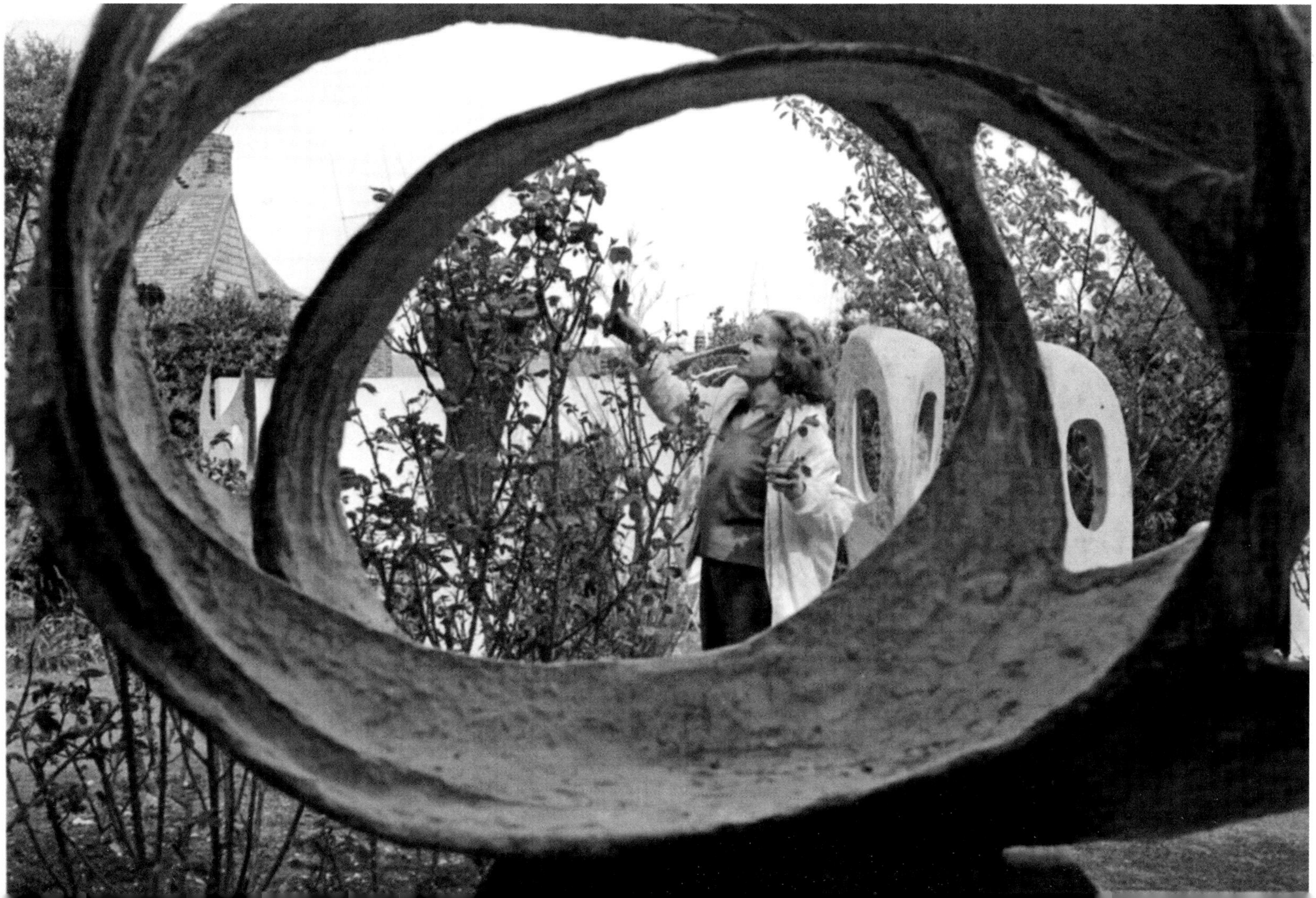

Assistants for Hepworth

In 1950 Hepworth had been invited to represent sculpture in the British Pavilion in Venice for the International Biennale. Also represented were the painters John Constable and Matthew Smith. Barbara Hepworth was the major British sculptor. She enlisted two extra assistants, Terry Frost and John Wells to help with the carving of *Contrapuntal Forms*. Two rooms were allocated to display 40 of her sculptures with drawings and paintings. Misome Peile visited Trewyn at 11 o'clock at night to view Barbara's work. '… the moonlight shone on a huge tarpaulin covering sculpture looming up in the garden. Inside and upstairs on the bare boards stood a number of carvings in wood and stone… the effect of tension, delicacy and strength was tremendous.'

Over the years Barbara recruited the help of many artists, such as Breon O'Casey, Roger Leigh, Brian Wall, Tom Pearce, John Milne, Michael Broido, Keith Leonard, Tommy Rowe, Dicon Nance; but her chief assistant for a period of 10 years from 1949 was Denis Mitchell, who was introduced to Hepworth by Bernard Leach.

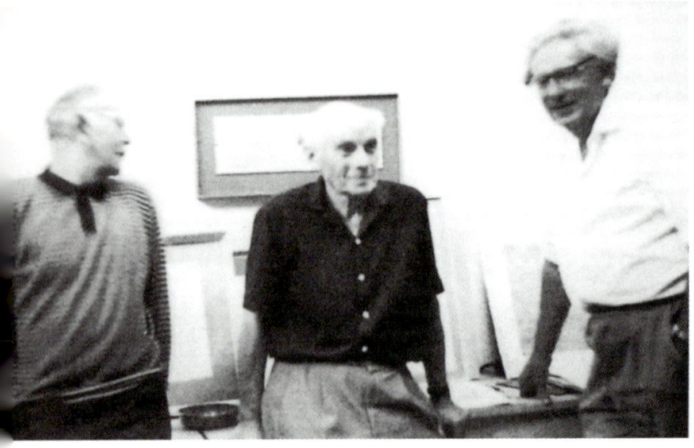

Terry Frost, Ben Nicholson, Denis Mitchell

Mitchell had worked as a miner at Pendeen, which was useful in helping him to handle tools and manipulate heavy loads. Roger Leigh said he and Hepworth trained the temporary helpers in 'grinding, drilling, tempering, polishing, packing and weight lifting.' Denis Mitchell left in 1959 to become a sculptor in his own right. He bought a house in Newlyn, La Pieta with his wife Jane, and shared a studio at Trewarveneth with John Wells.

In 1950 Tate Gallery, London, acquired its first Hepworth sculpture *Bicentric Form.* She described it as a 'fusion of two figures into one sculptural entity.'

The Festival of Britain

In 1951 several artists from Cornwall were invited by the Arts Council to exhibit large works for the Festival of Britain, among them were Peter Lanyon, Patrick Heron, Ben Nicholson, John Tunnard, Bryan Wynter, William Scott and William Gear. Barbara Hepworth was commissioned by the Arts Council to produce a sculpture, which resulted in *Contrapuntal Forms.* In this same year the Festival of Britain authorities commissioned a piece for the Thames-side restaurant. For this she submitted *Turning Forms*.

Alongside this, Barbara, Priaulx Rainer and Michael Tippett, Cornish born composer and conductor, set up the first St Ives Festival of Music and the Arts. Also involved in the music were Peter Pears and Benjamin Britten. This led Hepworth to design sets for the stage.

Following an inspiring trip to Greece a gift of Nigerian scented guarea wood arrived in her garden in 1955. *The logs were the finest I had ever seen – most beautiful, hard, lovely warm timber.*[7] During the fifties these huge pieces were carved and the motifs of holes and string were incorporated. They were dedicated to Greece and named accordingly, with Greek titles.

Sophie Bowness commented: *Titles always came later for Hepworth, after a work was completed, and were loose associations; it would be a mistake to take them too literally. Chun Quoit* [Single Form Chun Quoit] *is a Neolithic chamber tomb of the type known as quoits in the Penwith peninsula, and is the only example in perfect condition. It is between St Ives and Land's End, in a landscape that had a profound effect on Hepworth.*[9]

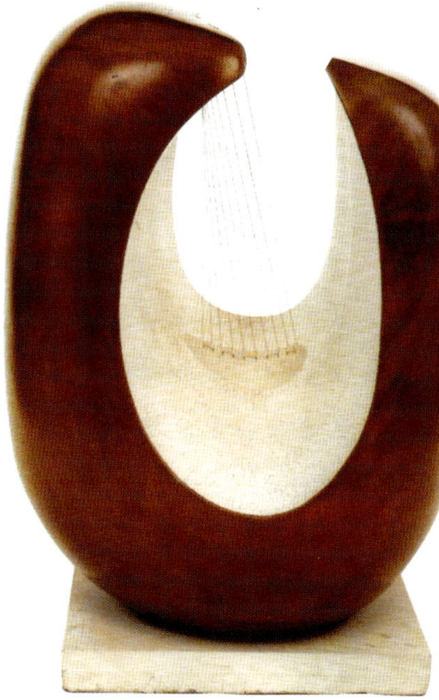

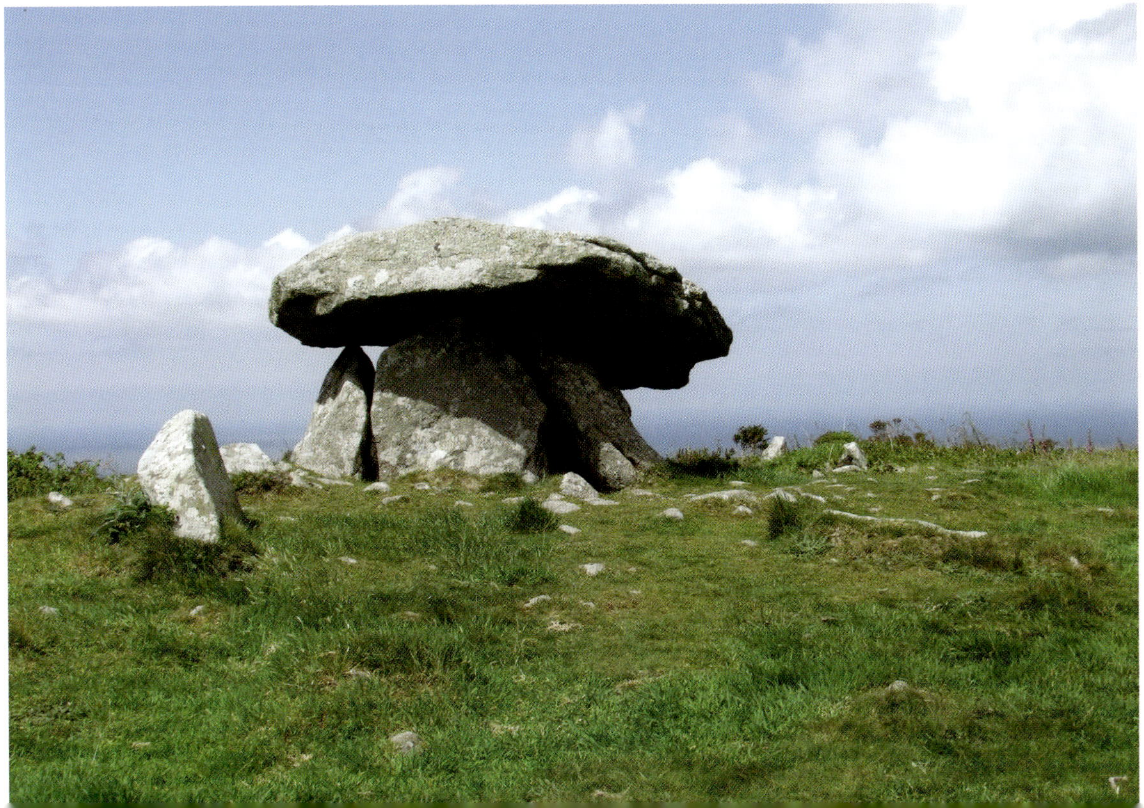

Above: 'Curved Form, Dephi', 1955

Left: Chun Quoit

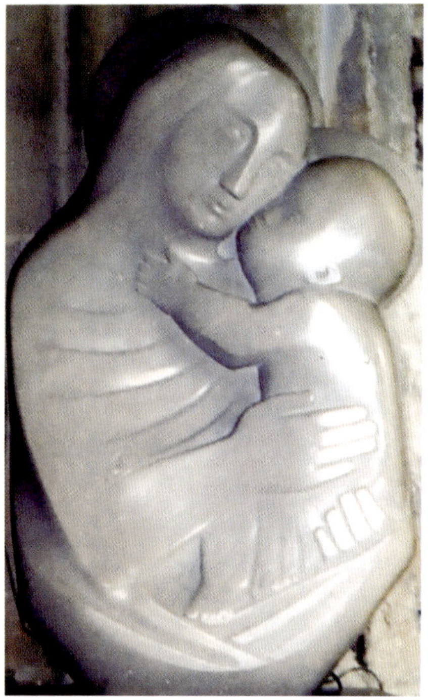

'Mother and Child' in St Ia church

Her love of landscape started in the Yorkshire Dales, sitting beside her father in his car as he travelled the countryside. Her desire to learn the techniques of carving were satisfied when, having achieved a scholarship, she spent a year in Italy. In Florence she met and fell in love with the sculptor John Skeaping. They studied the skill of carving together and travelled around Italy. She married him in Florence in 1925 and their son Paul was born in 1929.

In the Lady Chapel of St Ives Parish Church is one of her fine pieces, a sculpture in limestone of Mother and Child, carved by Barbara Hepworth in memory of Paul, who died in a flying accident over Thailand in 1953. What tender thoughts went into the carving and smoothing of that beautiful piece of stone.

The Hepworth Garden

Later in the decade Hepworth won a major prize at the International Exhibition of Modern Art, Sao Paolo, Brazil. She had sent a selection of work in wood carvings, bronze and drawings executed over the last 20 years in St Ives at her Trewyn Studio. She was also working towards a solo show in New York and some 30 sculptures were in preparation.

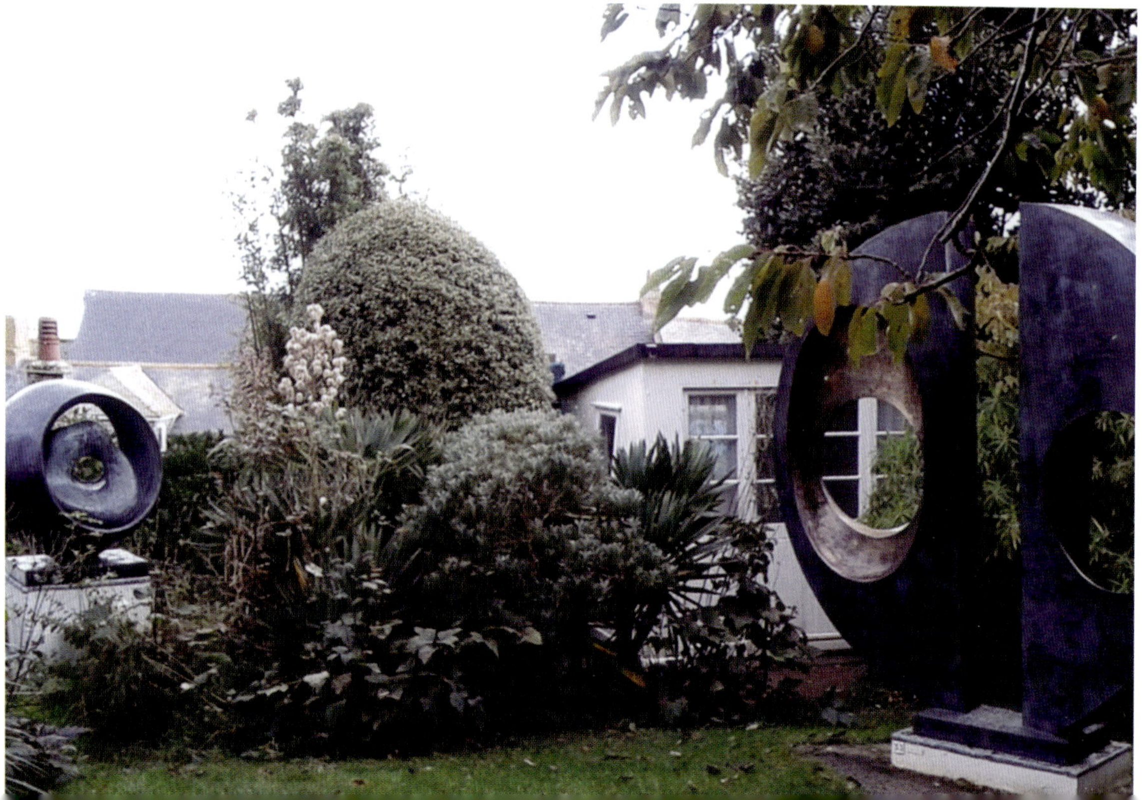

Left. *Sphere with inner form*, bronze, 1963. Right. *Two forms (divided circle)* bronze,1969

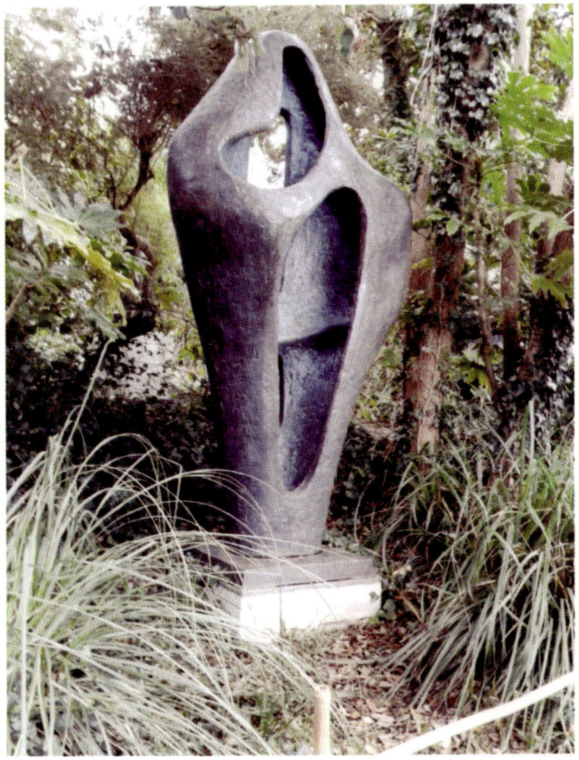

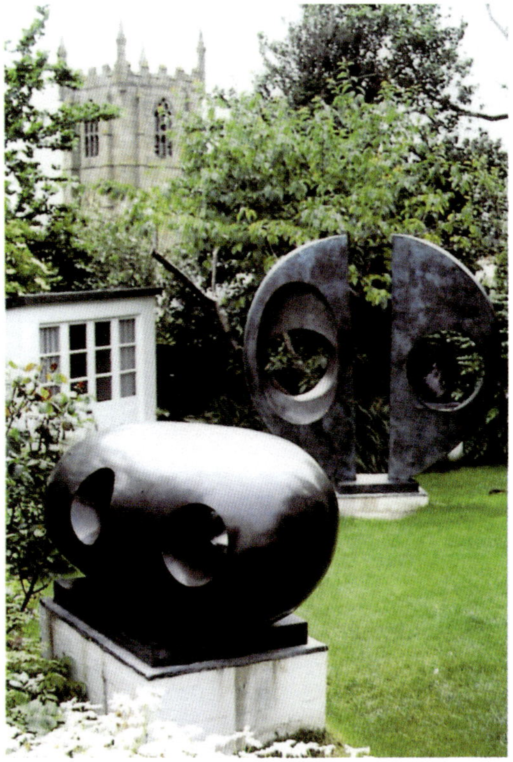

Far left: The Barbara Hepworth Garden 'Figure for Landscape', bronze 1960

Left: The garden with St Ia Church and her day chalet with the sculptures 'Riverform' and 'Two Form' (divided circle)

It seems Barbara Hepworth was interested in having her work in the public domain, rather than hidden in private collections. She therefore would have approved of 'The Plasters' 44 prototypes from the Hepworth Estate being gifted to the new Hepworth Wakefield Gallery.

Sculpture for St Ives

Her sculpture can be found in many public places in the town, as well as in her studio and garden, managed by the Tate Gallery. It stands as her permanent memorial to her artistic career and for her love and devotion to St Ives and Cornwall. The first pieces of her sculpture to be displayed in the open air were to grace the courtyards of Piazza and Barnaloft flats, which were replacement buildings for the old and dilapidated pilchard packing, salting cellars and studios on the site.

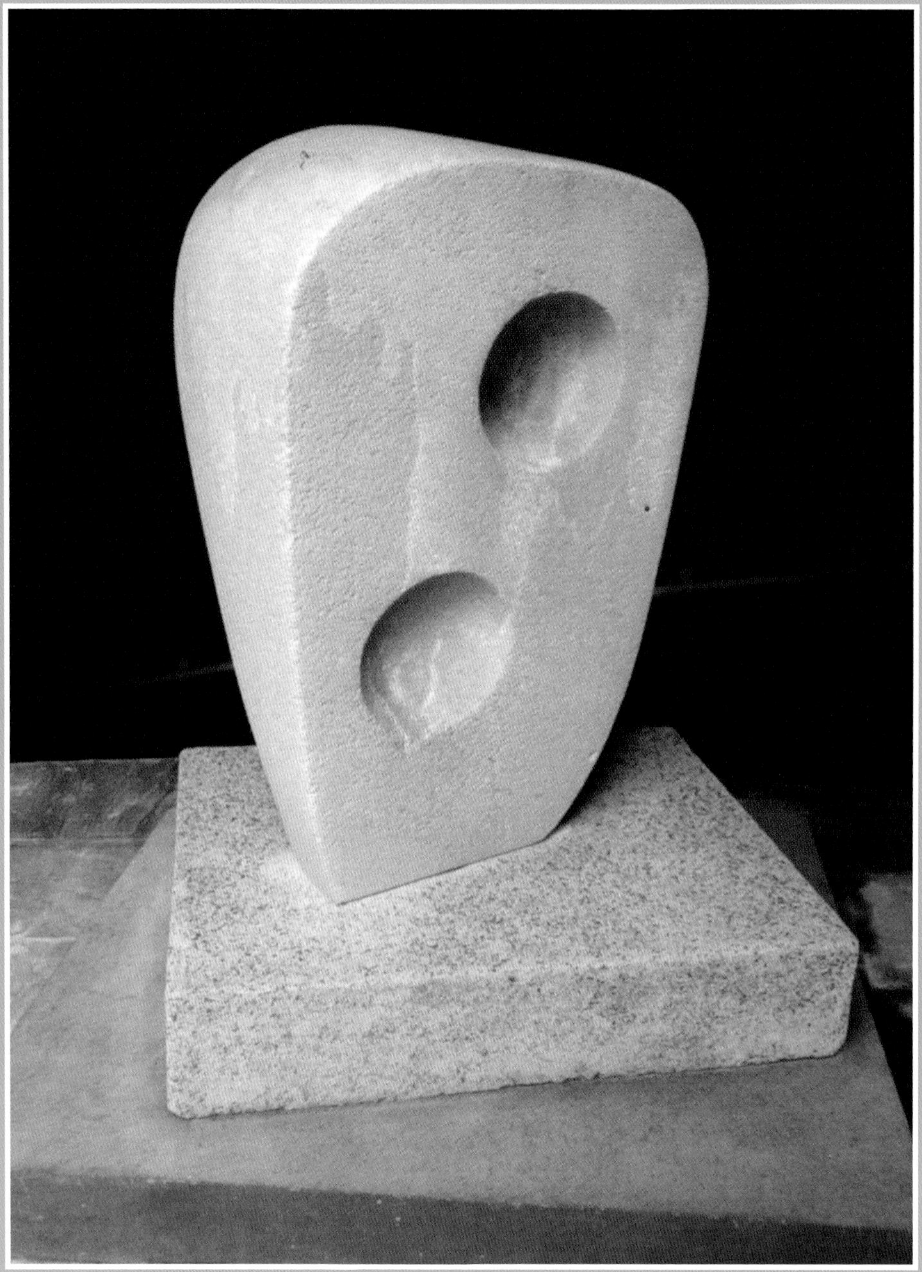

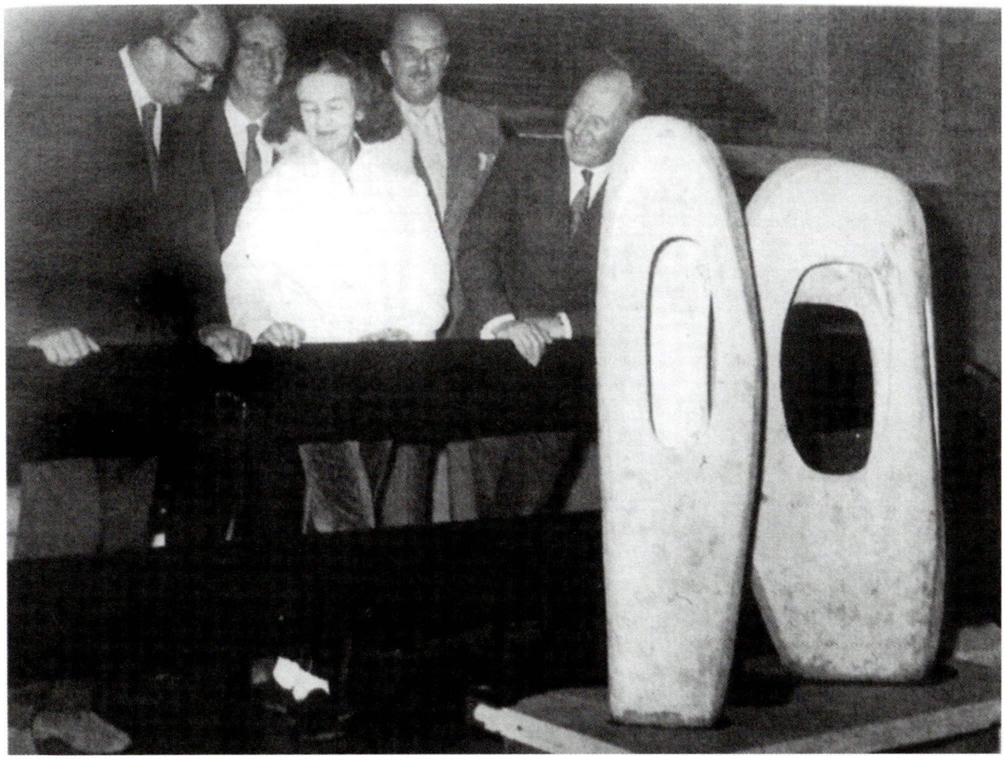

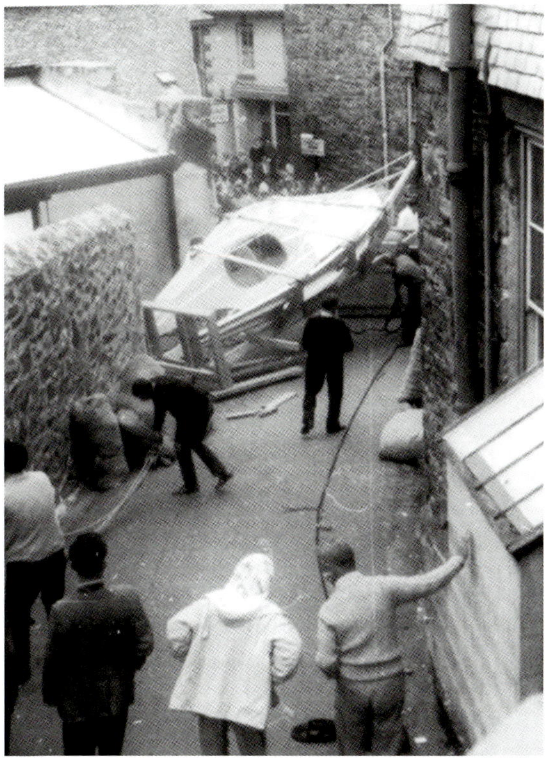

Above left: 'Two Forms in Echelon', bronze, Barnaloft

Above right: Sculpture 'Winged Figure' in transit from the Palais de Danse. Barbara Hepworth in white jacket

Opposite page: 'Single form with two hollows, Piazza'

Both buildings were the designs of Henry Cyril Gilbert (Gillie) and although, in part, were intended as flats and studios only a few artists took up residence and the majority became holiday lets for the tourist trade. However, it was through Gillie's friendship with Hepworth that she agreed to the idea of allowing her work to be shown in this environment. Here she assists at the unveiling in 1963 with councillors. Henry Gilbert stands behind Barbara Hepworth.

The Palais de Danse

In 1960 Hepworth acquired the Palais de Danse for a studio, a huge interior space and yard opposite the Hepworth Museum, where she could sculpt and carve her larger pieces. One of these was *Winged Figure* an aluminium sculpture with stainless steel rods, which was a commissioned piece for the exterior wall of John Lewis, the department store in London's Oxford Street.

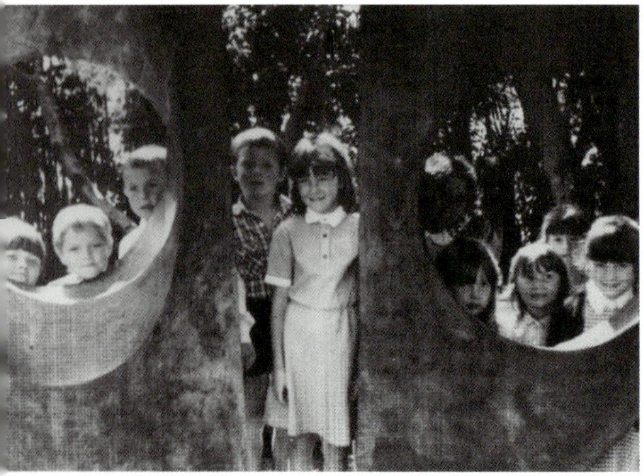

St Ives Infants School in Barbara Hepworth's sculpture garden 1985

It was at this time that Dag Hammarskjold, Secretary General of the United Nations, and she were discussing the idea of a sculpture for the United Nations building in New York and Barbara worked on the first stages of a design in her new large premises. However, tragedy struck when Dag Hammarskjold's plane was shot down over the Congo and he was killed. In spite of the personal loss of a friend, she started work on this piece, called *Single Form* which related to Hammarskjold's philosophy of life and creativity. The sculpture was eventually commissioned as a memorial and was unveiled in 1964. It stands at twenty one feet in height.

In her garden and her out-of-doors sculpture, Barbara encouraged people to touch and feel the sensation under their hands of her bronzes, stone and marble pieces. She would have enjoyed seeing the children's exploration of her work and their natural curiosity in seeing, touching and experiencing.

The Dynamics of Carving

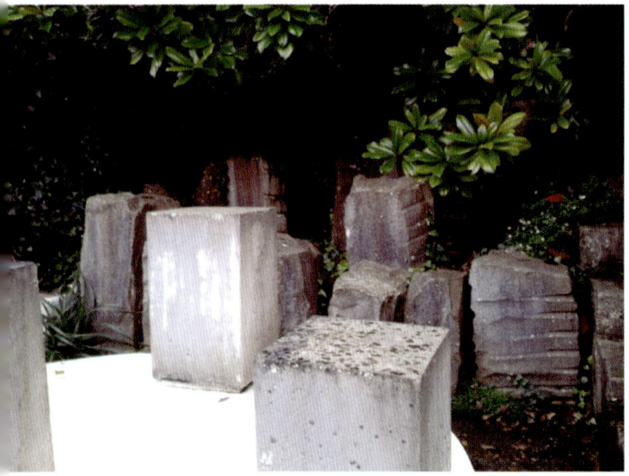

Dame Barbara's sheep

Hepworth was fascinated by the luminosity of marble and loved the painstaking process of carving by hand, ignoring any mechanical facility with its faster outcome. Her stone carving workshop in her garden was an ideal working environment. Outside, enduring the English weather, and waiting their turn to enter the carving area were her waiting blocks of marble from the Carrara mountains in Italy; she referred to these patient pieces as her sheep.

> *In sculpture there must be a complete realisation of the structure and quality of the stone or wood which is being carved. But I do not think that this alone supplies the life and quality of sculpture. I believe that the understanding of the material and the meaning of the form must be in perfect equilibrium.* [10]

Like many artists who live and work in the town, Barbara Hepworth took a civic pride in preserving the beauty, architecture and traditions of her chosen habitat. She often spearheaded and took action to protect the environment, or became involved with others of like mind. One important project was the saving of The Island from being turned into a public car park. It is an ancient site (as yet unexcavated) which had been granted a public space in 1907. She, Patrick Heron, and other artists and writers, co-operated and were successful in many campaigns.

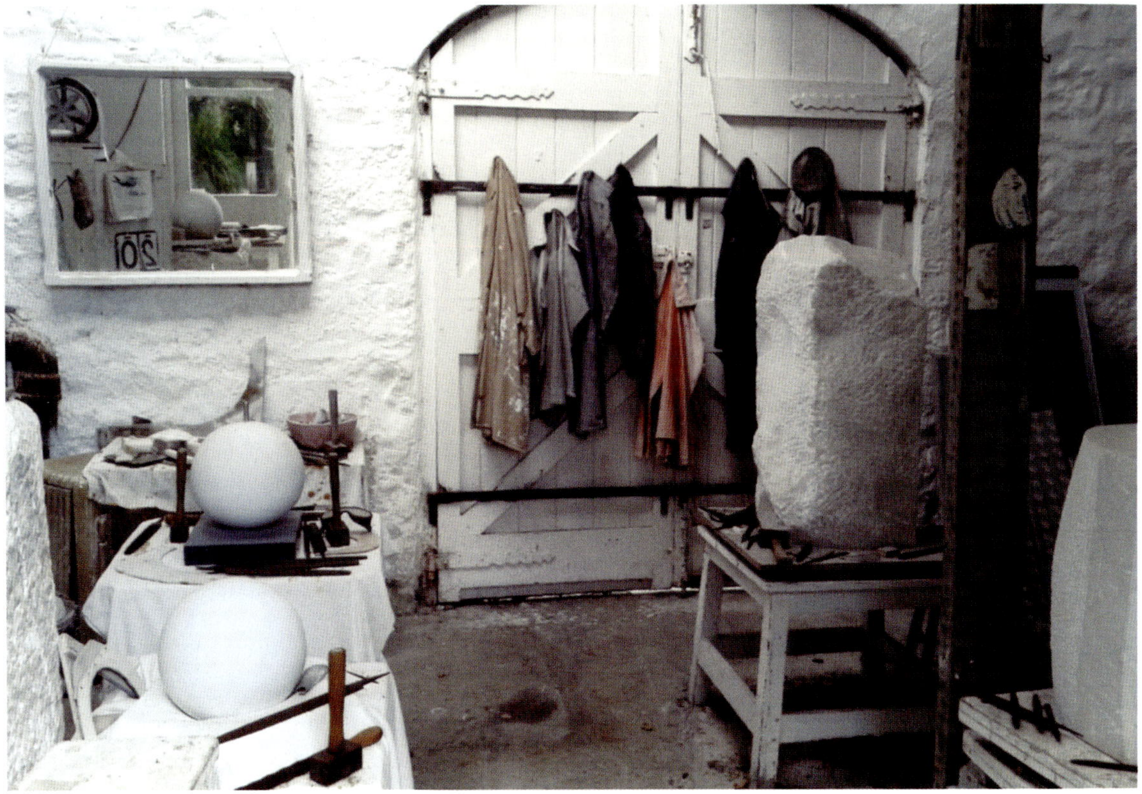

The carving workshop

Peter Lanyon

An event which created a great sadness in St Ives was the death of Cornish artist, Peter Lanyon in 1964. He died as the result of a gliding accident. This gliding activity had an enormous impact upon his paintings. He described the thermal currents of hot air in which he floated, as a world of activity as complex as the sea. He made the invisible, visible in his paintings.

Find me a thermal to speak and soar to you from
Over Lanyon Quoit and the circling stones standing
High on the moor over Gurnard's Head where some
Time three foxglove summers ago, you came.

The Thermal Stair (for the painter Peter Lanyon)
Excerpt from the poem by W.S. Graham

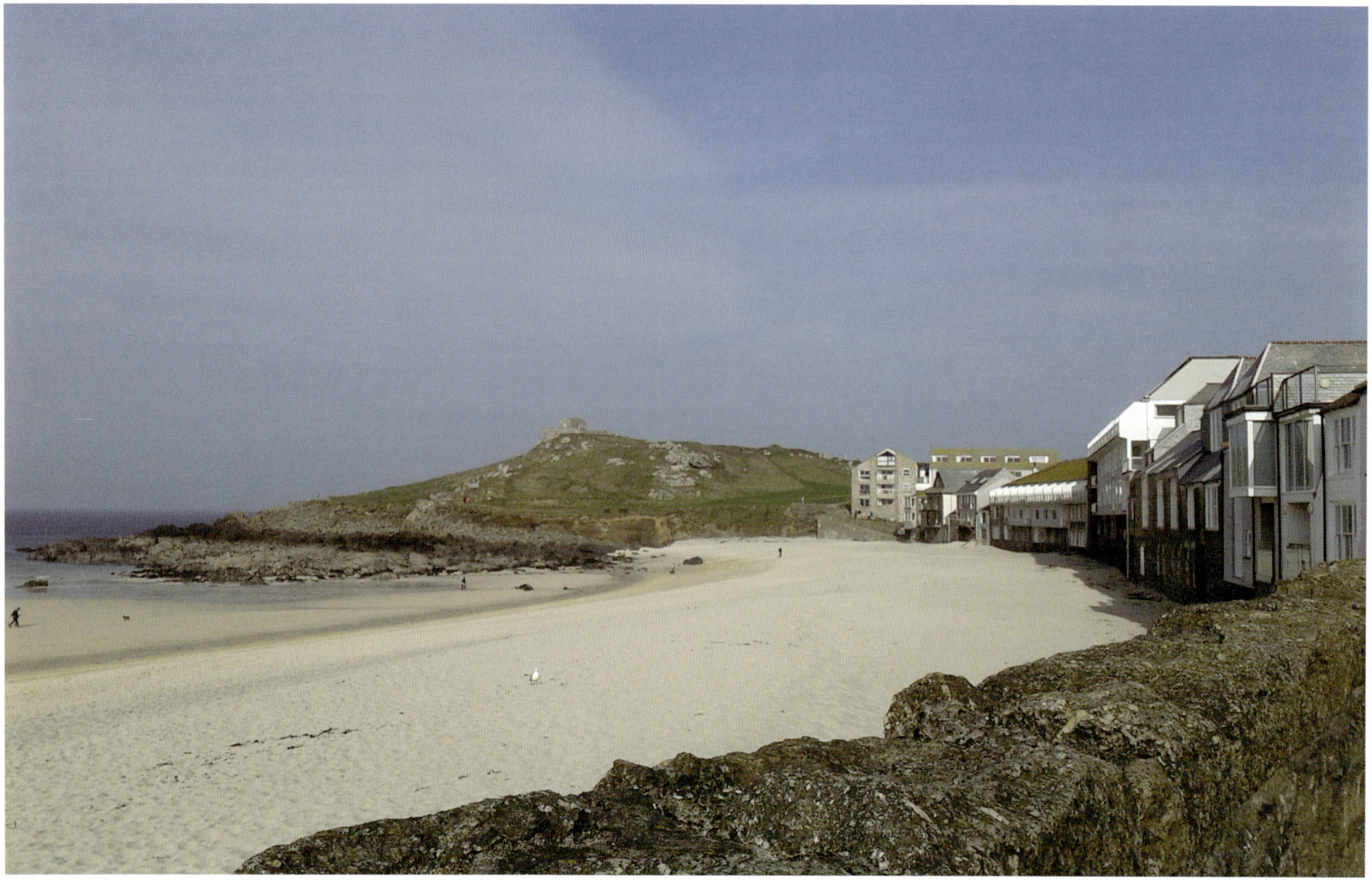

The Island and Porthmeor beach

Barbara Hepworth said at his funeral, 'He was a unique spirit. I don't suppose he knew how much we all thought of him, but we did love and admire him tremendously.' Patrick Heron said he was a Cornishman whose reputation was truly international. An oil painting by Peter Lanyon *Two Place 1962* was presented anonymously to the County Council for hanging in the new County Hall building in Truro. This same year the Tate Gallery held an exhibition *Painting and Sculpture of a Decade 1954-1964*. It included the work of Lanyon, Hepworth, Heron, Nicholson, among other European and American artists.

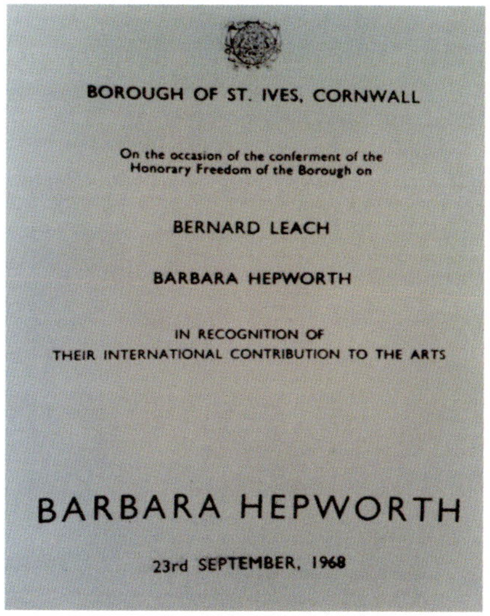

Dame Barbara

In 1958 Hepworth was given the CBE and in 1965 Barbara Hepworth was granted the honour of Dame Commander of the British Empire. She was also the first woman trustee of the Tate Gallery in London and served for seven years. She received many more honours from universities and other prestigious organisations.

Freedom of the Borough of St Ives

In 1968 The Freedom of the Borough of St Ives was granted to three major artists in the town, Bernard Leach, the potter, Ben Nicholson, the painter, and Barbara Hepworth, the sculptor, in recognition of their contribution to the arts. Nicholson was unable to attend because he was living in Switzerland. On receiving the award Barbara said:

> *I owe St Ives a tremendous debt: living here has meant a very great deal to my work. It is not just landscape, but the community, the town and everything about the place.* [11]

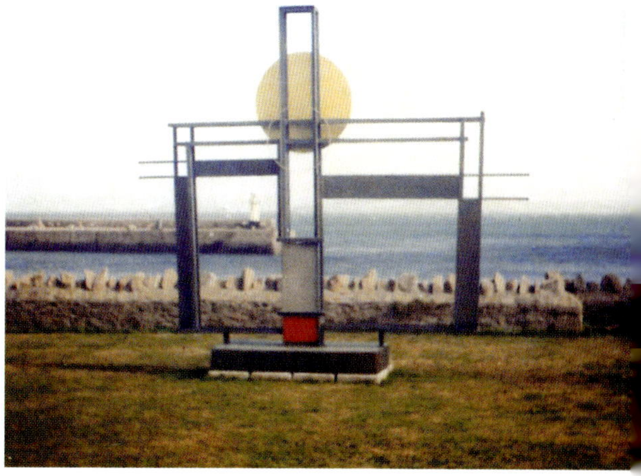

Barbara Hepworth sculpture 'Crucifixion'

To celebrate the occasion, the work of the three artists was exhibited in various venues around St Ives. Barbara Hepworth sculpture *Crucifixion* was beautifully sited in the Parish Churchyard overlooking Smeaton's Pier and St Ives Bay.

In this same year Barbara Hepworth received an Honorary Degree from Oxford University. She was also nominated a Bard of Cornwall in recognition of her international contribution to the Arts.

I chose the name Gravyor (sculptor) *and it was a memorable moment when this was conferred upon me by the Grand Bard of Cornwall at an unforgettable ceremony at St Just in Penwith.* [12]

The Hepworth Museum

Barbara Hepworth was resident in St Ives until her death in her Trewyn Studio in 1975. In 1976, according to Barbara's wishes, the Hepworth Museum opened to the public. The lower ground floor was given over to memorabilia, the first floor to works through the different periods of her life and in the garden various large works were displayed among the trees and flowers. Her workshop remained untouched from the time of her death. Hepworth's daughters, Sarah and Rachel, were able to relinquish their obligation to their mother's wishes to open her home to the public when, in1980, the museum was offered to the Tate for the nation. The Museum is a lasting tribute to Dame Barbara Hepworth's great accomplishments.

'Epidaurous', Barbara Hepworth bronze sculpture on the Malakoff

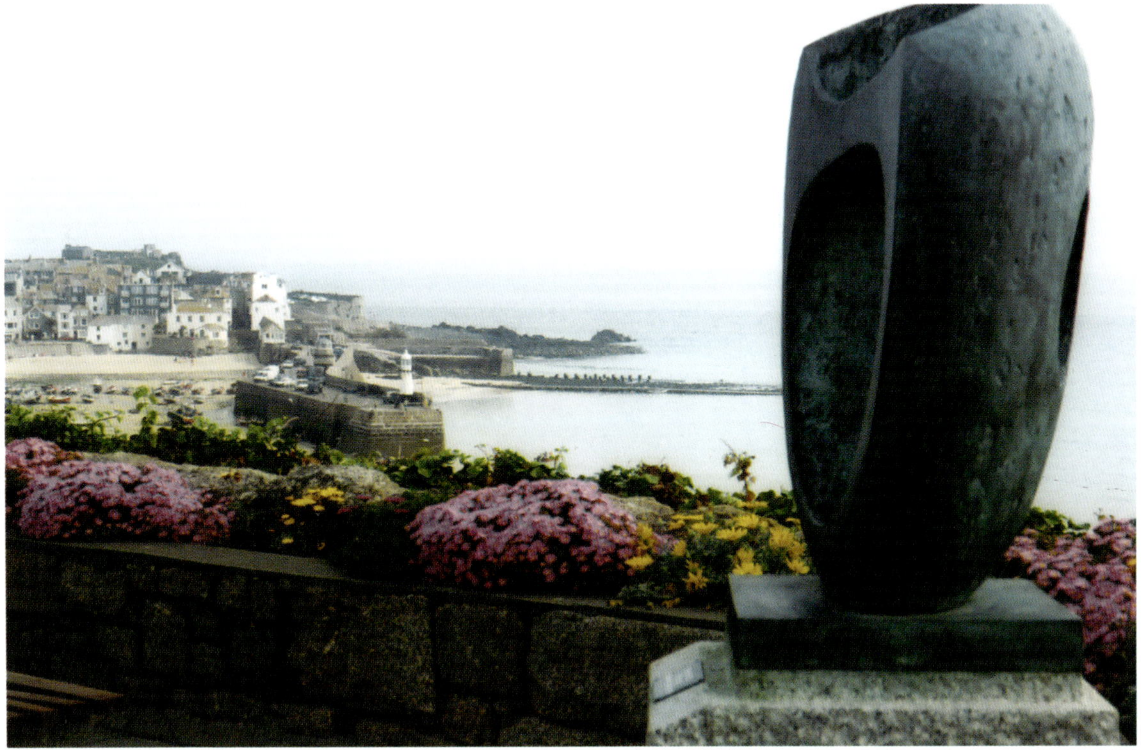

SMART REGENERATION

Borlase Smart John Wells Trust

THE BORLASE SMART John Wells Trust worked for many years to raise the money to repair and renovate the buildings on Porthmeor beach so that work places for fishermen, artists and the St Ives School of Painting could continue in the heart of Downalong. The newly established *Smart Regeneration* committee raised £70,000 from a local appeal, which helped the Trust to reach its £4 million target.

Borlase Smart John Wells Trust. Porthmeor Studios Manager, Chris Hibbert; Vice Chairman, Jane Val Baker, Director; Construction Manager, Chris Symons; Architect, M J Long; Construction Partner, Paul Whiston and Cornwall's Capital Projects Officer, Tamsin Daniel

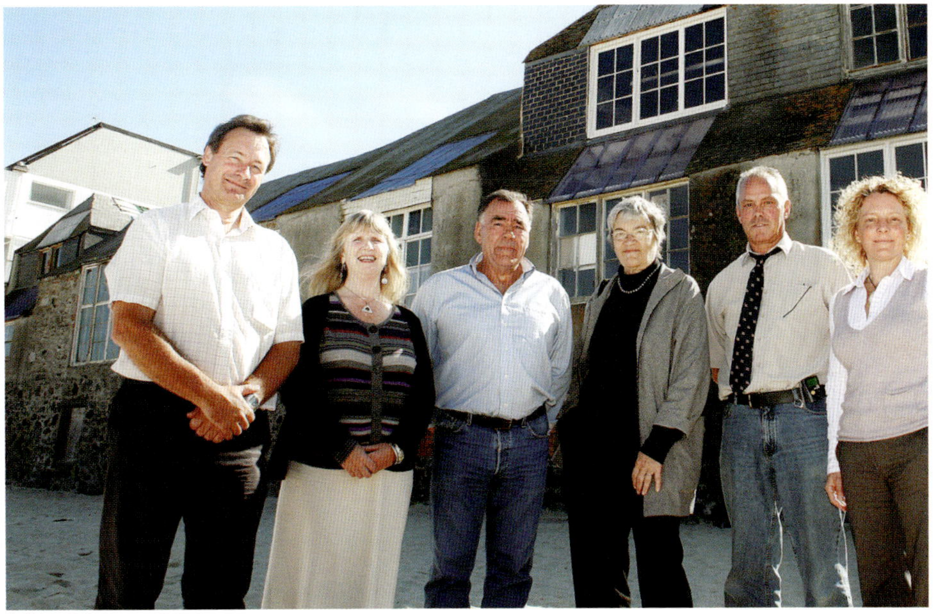

The studios and fish lofts acquired major funding for a total regeneration of the buildings and to save the site being turned into luxury holiday flats. It was time for the local fishermen and artists to reaffirm their traditions of living and working together to save the building for the town and the livelihoods of both occupations. They were united under a fund-raising committee. The buildings were frail; the hope of them surviving for much longer was a serious concern.

However, in the reliability, trust, determination and gallant efforts of a handful of people, who recruited a much larger group to carry out their plans, the Porthmeor Regeneration programme was completed in 2012; on time, on schedule and on budget.

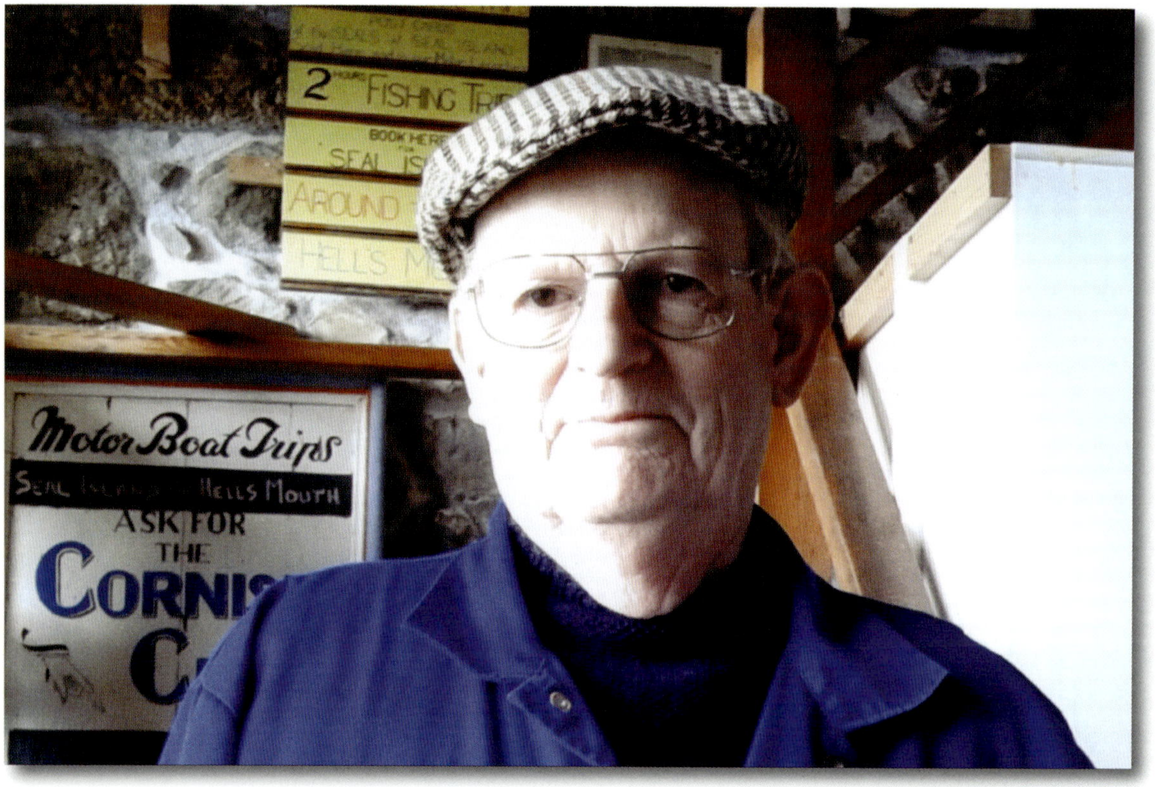

Brian Stevens

St Ives born and bred. I am the Honorary Curator of the St Ives Museum and recorder for the St Ives Old Cornwall Society. Having such a love for my own town I regret that so much is now devoid of the old traditions and industries which were associated with the Port and Town; the Fishing Industry is just one of these researches.

When the plight of the Porthmeor Studios became so serious, I wrote several articles in *The St Ives Times & Echo* that highlighted their importance; stressing then that it was the ancient pilchard fishery that built Downalong, and later these Studios over the great Fish Curing Cellars beneath, proving that Artists and Fishermen have worked together in harmony there for 120 years. Helping save this vital piece of Art and Maritime history is the aim, and I look forward to it continuing.

Meanwhile, as the Museum's Curator, I have worked over the past few years to restore an original Fish Curing Cellar within its interior and have lectured on the heyday of Seine-net fishing for pilchards on many occasions, emphasing that if you do not gather up the fragments which remain then they will be lost. At the Museum my task carries on to glean and gather together the town's history to pass on to future generations.

Jane Val Baker

I have had a long affinity with the studios as I grew up on Porthmeor beach in an artistic family, my mother Jess was a potter and my father Denys an author of over 100 books and editor of the *Cornish Review.* Our house was the hub of the artistic community. When I was 10, I climbed a ladder from the beach to a studio and met Wilhelmina Barns Graham, I was in awe I did not know there were women painters. I would often visit; she called me her 'water nymph' as I was invariably in a wet bathing suit. We kept in touch and in the last years of Willie's life she trusted me to help her regularly in her studio.

I returned to Cornwall after a career in film editing at the BBC where I was also involved in equal opportunities. In my last year I developed a conference for the European Union on Equality in Broadcasting.

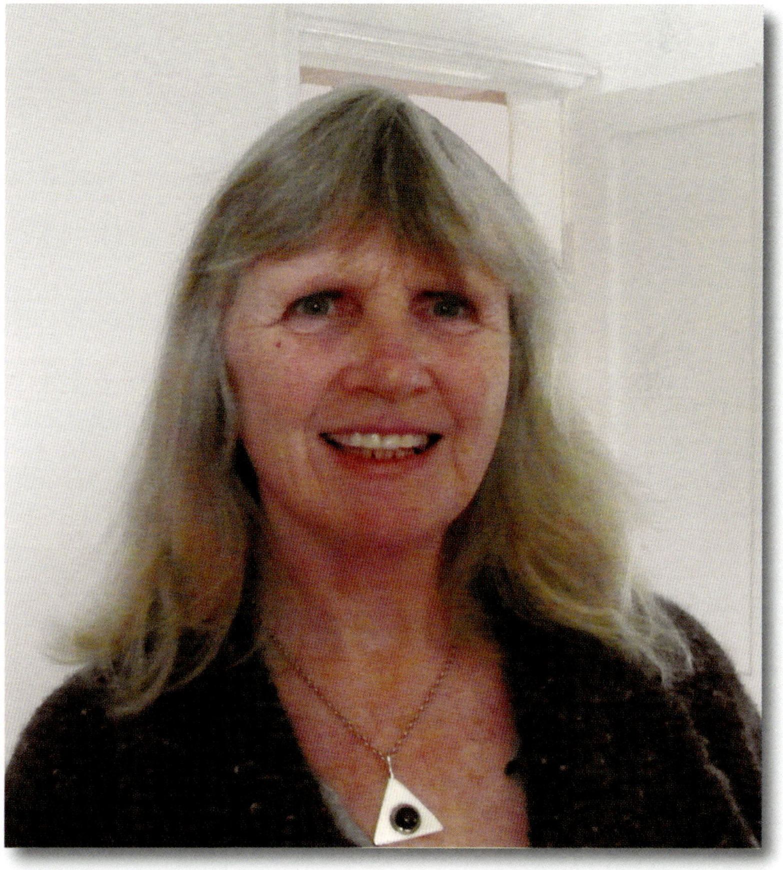

I always maintained an interest in the arts in Cornwall and was honoured when Sir Nicholas Serota asked me to become a Trustee of the BSJW Trust. I have been responsible for producing 2 Portfolios of our tenants work and co-ordinating art shows and events to raise funds and awareness. I am now Vice Chair of the Borlase Smart John Wells Trust.

Right: At work in the fish cellars

Below left and right: Trustees of the St Ives School of Painting inspecting the work in hand. Original ceiling to be protected by internal cladding and new roof

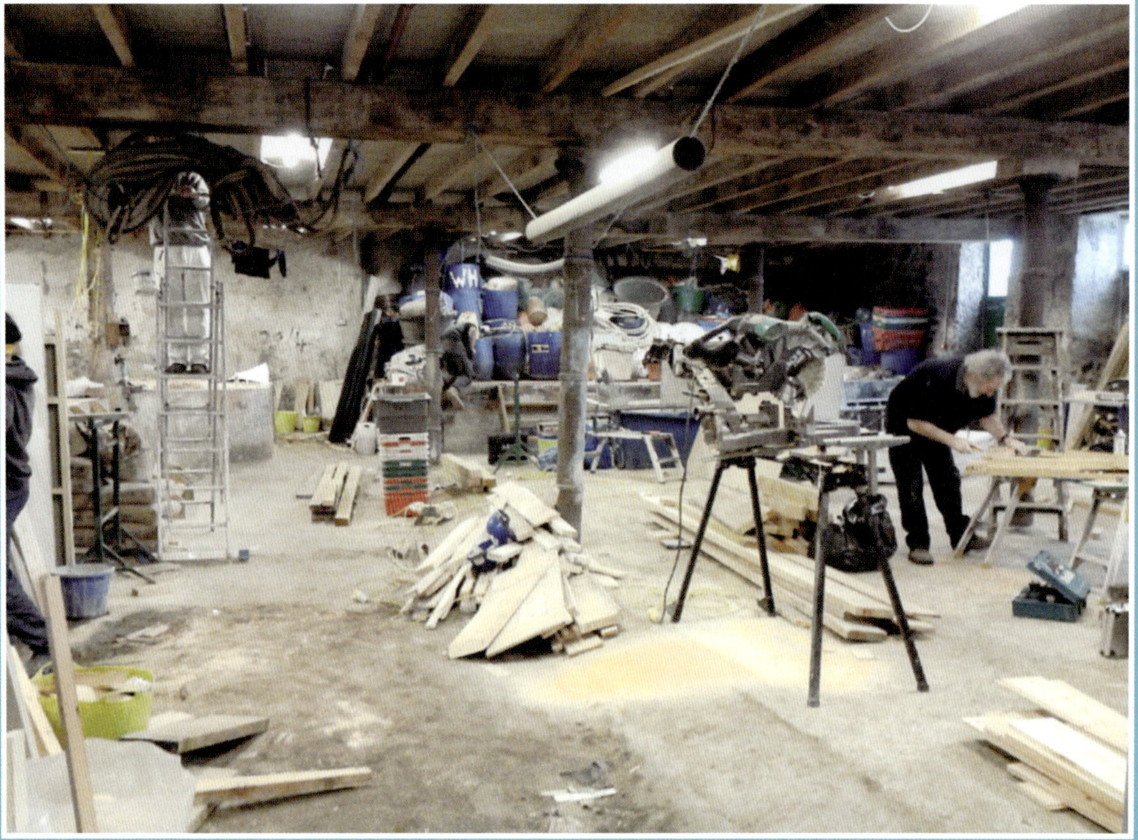

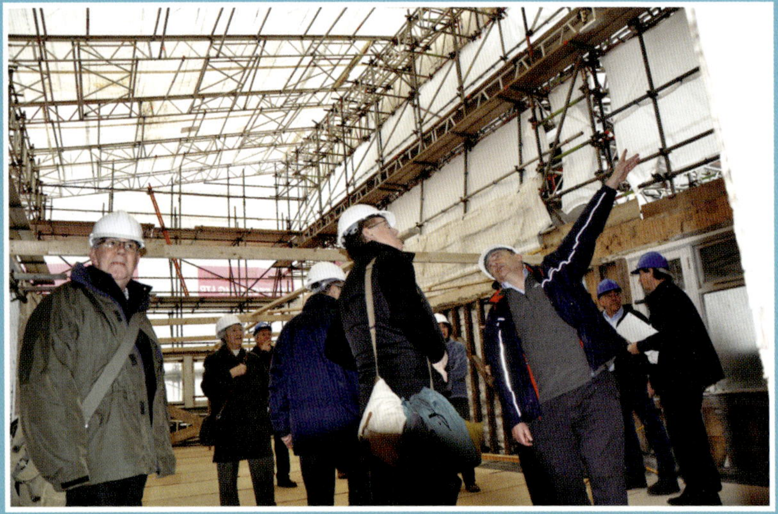

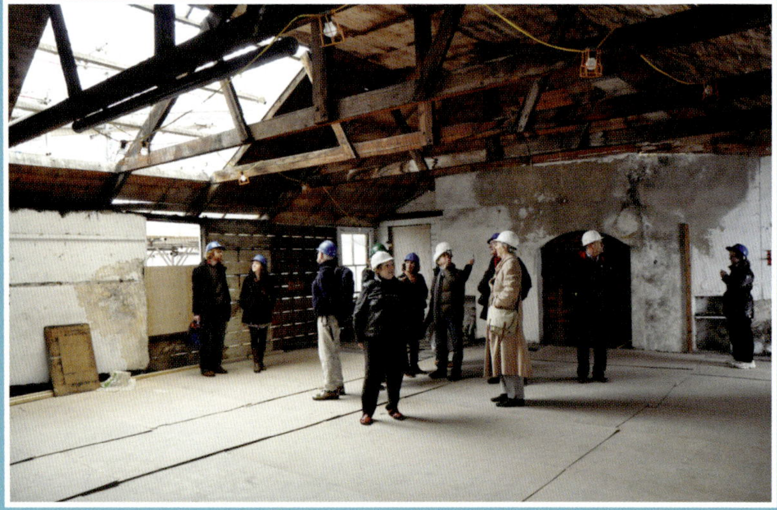

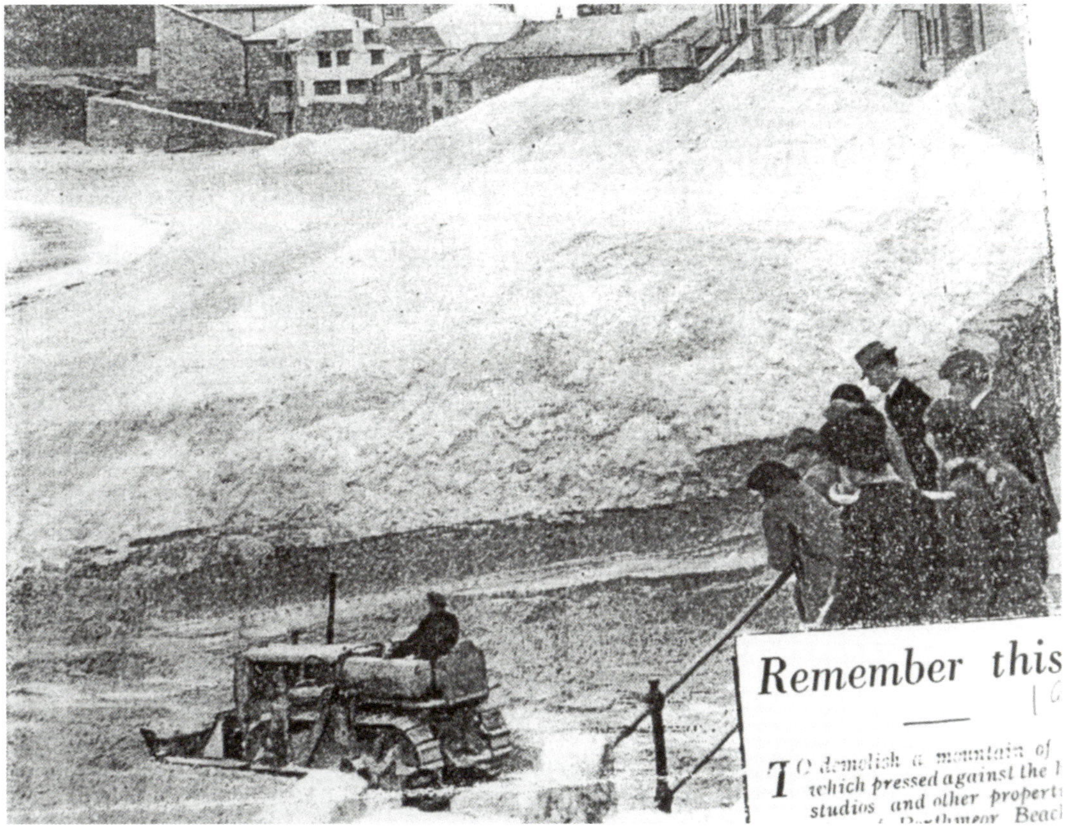

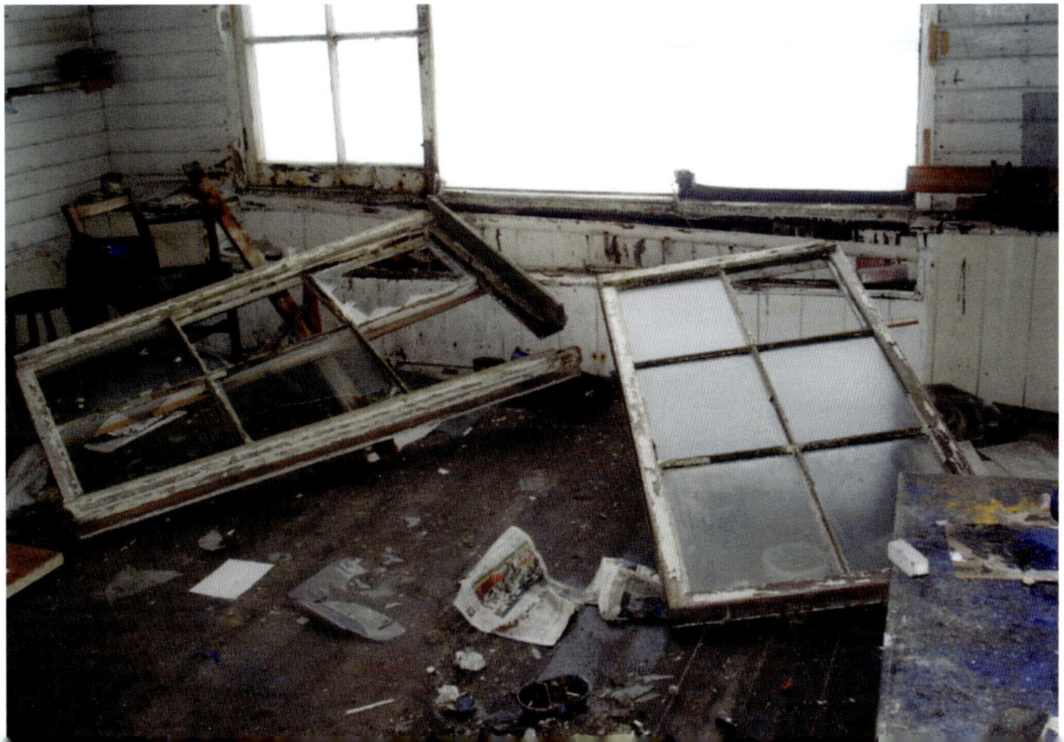

The Old and the New

An invasion of sand on Porthmeor Beach 1952

John Emanuel's studio after a storm in 2008

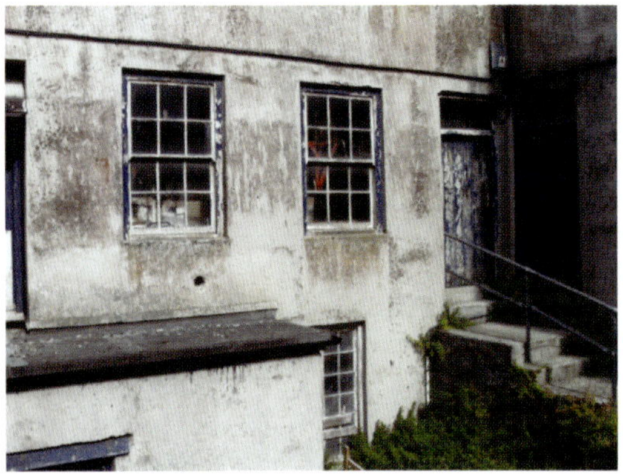

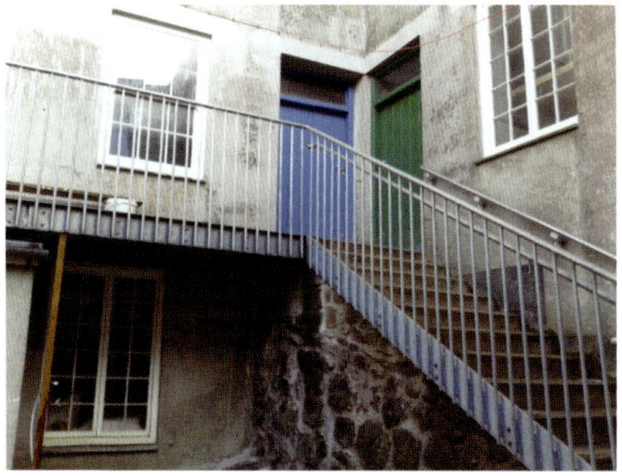

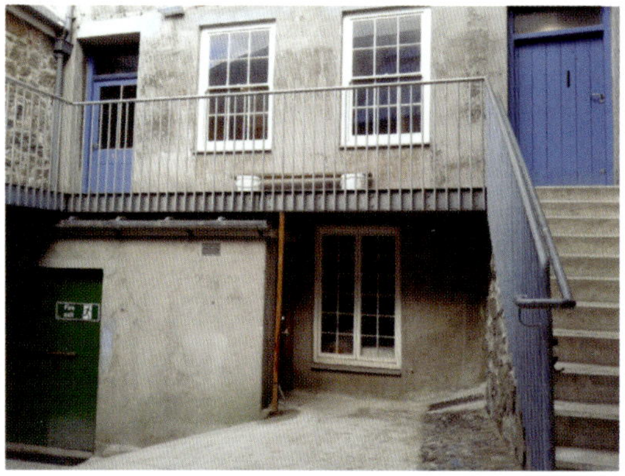

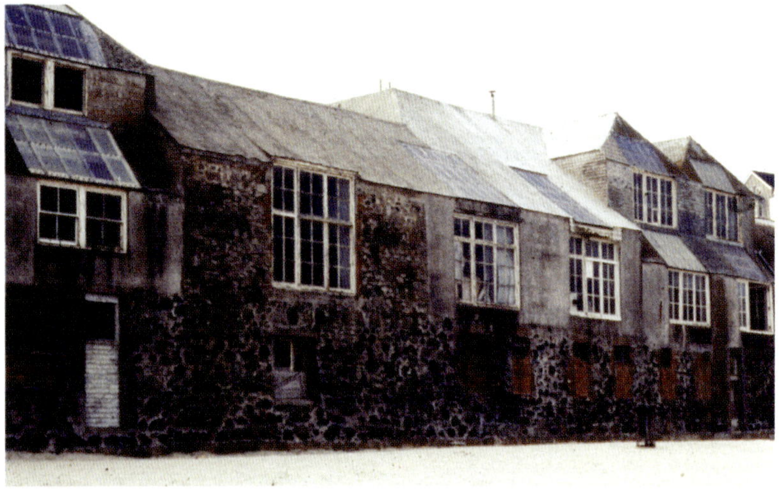

Top left: The old courtyard. Above left and right The new inner courtyard

Left: Porthmeor studios before renovation

Opposite page, top left: From Porthmeor beach before renovation
bottom left: After renovation with extra studios

Far right: 'Porthmeor Beach' by Kim Lynch

Porthmeor Studios and Fish Lofts with Improvements

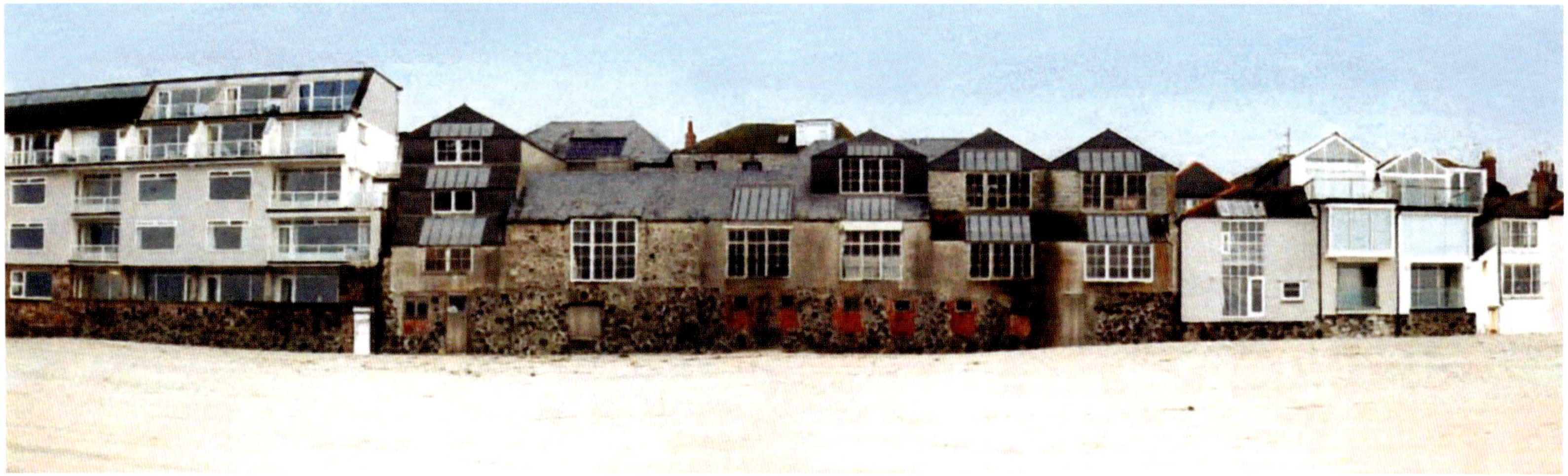

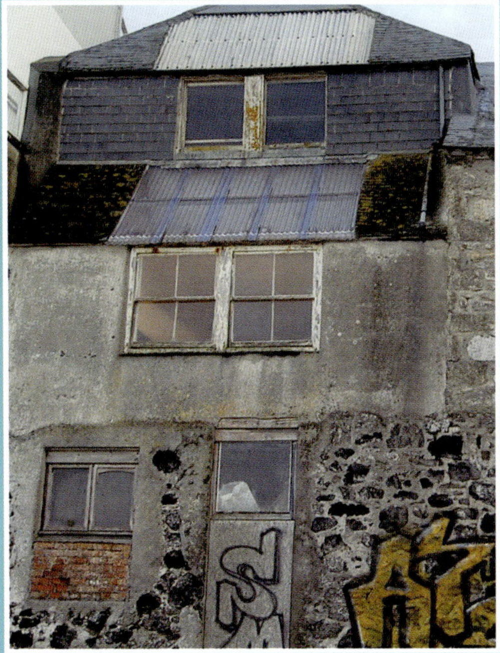

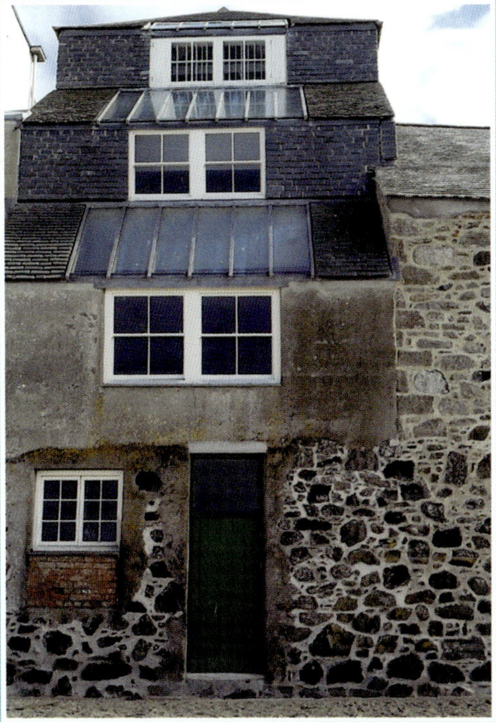

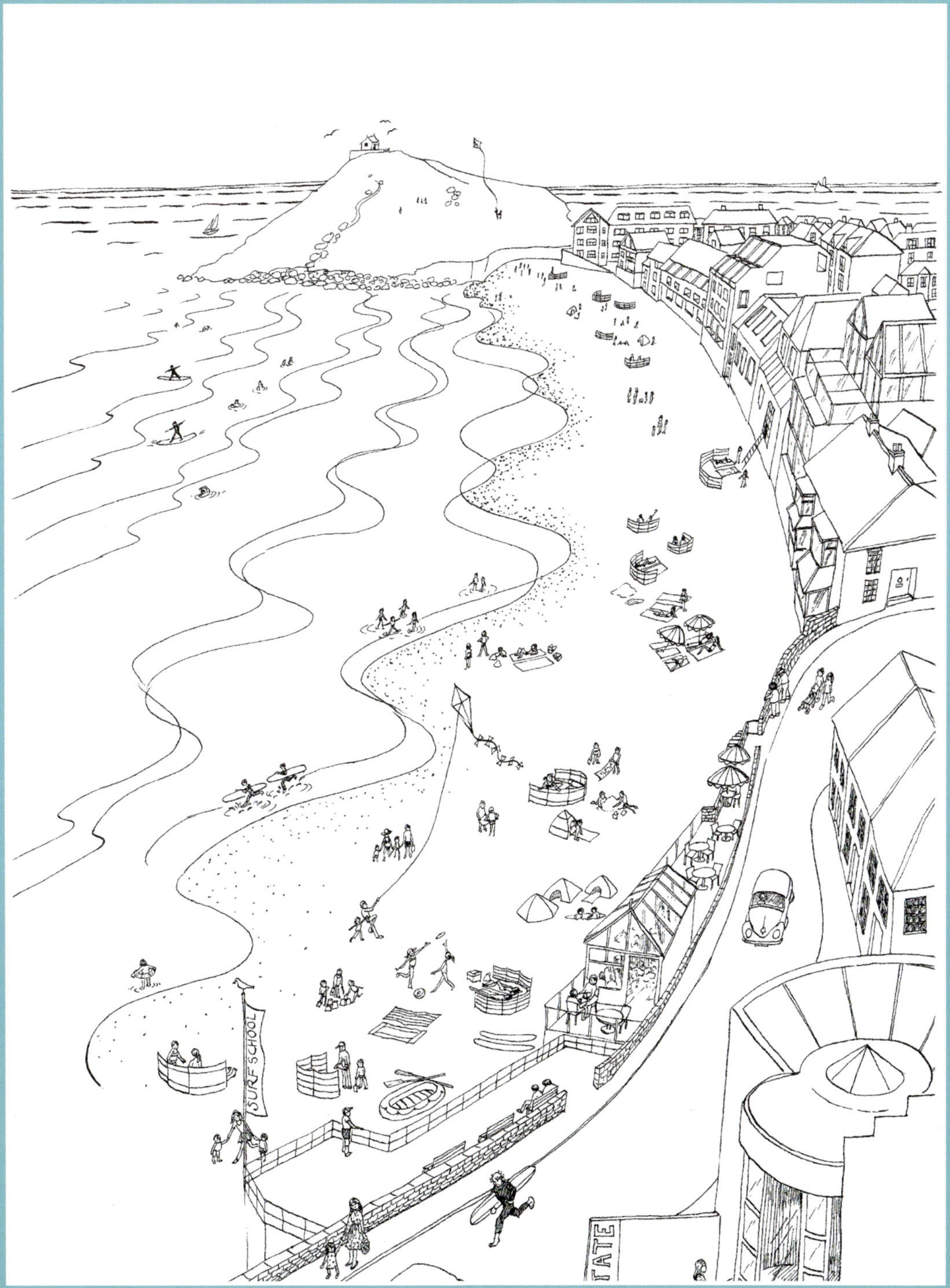
SURF SCHOOL
TATE

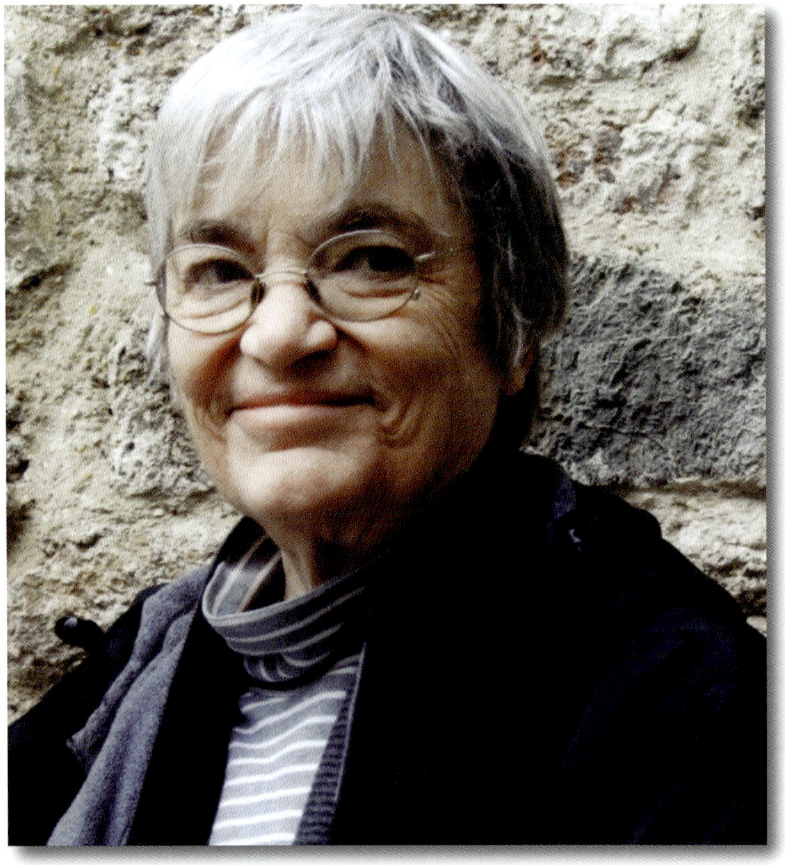

Architect M J Long

I would describe the experience of entering one of the huge Porthmeor studios for the first time as a 'through the looking glass experience'. Especially at high tide, and during one of the frequent Atlantic gales, a Porthmeor studio could be the quarter deck of a ship at sea. The groans of the timber were atmospheric, but also symptomatic of a building at risk, and the painter tenants testified to the number of paths used by rain and sea to get into the building.

Our challenge was to repair the building, and increase the number of studios, but it was agreed that the work would have to be done in a sympathetic manner if the fragile beauty of the place was to be preserved.

The architects took great pleasure in measuring and drawing by hand every board and brick in the building.

We devised a method of inserting the necessary insulation and fire separation while keeping as much of the old fabric in place as possible.

Architect Rolfe Kentish

When walls had to be stripped to restructure, repair, or insulate, the boards were numbered and reinstalled in their original location.

Improvements were made; glass skylights replaced the plastic ones that had been installed, and wood stoves were specified to replace the ones that had been removed. Lighting track was provided to allow some flexibility for painters to choose their own way of lighting their work places.

Rolfe Kentish made it his particular business to become an expert in the reinstallation of wet laid scantle slate roofs.

I invented an almost undetectable method for introducing ventilation into the roof without changing its appearance. And I enjoyed working with washed sand from the beach as the original builders had done.

Both Long and Kentish found the project one of the most satisfying of their long careers.

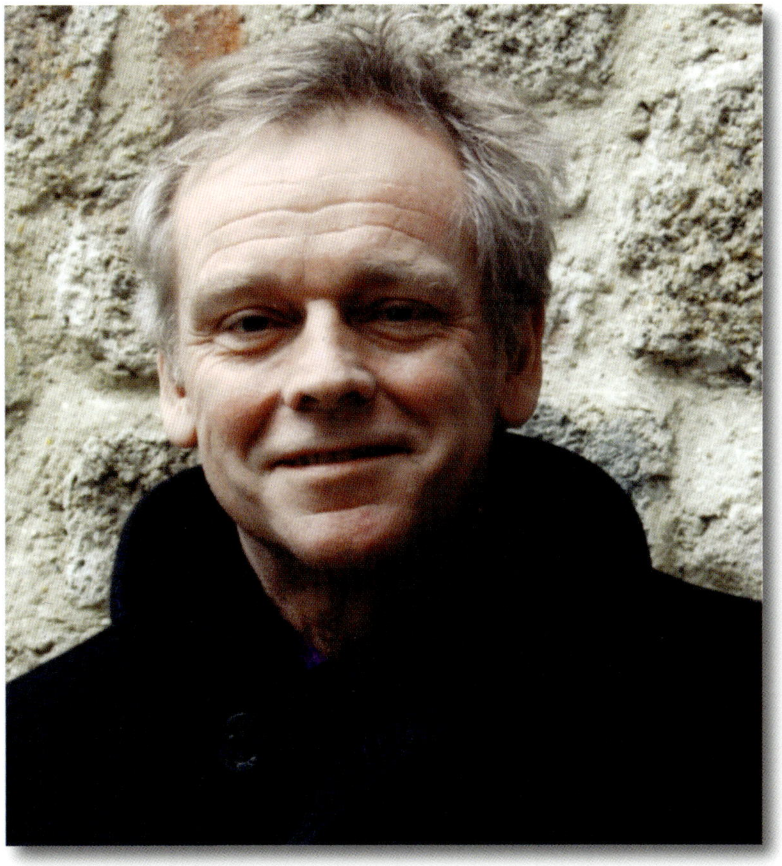

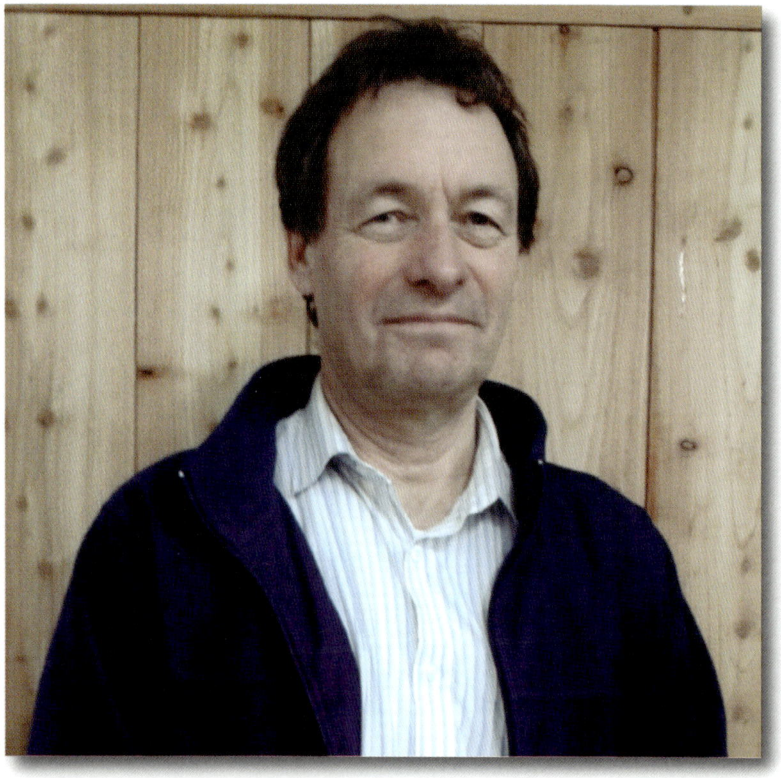

Chris Hibbert

Chris Hibbert was appointed Trust Manager in 2005, and his main priority was to develop and fundraise for the repair and renovation of Porthmeor Studios and Cellars.

Through working at Trebah Garden, I had built up experience of working with a number of arts and heritage projects, and this understanding has been invaluable. This was a complex project with many different funders, and it has taken a long time to come to fruition. However this delay allowed us more time to work with the tenants and better understand the needs of the building.

Working on a Grade II* listed building calls for exceptional care and sensitivity, and we are indebted to the design team led by architects Long & Kentish, Project Manager Trevor Humphreys, who made sure that it was completed on time and within budget, and the exceptional skills and workmanship of St Ives-based contractor Symons Construction. It is very reassuring that all the skills needed to look after this building are in the local workforce. I have particularly enjoyed working alongside the artists and fishermen, and learning more about the amazing heritage of the building, the fishing industry and the artists who have worked here. It's been a real education.

Ross Williams

Ross Williams became a trustee of the Borlase Smart John Wells Trust in 2004 and has been its Chair since 2005.

I grew up in Redruth, but have had close links with St Ives for many years – my family were involved in building projects including Barnaloft and Piazza from the 1950s onwards and my father chaired the Penwith Society of Arts in the 60s. Seeing the Porthmeor Studios restoration through to its completion has been a hugely rewarding project – there were times when it seemed like an impossible task, but we have had amazing support from our funders; from a great team of designers and builders; from our own very small staff team; and from the artists, fishermen and wider community of St Ives.
Our thanks are due to all of them.

In my day job I manage an arts organisation in Redruth which amongst other projects runs Krowji, a studio complex which houses about 100 creative practitioners. I feel that being involved with the capital schemes at Porthmeor and the BSJW's other studios in Newlyn has been a hugely useful process.

Cornwall is a small and very well connected place and it's great that everyone can work together in a collaborative and mutually beneficial way.

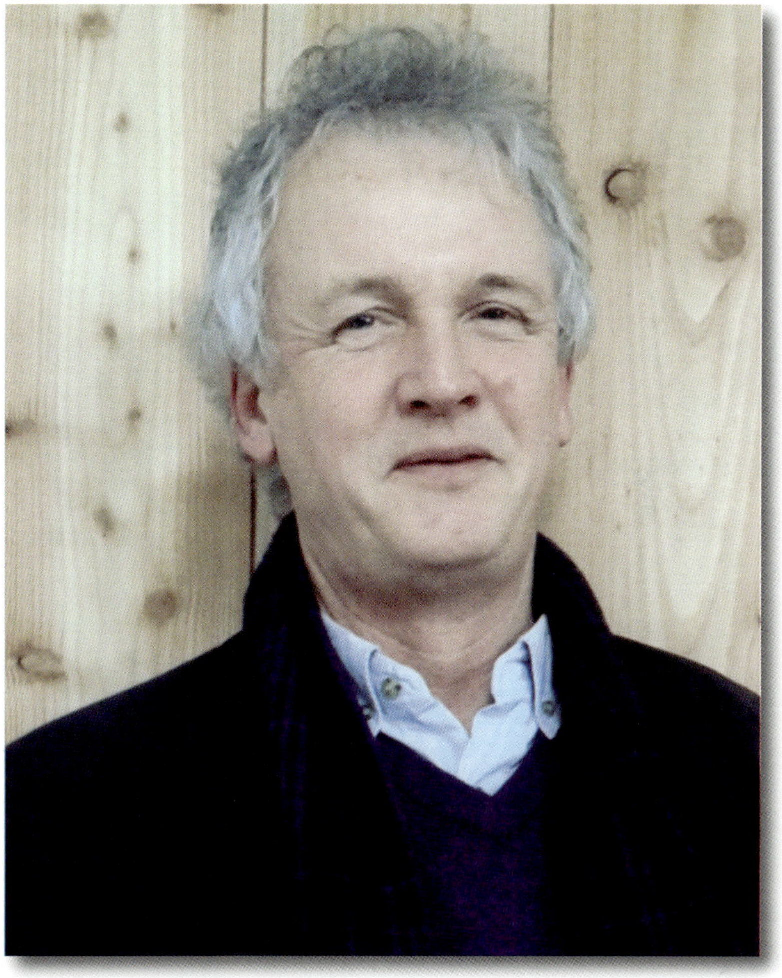

Celebrating the completion of the Porthmeor Studios Project in 2012 Jane Val Baker, Chris Hibbert, Janet Street Porter, Ross Williams, Sir Nicholas Serota

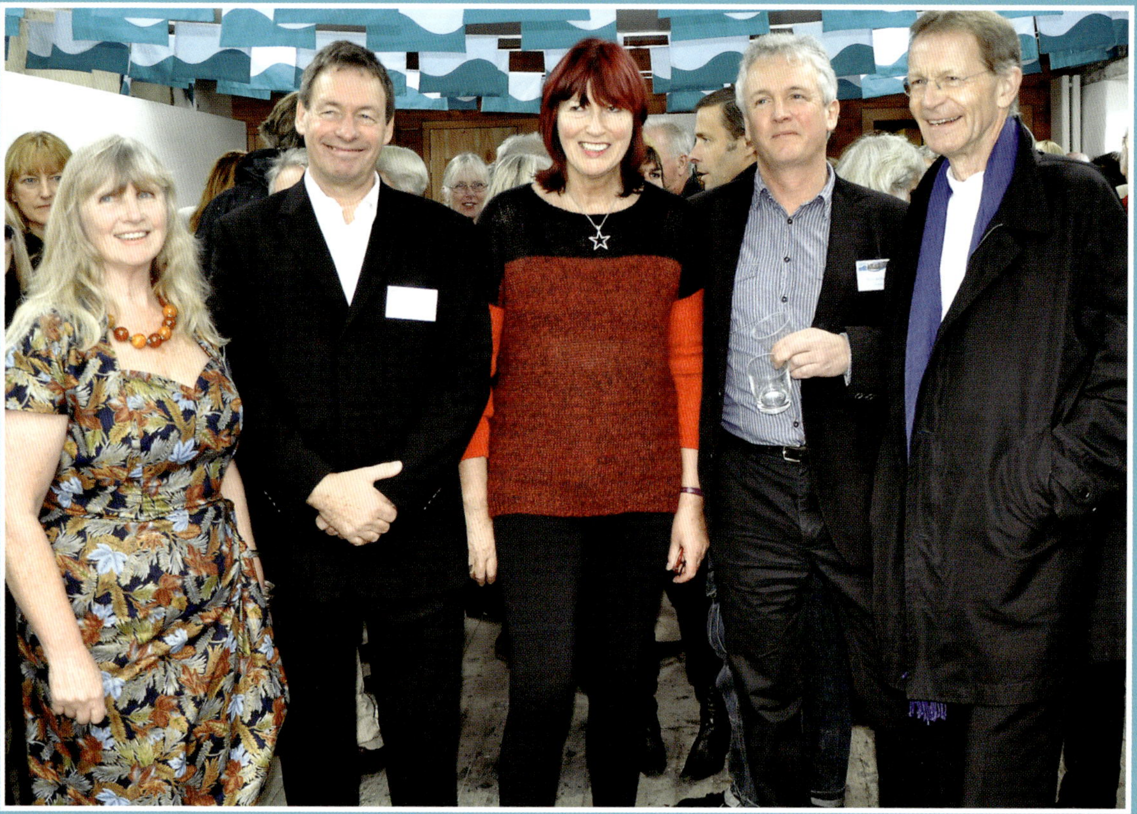

Below: Addition of a lift and staircase; The old and the new

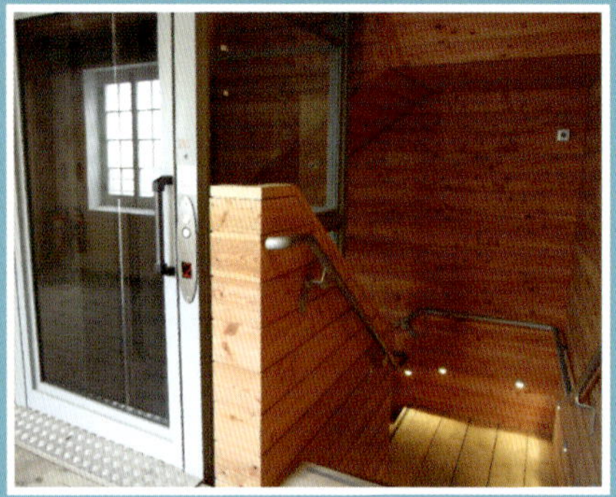

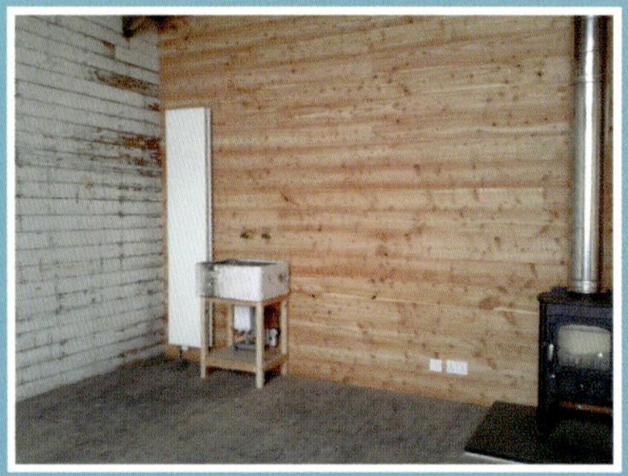

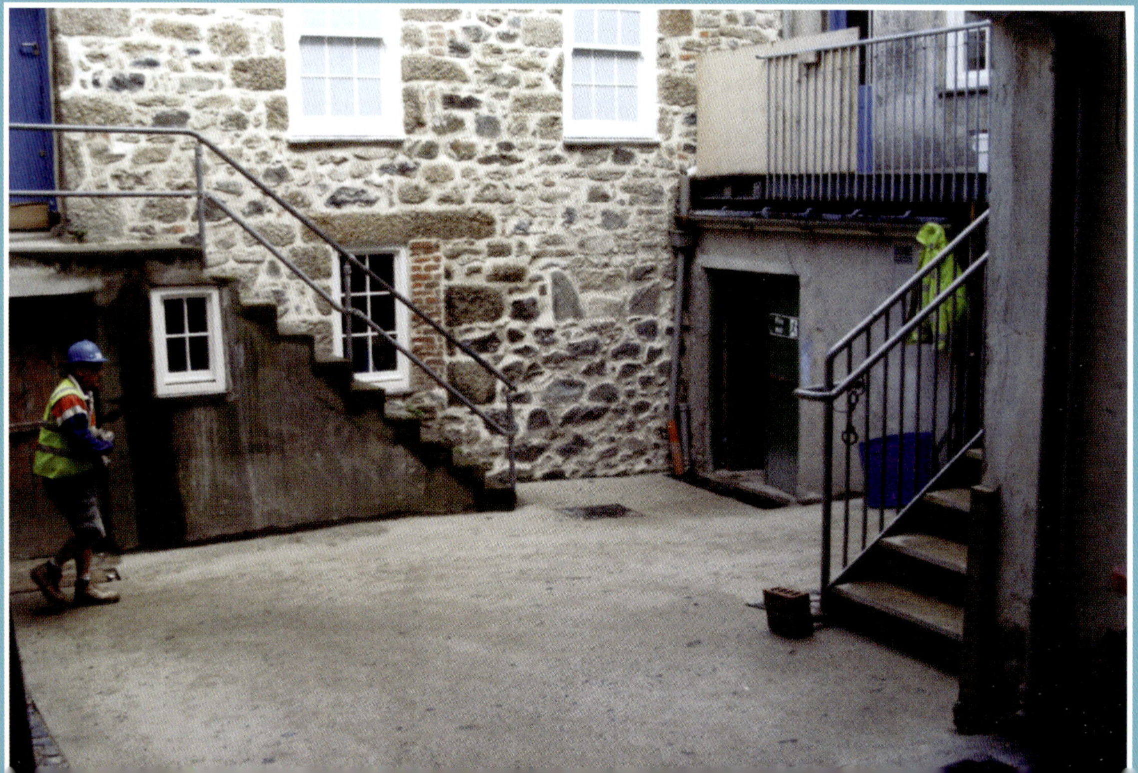

Newly surfaced entrance to fish cellars and studios

DOWNALONG

THIS IS THE area where the fishermen lived. The cottages processed fish and housed fishing gear on the ground floor with living quarters above. It is close to the harbour where boats would be moored and fish were gutted, salted and packed in barrels for export to Italy. It is true to say that the arrival of artists in the town of St Ives in the 1880s, and continuously, re-floated the economy. As fishing declined the artists flourished, and the local population was ready to adapt to a new lifestyle. Artists began occupying large premises, which had usually housed fishing gear and skylights appeared on the roofs in Downalong.

Sail lofts appeared on the sands around 1850, as part of a group of lofts extending the length of Porthmeor beach. They housed the fishermen's boats, tackle, fish nets and a huge area where they could work at making nets and repairing equipment during the winter months. This is still true today. Fishermen and artists reside together with neither encroaching on the others' territory, and respect is accorded to both occupations.

One remarkable story, to show how these two communities interact, is that the artist, Sam Bassett, who occupies Studio 18, is the son of a fisherman. That man is Stephen Bassett, who was a fisherman for 30 years before achieving the job of Harbour Master.

He comes with a legacy of family fishermen in the previous generation who worked in the Porthmeor cellars. These are the only surviving sail lofts still in existence on Porthmeor beach; they face the Atlantic, and back onto the old fishing quarter of the town.

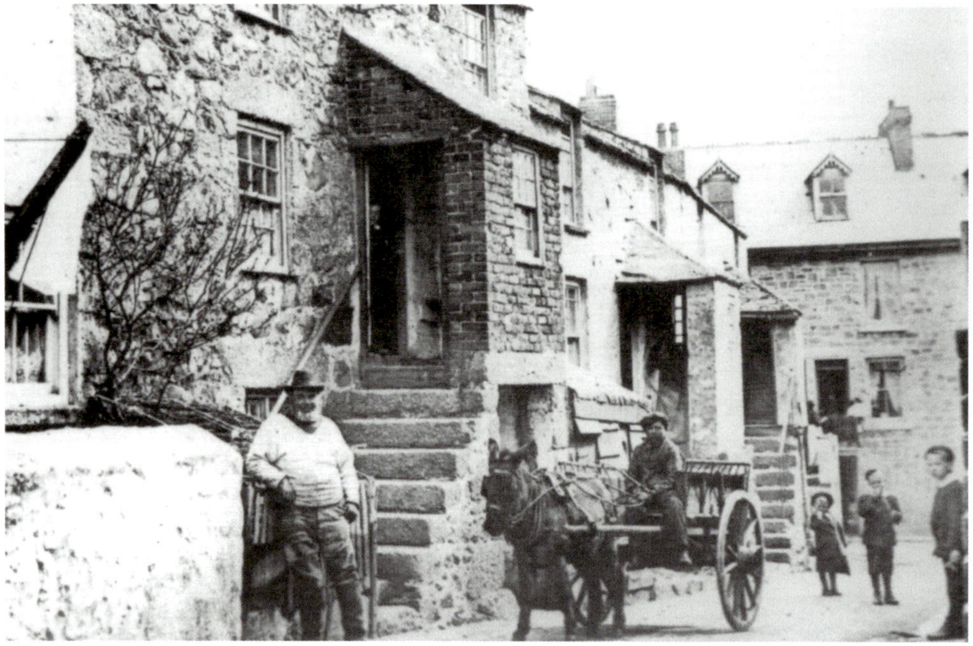

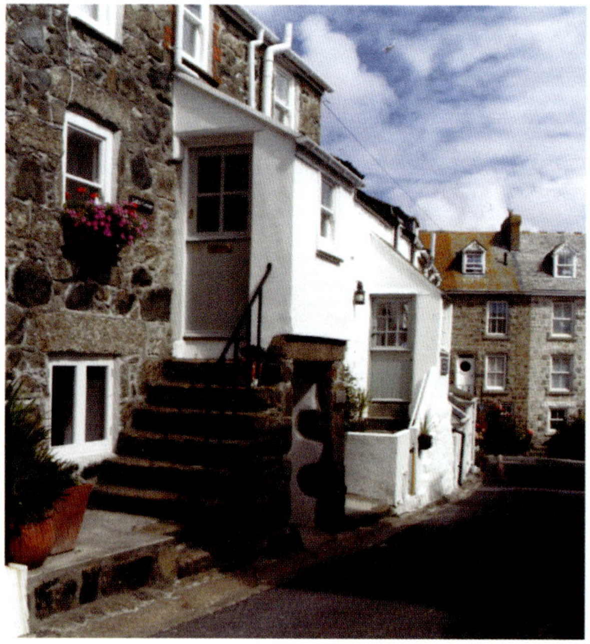

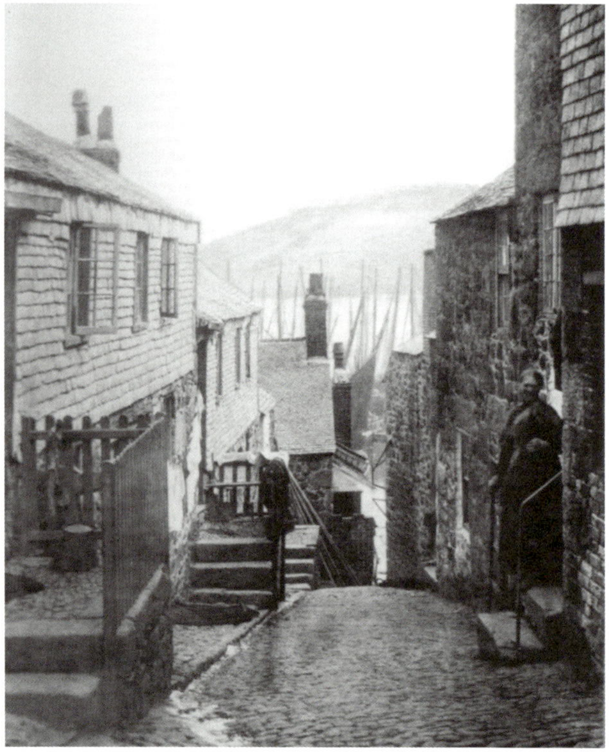

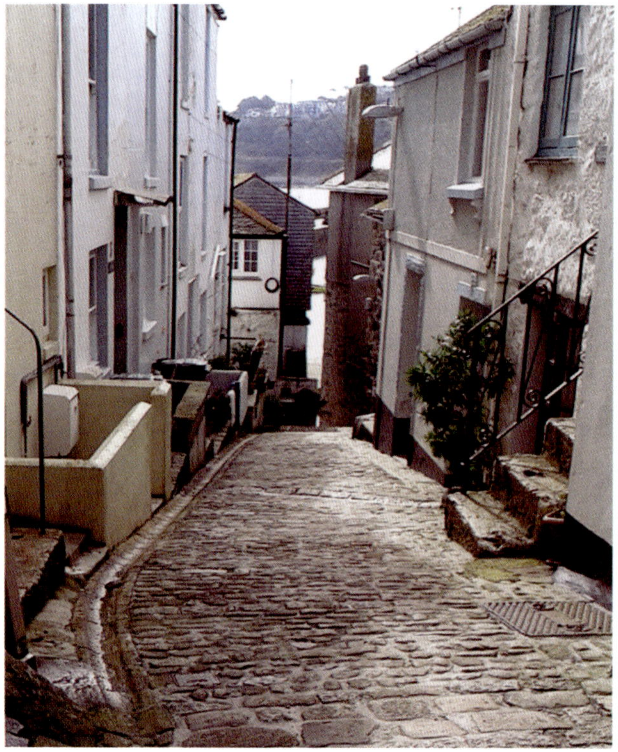

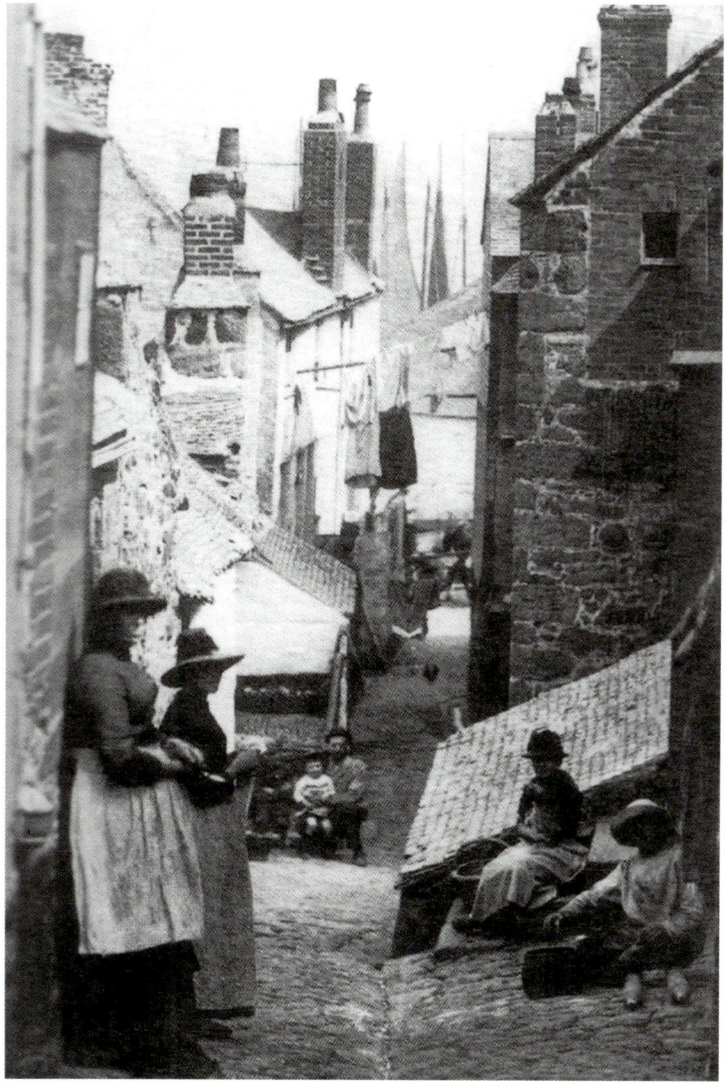

Bailey's Lane 1890s

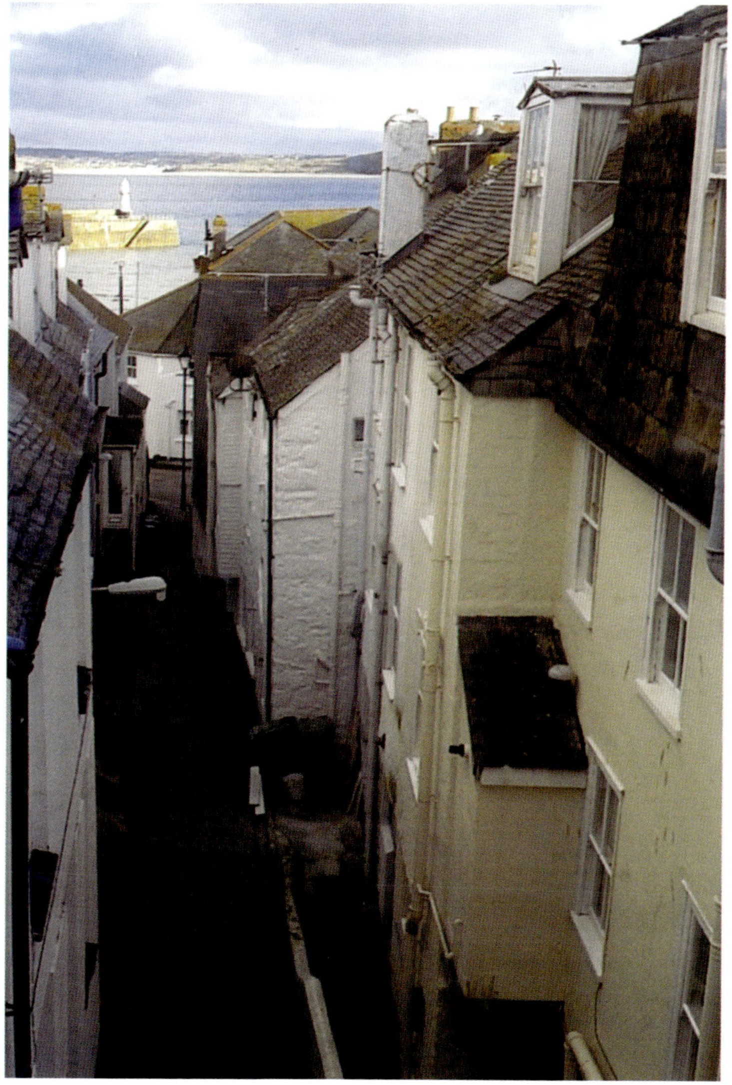

Bailey's Lane 2013

Opposite page:
Top, left to right: Back Road East Early 1900s; Back Road East 2013
Bottom, left to right: Bethesda Hill 1890s; Bethesda Hill 2013

When housing estates were built above the town many Downalong families moved to accommodation that could offer gardens back and front and all facilities for comfortable living. However, these same fishermen's cottages still huddle against wind and tide but the pilchards are gone and the basements are now equipped with kitchens and bathrooms and welcome the tourists.

The Commonality of Artists and Fishermen

I've often wondered what artists and fishermen have in common, that they should be so tolerant of each other, although not on intimate terms. They respect each other and that is because they have a shared independence of spirit that allows them to pursue their individual work. That seems to be the key factor in their relationship. They are self-sufficient, a law unto themselves and are beholden to no man.

Fishermen prefer to be their own boss. They relish the freedom of going to sea, being out there with the elements, battling to bring home a catch of fish; delighting in having their own boat and practising their skills. Making decisions about how they should organise their life is a liberating experience.

The artists in their studios are battling to come to terms with what drives them to develop their ideas, express their emotions, their feeling for the environment, their creativity and enjoyment in using their artists' materials and the space which is theirs. They cannot be told what to paint. They are individual in their choice of subject matter.

The loose relationship between fishermen and artists is an unlikely symbiotic co-existence, but it has worked for over a hundred years.

PORTHMEOR FISHERMEN

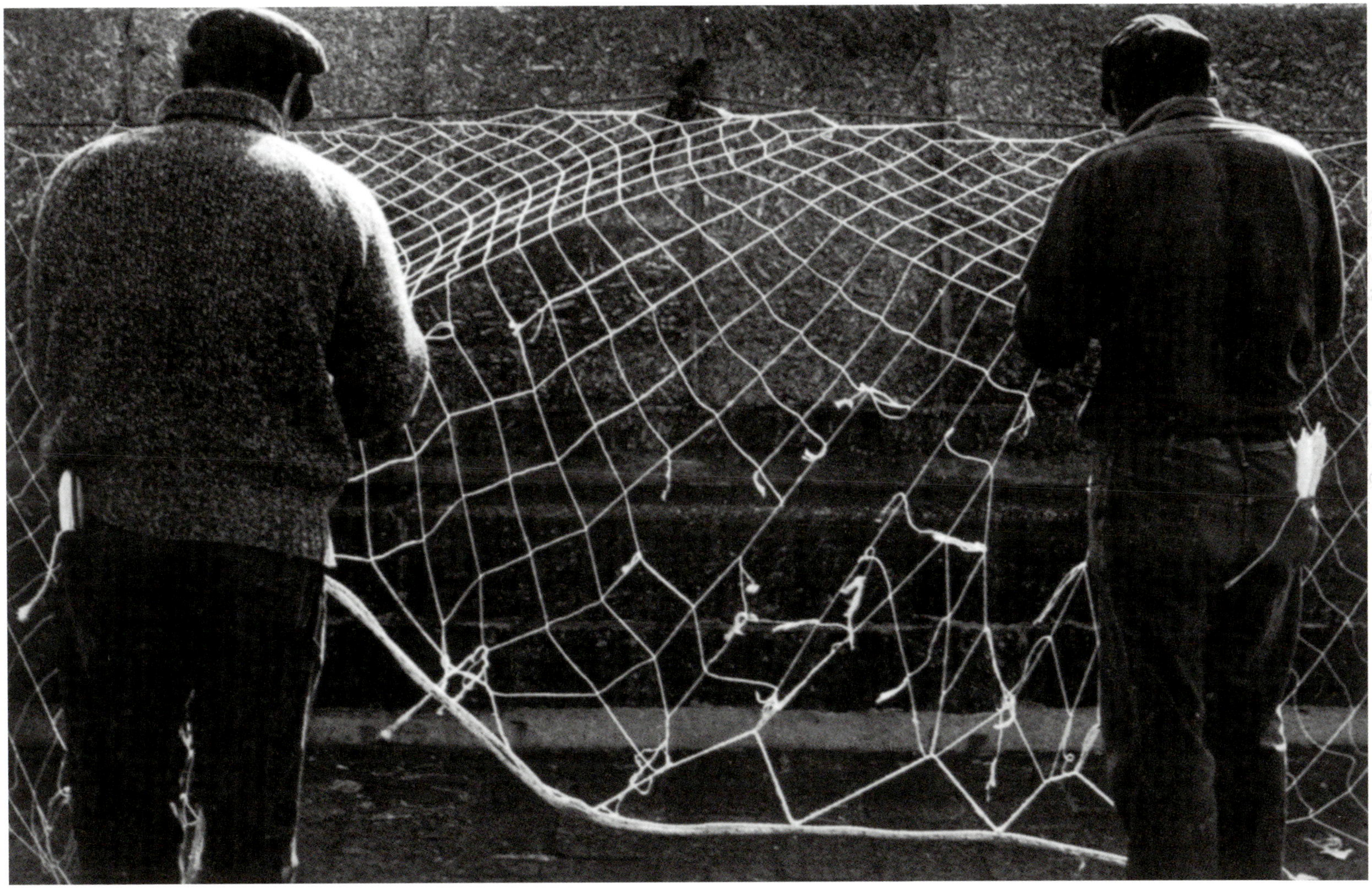

Brothers Sam and Eddie Bassett mending nets on Smeaton's Pier 1988

THE HARBOUR MASTER – FISHERMAN AND MASTER MARINER

Stephen Bassett

Stephen Bassett *was fishing for about 30 years on a variety of vessels experiencing many different methods of fishing activities.*

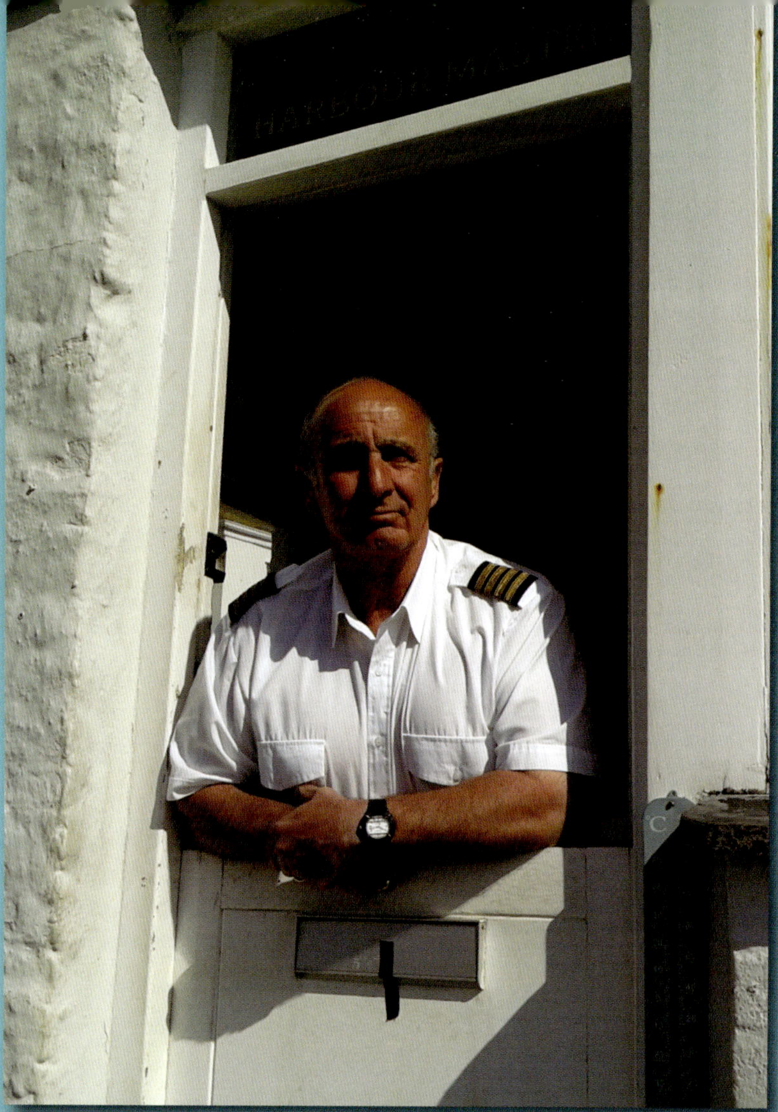

The last vessel on which I was skipper for a number of years was the *CKS*, which came from Whitby. It was named after Colin and Karen, the two children of the original owner. The main types of fishing for the *CKS* was gill nets, fishing for hake during the summer and wreck fishing for pollock, cod and Dover sole in the winter. The months of May, June, July we worked approximately 250 miles west of Newlyn on the edge of the continental shelf. Working a long way from our home port of Newlyn we landed at ports in Ireland, France and this country.

I have had a diverse working life at sea on supply ships in the North Sea, and on oil rigs but fishing has been my main occupation. Whilst at sea I have gained my Class 1 Fishing Certificate of Competency and Master Merchant Navy in five classes of vessel.

My family has been in the fishing industry for many generations and I started with my father Eddy, and uncle Sam on the *Heather Armorral*. The Porthmeor net lofts were used for the storage and rigging of fishing gear by my family for many years before me.

Stephen Bassett has been the St Ives Harbour Master for 10 years. The role of Harbour Master is like being Master of a ship. There are a lot of responsibilities to deal with, good communication is vital as is experience in the maritime industry. A knowledge of Maritime Law, Health and Safety regulations, Rules of the Road, enforcing Bylaws, Accounting, collection of harbour dues, laying moorings, berthing vessels, giving advice, compliance with the Port Marine Safety Code, maintenance and upkeep of the harbour are but a few.

Born: St Ives.   Lives in St Ives

THE PORTHMEOR FISHERMEN

Chris Care

***Chris Care (Bish)** was born in St Ives. He has worked at his net-setting for 15 years in the same loft and reckons he walks 2 to 3 miles a day.*

This was formerly a cooperage where they made the barrels. They used to have salt cellars and the big cellar was where the tanks for the storage of fish was situated, but they were never used. Most of the pilchards were exported to Italy. The gill netting I'm working with is for 8 or 9 boats. I supply nets for boats working out of Hayle, Newquay, Cadgwith, Newlyn, Padstow and for St Ives.

All St Ives fishermen have a nickname. Our family nick name was *Bish*. When we were younger father had a big cellar but we always called them lofts. He was a fisherman, he and his two brothers. They had a boat called *SS40 Moss Rose*. In 1956 they had a new boat built in Falmouth. She was called *SS45 Lamorna.* She was built for long-lining and pilchard catching. I believe the fishermen have been working on this site for 200 years. These are wonderful buildings. I'm glad we're going to be here a lot longer.

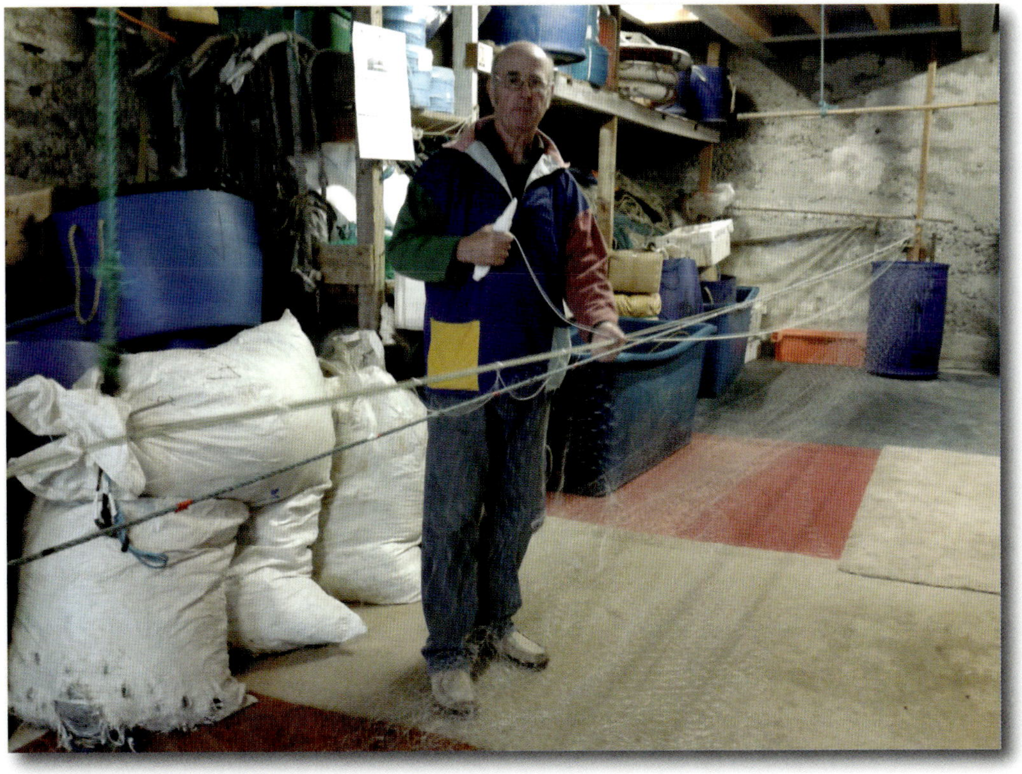

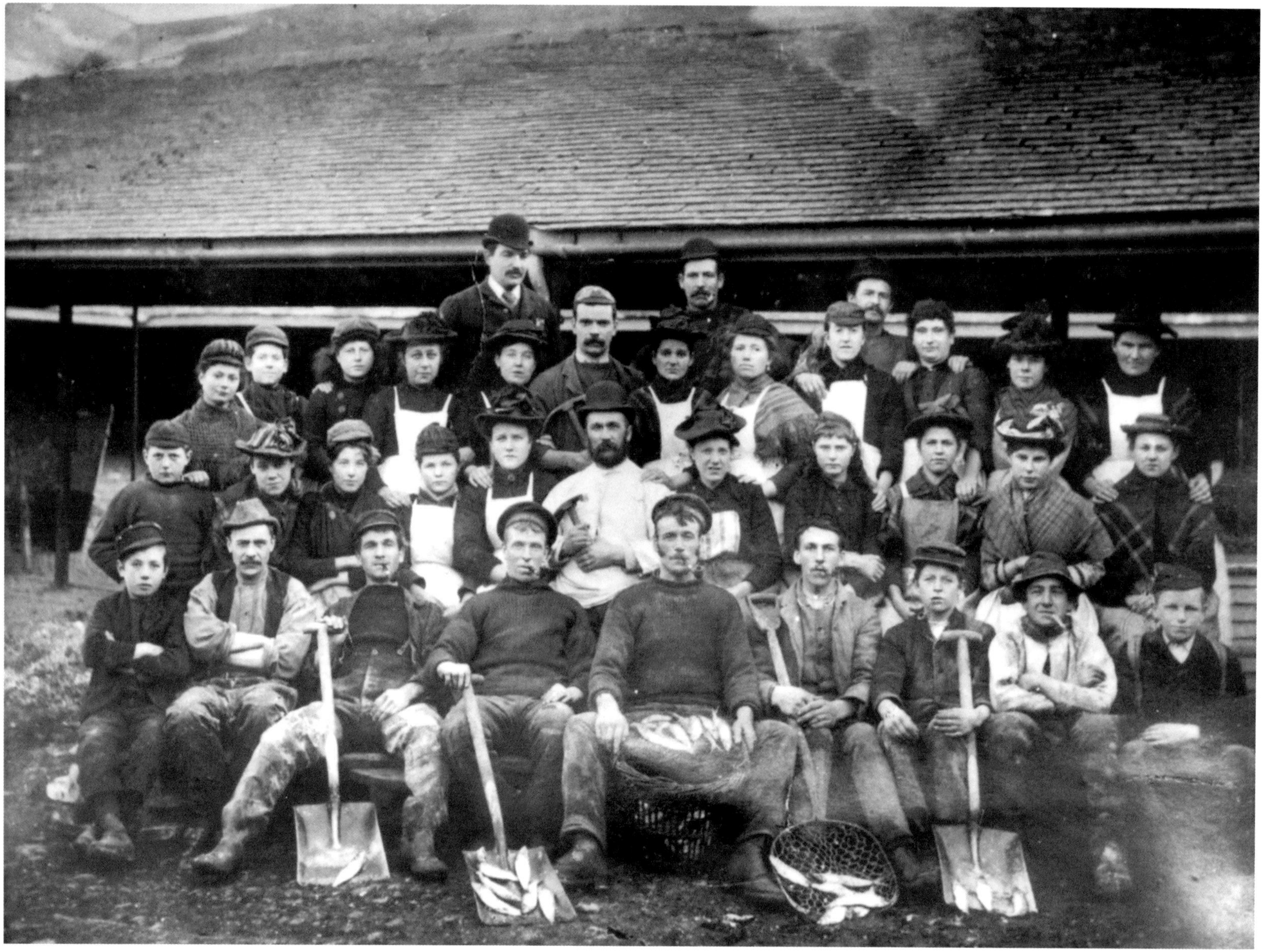

Workers in the pilchard cellars

Packing fish in barrels for export to Italy 1900s.

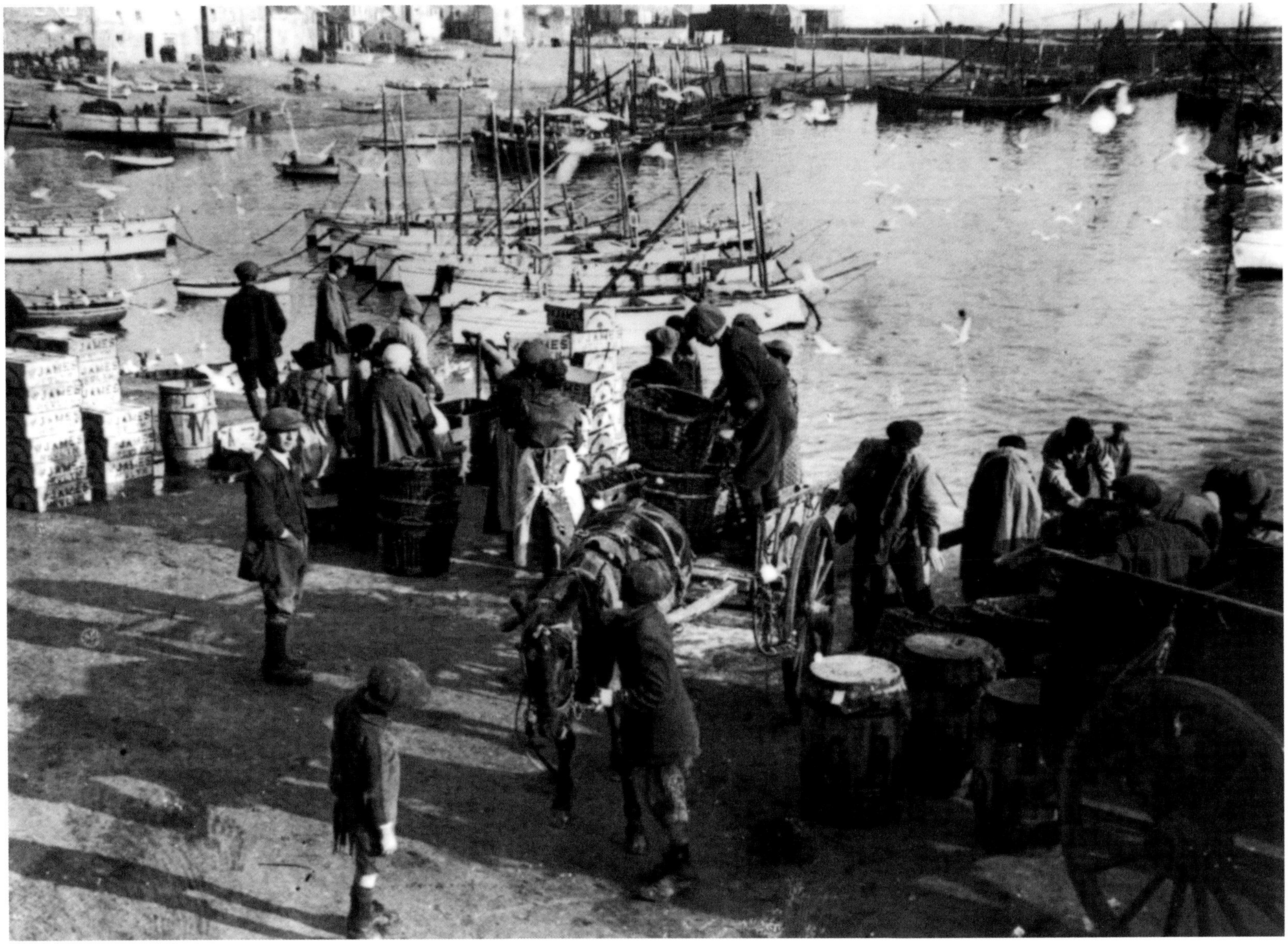

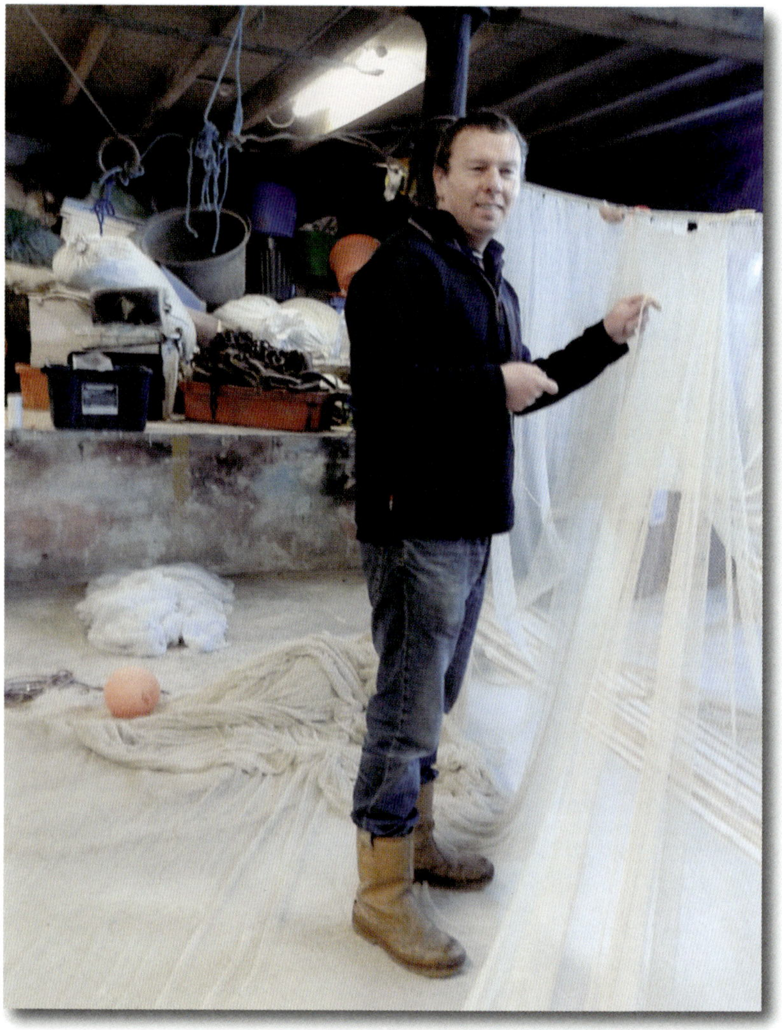

David Prisk – Fisherman – (Prisky)

I'm mending my sand eel nets ready for the season. I'm semi-retired now and work in the spring and summer. I make nets for myself, but help out when there is an urgent call for other nets. There are the 'wreck nets' for fish that live over wrecked boats, like ling, pollock, cod, black jacks and others. Mine is a seine net. It is very labour intensive to work with because the mesh is so fine, which it has to be to catch sand eels. They are about 10 inches long and very thin. Sand eels are sold as angling bait to Tasty Macpac. They are sorted, frozen and put into packets and then shipped around the country.

The net weighs 40 stone. Very heavy. It is 36 foot deep and 120 yards long. It takes two hands to haul it in. My crew mate is Terry. I've worked on my own boats mostly. The one I have at the moment is called the *Osprey.*

My dad was an engineer at Holman's in Camborne.
They made equipment for the mines, pumps, compressors, drills; all that was needed.

Born in St Ives. Lives in St Ives

Roger Phillips – Retired Fisherman

I've worked on quite a number of boats working out of St Ives; one of them was the *Asper*, which means rough and ready in Cornish. When we weren't at sea we were working in the lofts preparing our gear for the right time of the year and net mending. There are hundreds of different nets for the many fish they used to catch. You name a fish and there's a net for it.

The only boat I haven't worked on is beaming. They trawl for everything, which destroys the sea bed. They are deep sea boats and take whole shoals of fish. I worked on day boats and fished 10 or 15 miles out of the bay, always returning to harbour after a day's work.

We never wore life jackets because there isn't one that is designed to allow a fisherman to do his work. They are good for saving lives, but not for working in.

My father was a miner. He went to America and worked in every kind of mine from tin to gold mines. He used sticks of dynamite to blow the rock up and extract the ore.

Born in St Ives. Lives in St Ives

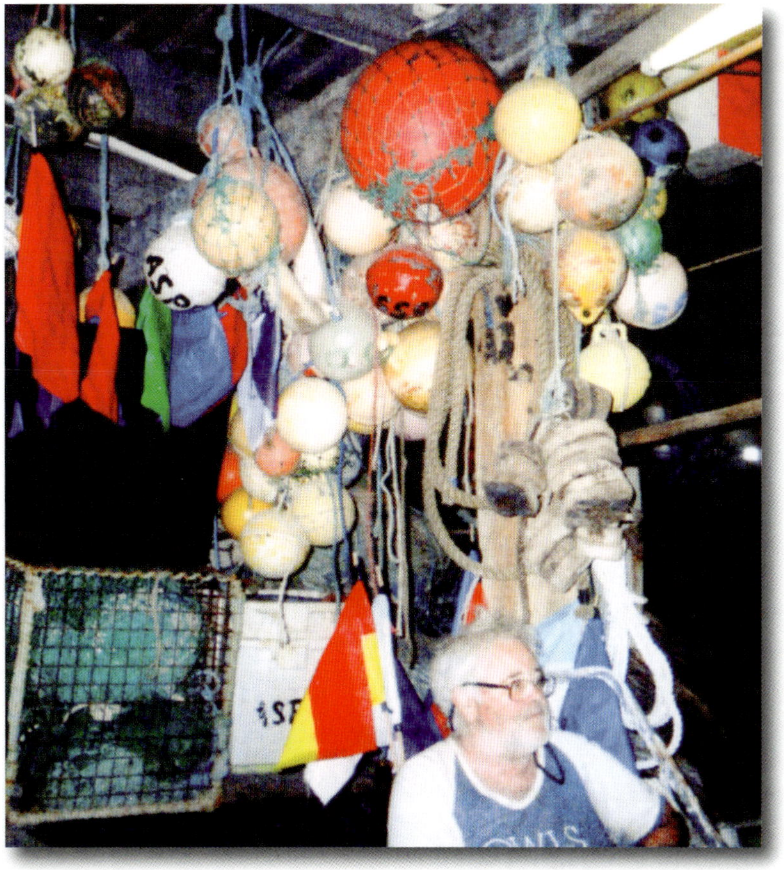

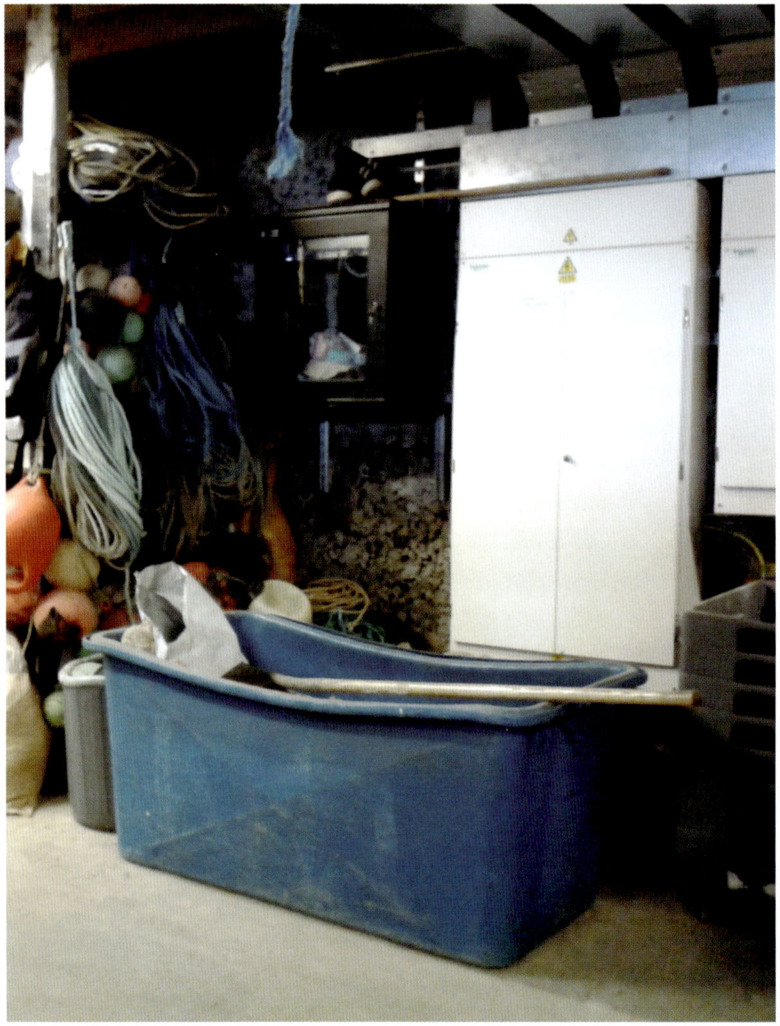

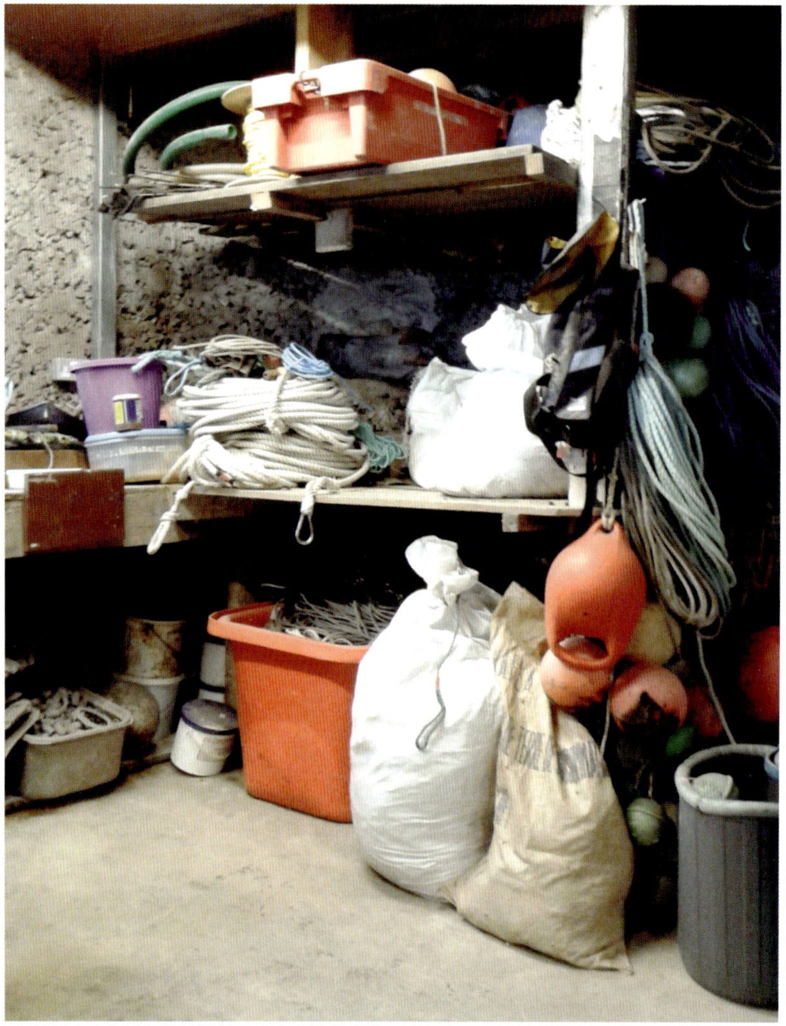

Fishing gear in the Net Lofts

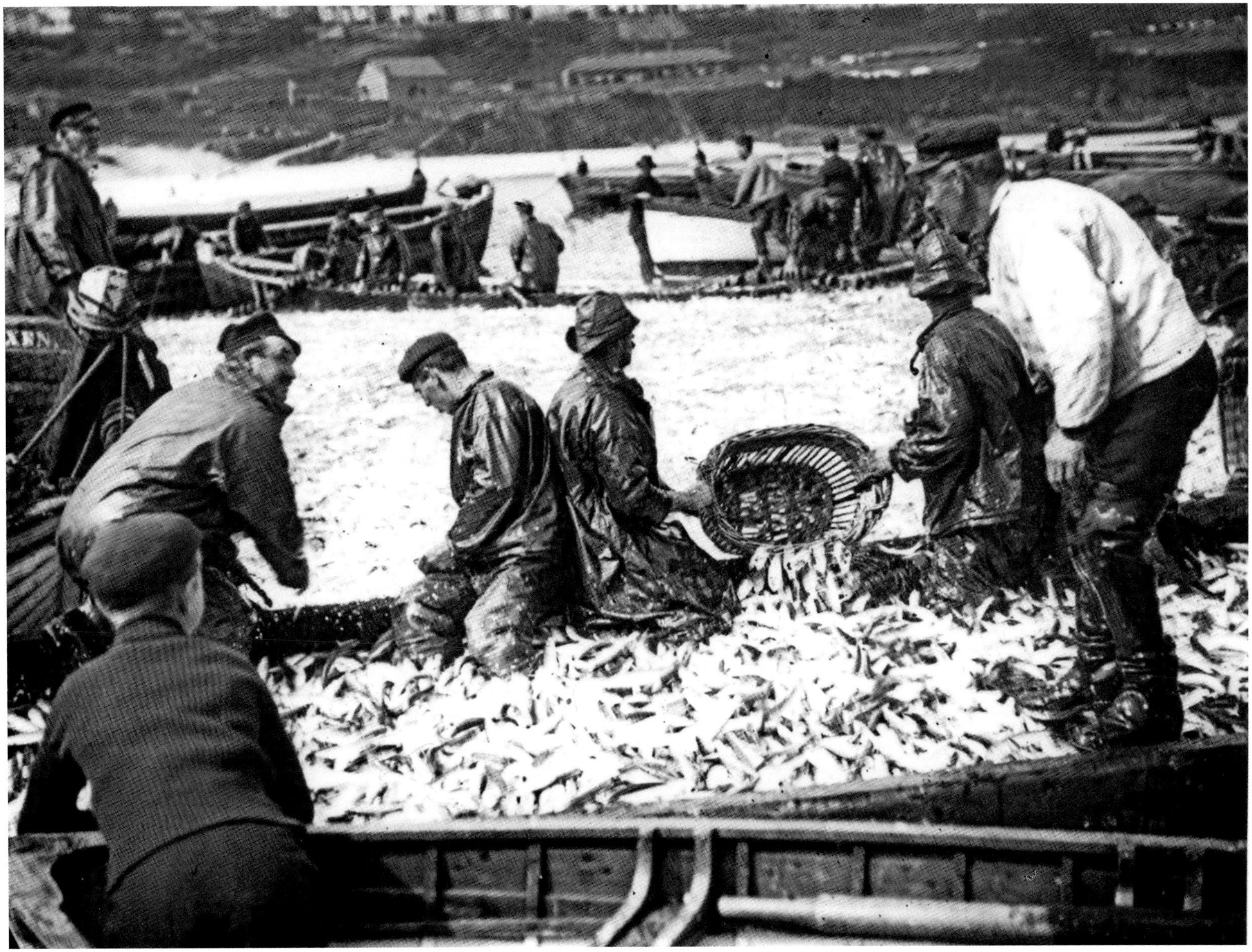

Seine Fishing. Dipping out pilchards from the tuck-net 1905

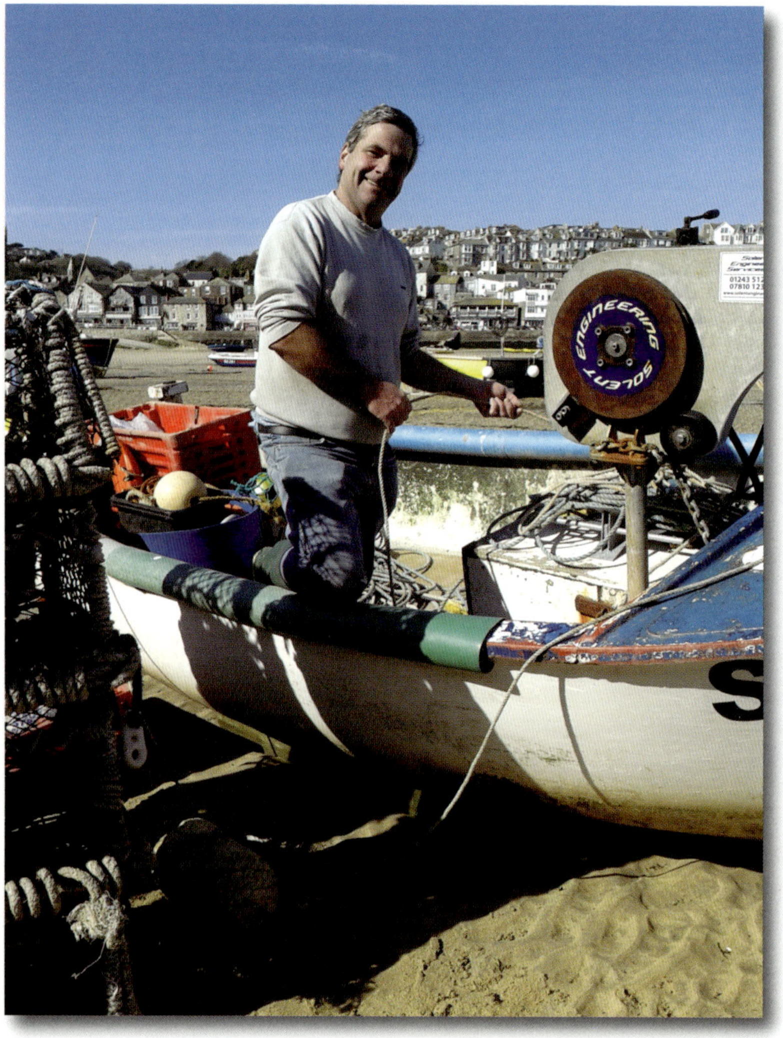

Simon Rouncefield – Fisherman (Rounce) St Ives Harbour

I fish out of St Ives all year round. Been fishing all my life. I started fishing from the quay at the age of five and haven't stopped since. I'm out nearly every day working for about eight hours. Mackerel and crab are always available. Other species, depending on the time of year, are bass, cod, plaice, pollock, whiting, ray, bream, herring, turbot, and last, but not least, lobster.

I am building up a list of fresh fish lovers. When I am still out at sea I send them a text from my mobile to tell them what fish I have caught and will meet them on the quay where they can buy my fish 'caught today' at very reasonable prices. Or I can arrange to deliver the fish locally. I give people a chance to buy and take what is left to market. There is nothing like fresh fish straight from the boat. Beautiful.

I was born in St Ives and have never found anywhere else I would rather live. There were three dolphins playing outside the harbour as I set off to sea and I managed to video them and select a good photo of one of them.

My family have always been fishermen and I love being able to carry on in the trade. When there's a bitter northerly wind it gives me time to make new nets and prepare my gear. This spring I'm going to give my boat SS170 *Jen* a new coat of paint.

Born in St Ives. Lives in St Ives.

Stuart Noall – Fisherman – (Boco)

I have a boat, *Gemma,* in St Ives and work on a boat in Newlyn called *Bethshan*. I fish all year from both places, mostly for herring and mackerel. These nets I'm making are for that type of fish.

In the summer time I team up with Karl and Gary. We're separate businesses but come together when necessary. We work three boats between us. The third boat is the *Athena Fay.*

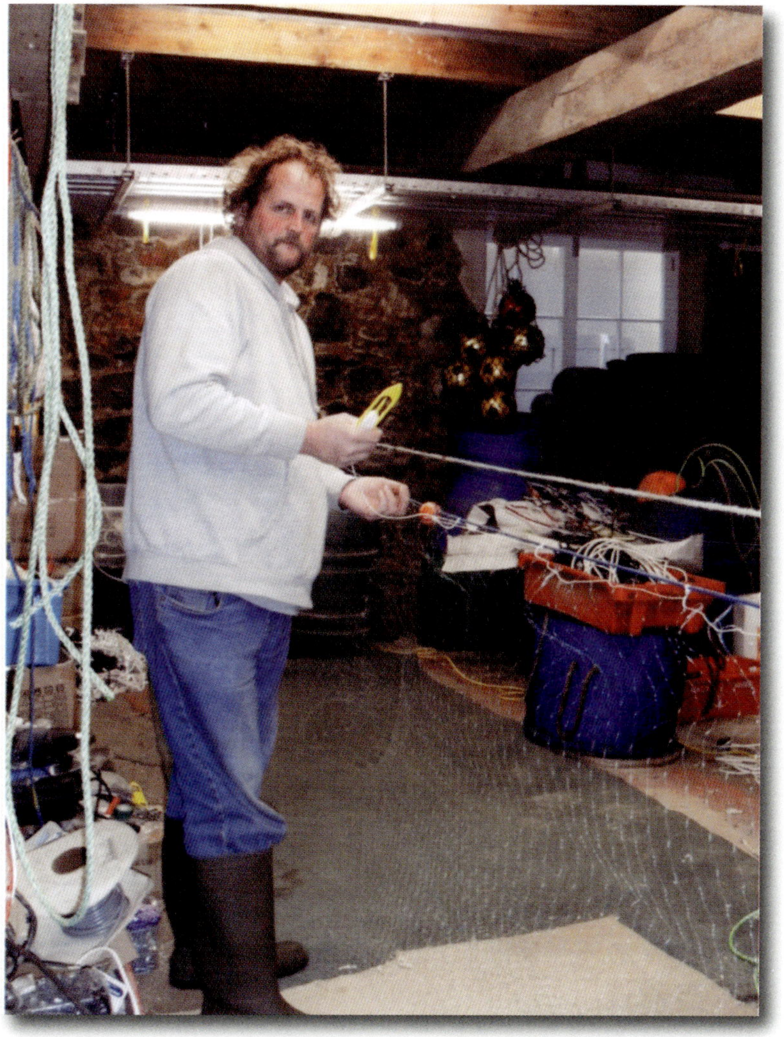

I used to work part time at fishing but my dad, Richard Noall, bought me a boat and that was when I decided to become a full time fisherman. Dad has always fished and had a net loft here in the Porthmeor cellars for many years. He used to work with his fishing partner Jack Murt.

I sell my catch locally to the pubs, markets and restaurants and people who like to buy direct from the boats that fish out of St Ives.

Every year I install all the Christmas decoration lights on the harbour and on the fishermen's lodges.

Born in St Ives. Lives in Hayle

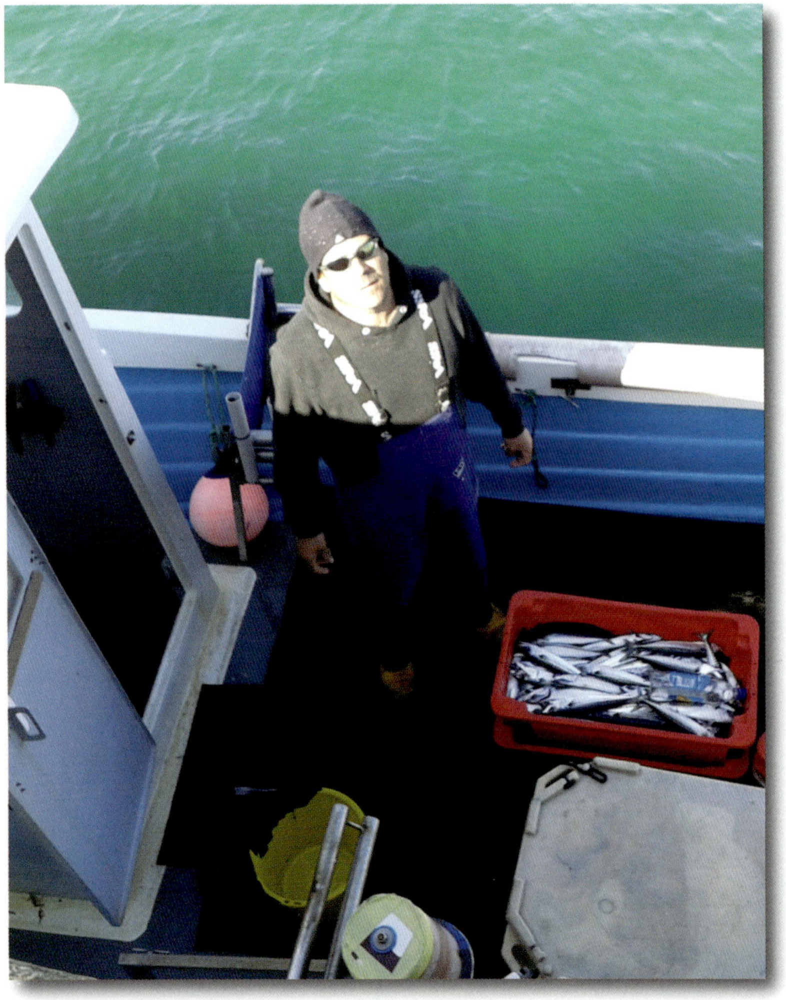

Karl Laroche – Fisherman

I love going to sea and being your own boss and working with a good experienced crew who knows what you're doing. Stuart McClary was the first fisherman to talk to me and teach me about fishing and we've been mates ever since. When I came to St Ives from Derby 29 years ago I wasn't given a warm reception but gradually I was accepted into the fishing community. We were crabbing for a number of years. When you're dealing with pots you can tell your wife what time you will be home, but when hand lining for mackerel, or fishing for herring, pollock and sea bass you don't know if you're going to catch anything; you just have to stay at sea and hope for the best.

We fish out of Newlyn in winter and have boats in both ports but we're now back in St Ives for the summer. This boat *Athena Fay*, PZ49 is named after my wife.

We abide by the rules and the bye-laws, of which there are many, regarding size of nets and fish and we stop fishing when the migratory birds arrive in the bay.

Born in Derby. Lives in St Ives

Ian Kemp – Assistant Harbour Master

I've worked mostly for my father, Eric Kemp, as a pilot, taking the bigger ships in and out of Penzance and Newlyn in Mounts Bay. Dad was a Master Mariner in the Merchant Navy. Grandfather was also a Master Mariner and went to sea with the Hain Steamship Company of St Ives. I've worked on ships in the dry dock at Penzance when they came in for a refit.

My stepson, Simon Freeman, built his own fishing boat *Keira* SS61, which is having a refit. It was built in my workshop where I'm restoring a 1930s fourteen-and-a-half gaffrig yacht. There's also my wooden rowing skiff, built in the 1950s from the builders yard of Tom Thomas on the harbour. All Mr Thomas's boats were built entirely by hand.

Born in St Ives. Lives in St Ives

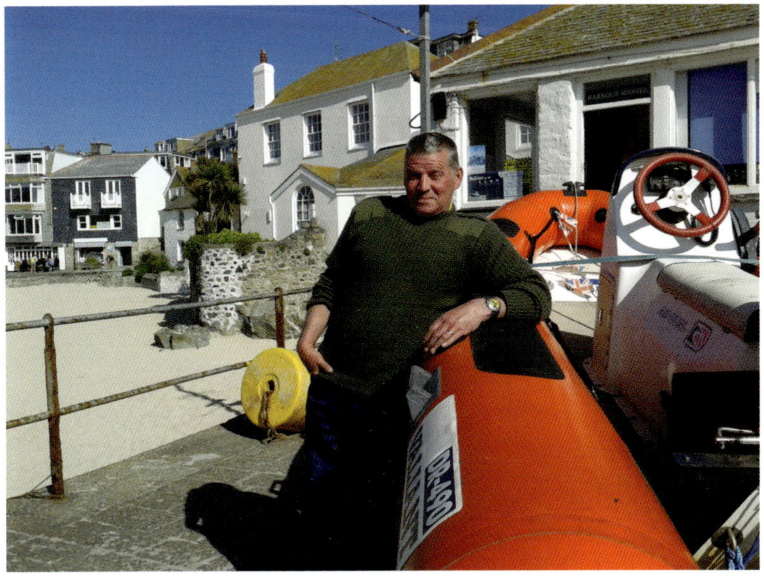

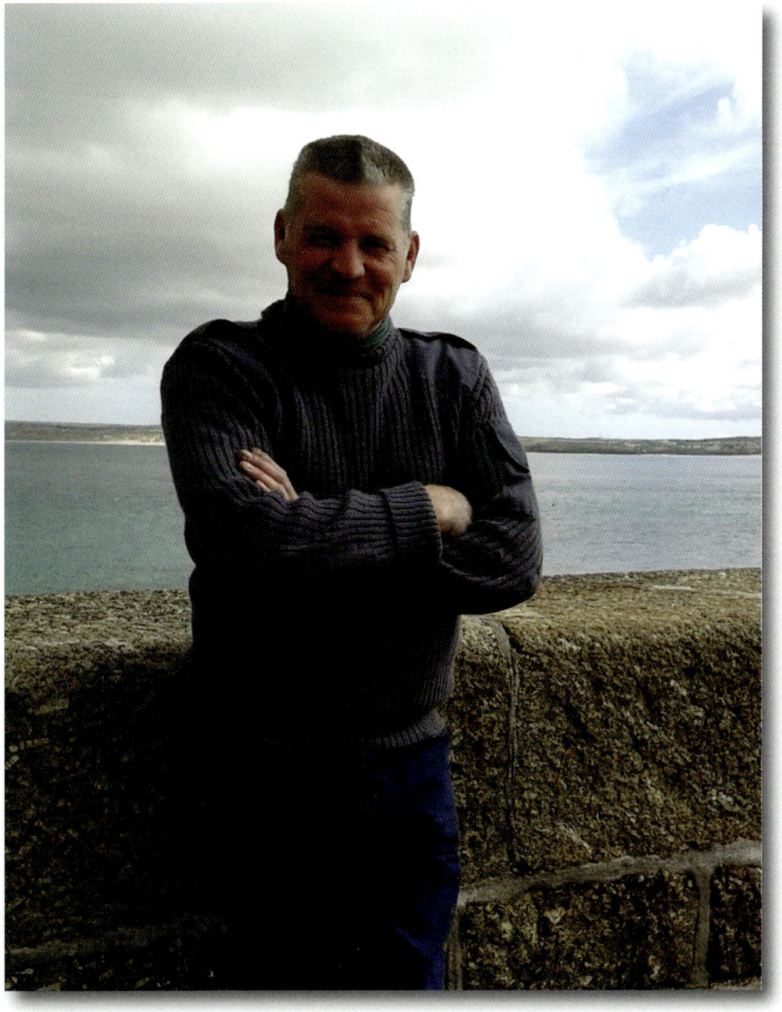

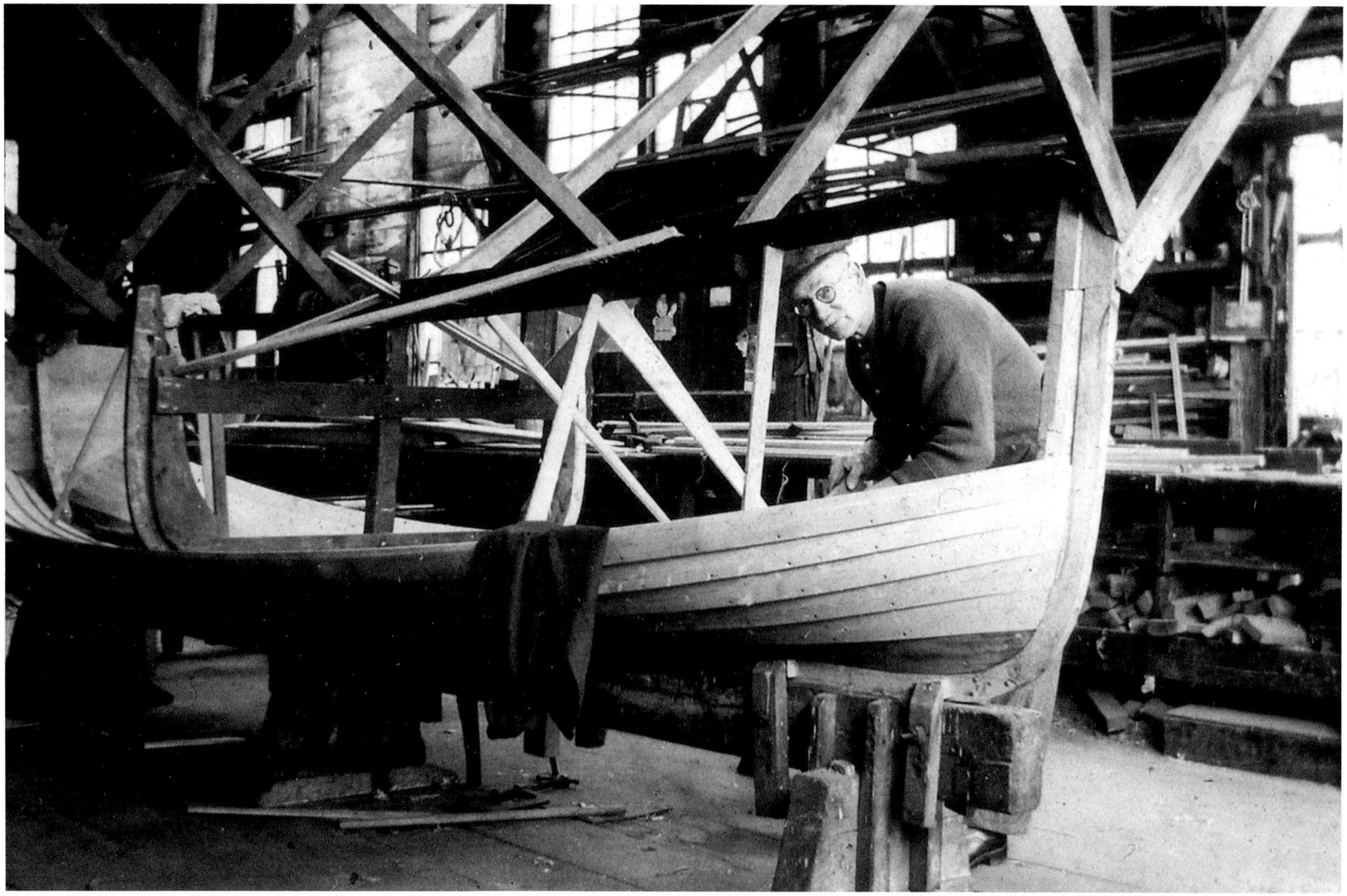

Tommy Thomas planking up a new skiff in workshop on Wharf Road. Est. 1908-1950s.

Stuart McClary – Fisherman – (Flakey)

I was born at Hellesveor Farm, St Ives. My father was working on the farm before he became a lighthouse keeper. He was on the Seven Stones and the Wolf at Land's End.

When I first went fishing I was in deep waters from Newlyn catching ling, cod, congers, everything. I came back to St Ives and worked on the *Unity* and *Harmony*. My own boat now is *Little Christina* SS80, named after my daughter. I've got pots and catch lobsters and crabs. We drop the pots overboard tied to buoys and ropes and come back several days later.
My nephew Dan works with me.

Daniel McClary

I've finished college where I was studying construction, but I want to carry on the family tradition of working at sea. I want to be a fisherman. I've already taken my exams for my fishing course and have certificates in First Aid, Fire Fighting, Health and Safety, Sea Survival and everything necessary.

Born in St Ives. Lives in St Ives

Daniel McClary is pictured overleaf

Stuart McClary

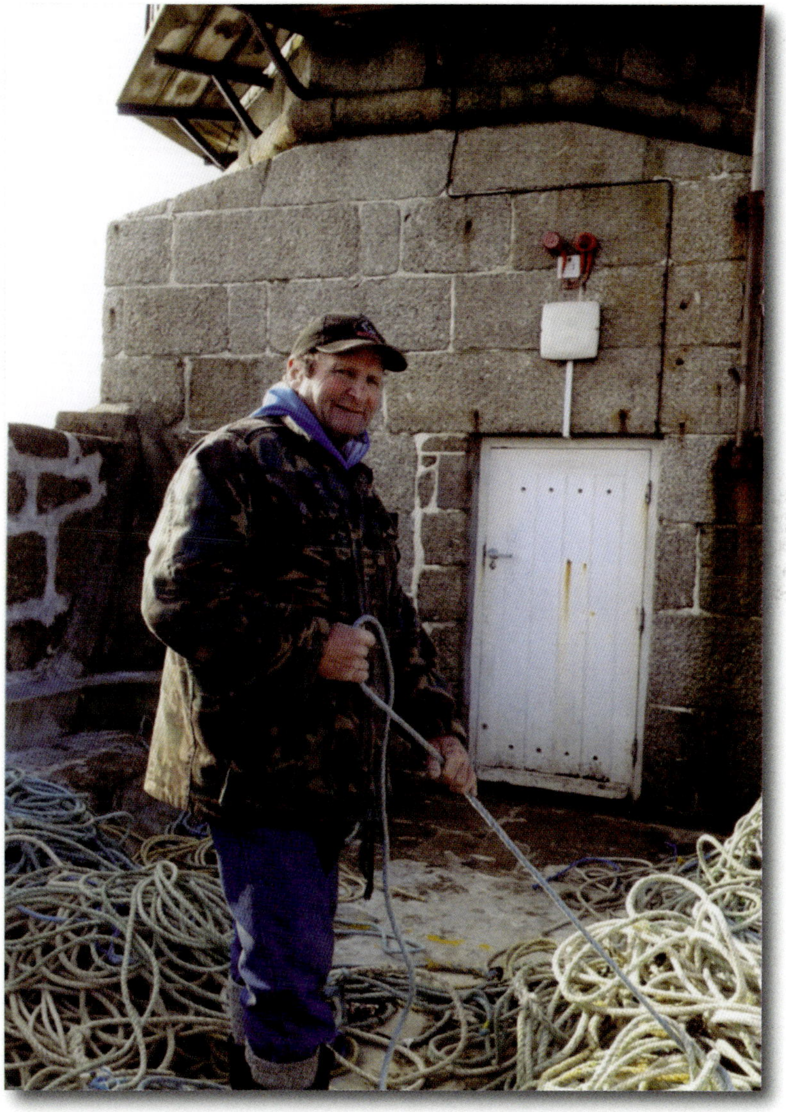

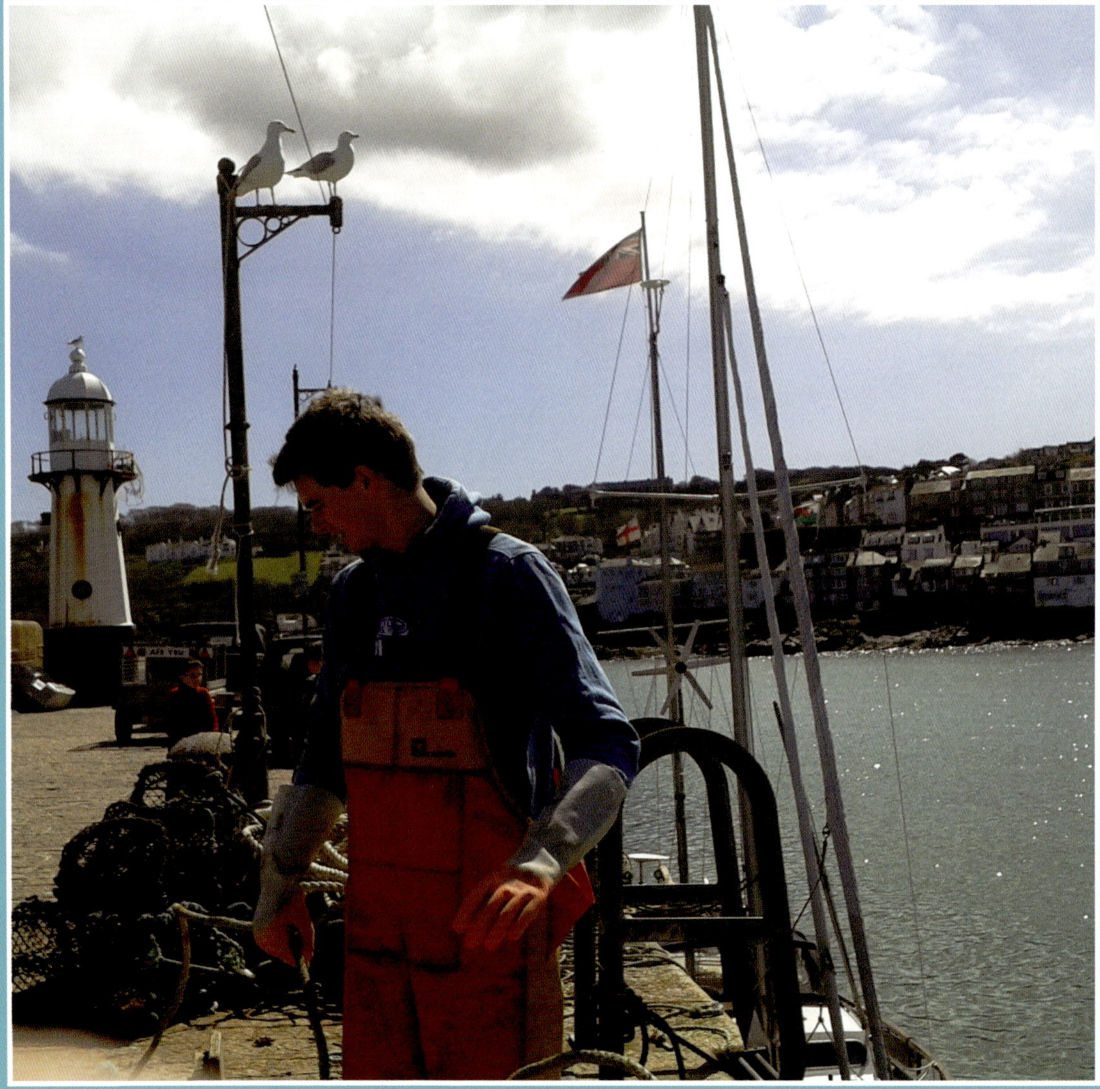

Dan McClary loading pots on the *Little Christina* before dropping them at sea

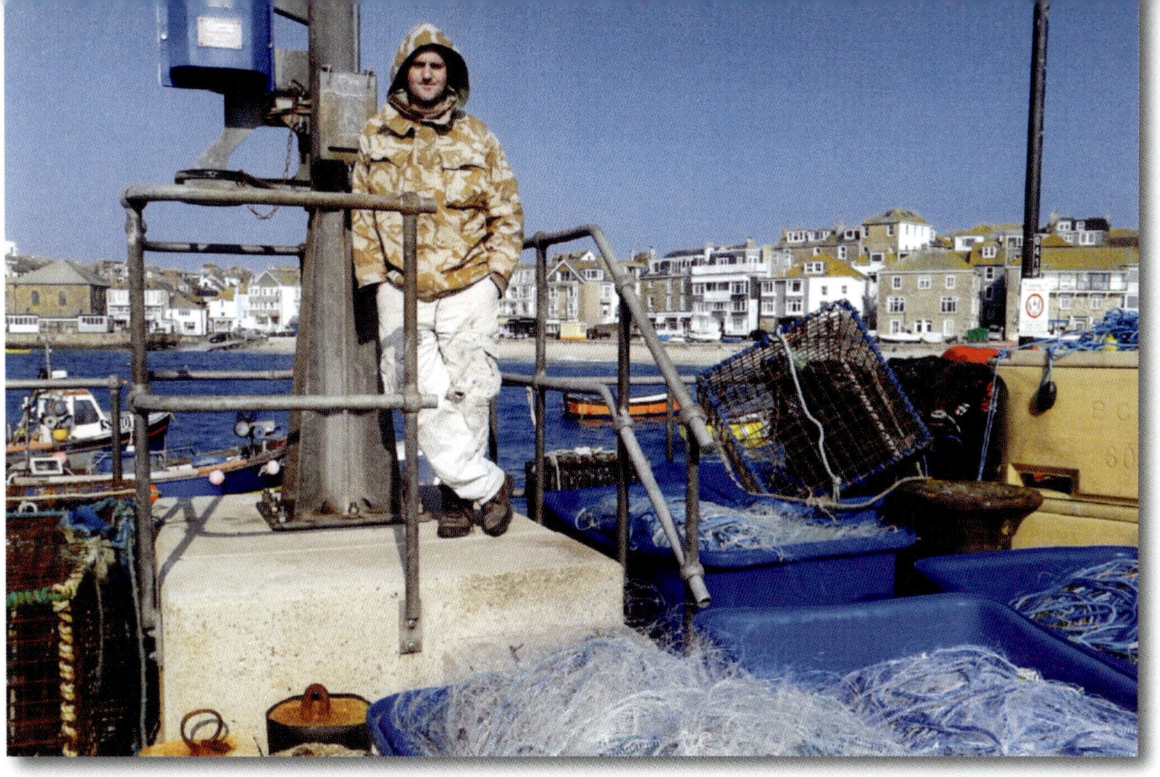

Simon Freeman – Fisherman – (Freemo)
St Ives Harbour

My boat, *Keira,* is a nineteen foot fast boat, which I built myself. My cousin Robert Jenkins works with me on the boat. We catch mackerel, herring and whiting, pollock and cod. In the winter we usually work on our netting, but when the mackerel arrive we will go lining. Mackerel often come to Falmouth first, then Newlyn and around to St Ives. I have a mechanism which releases the fish from the hooks. It's called stripper fishing. The fish are separated and funnelled down a shoot, which saves you from picking off the fish by hand.

Sometimes, when the fish come to St Ives first you get 'ring netters.' Their boats measure about 40-45 foot. They take a good percentage of the fish, leaving us very little. It is not good for us and not a sustainable way to fish.

When days are calm in the bay I will go fairly deep, up to about 20 miles, to fish for pollock. I fish for about eight months but do a year's work in that time. Robert and I will often work an eighteen hour day in the summer. We often land a catch and turn around and go straight out again. First light in the morning is when we can catch the most mackerel. When the tide is going out is another good time to fish.

I'm one of the younger fishermen, but I know there are a couple of men younger than me coming along, taking their exams before they can take their boats to sea, and they are keen to carry on the tradition of fishing.

Born in St Ives. Living in St Ives.

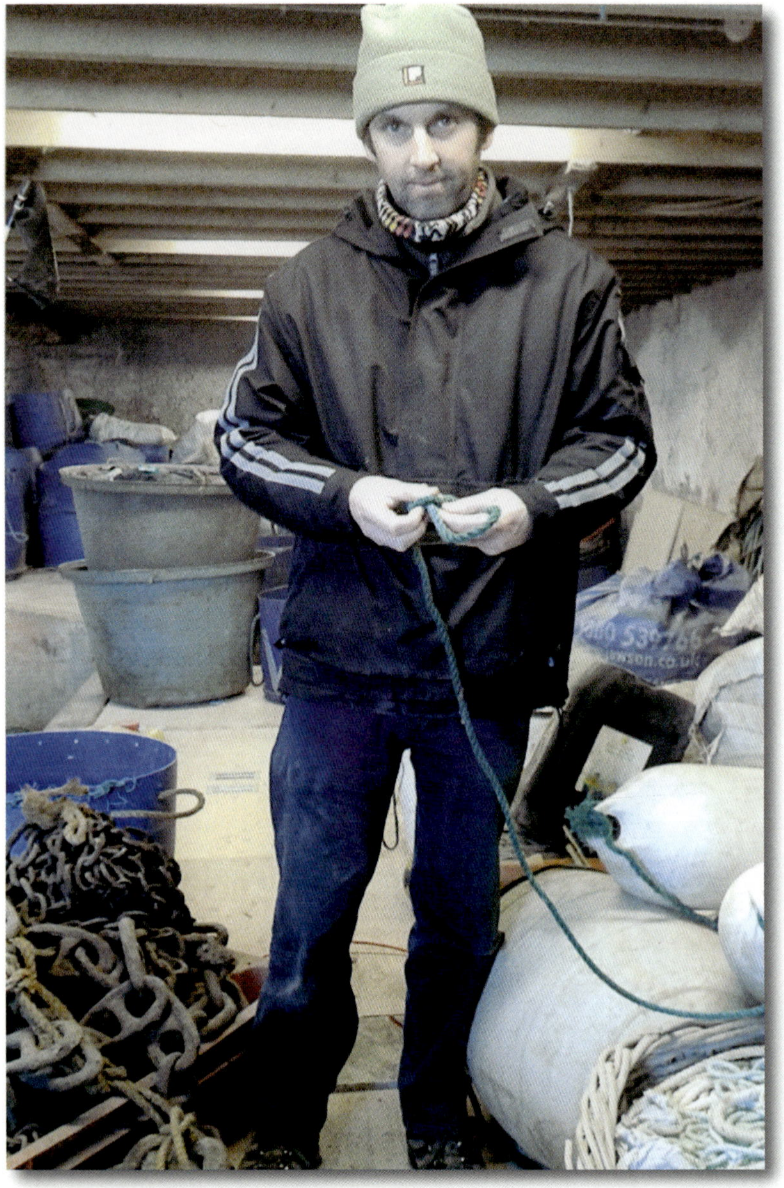

Nathan de Rosarieux – Biologist

I am a marine and fisheries biologist, working from on shore talking to people, dealing with problems and queries and engaging in desk-top research. I am a freelance consultant for many companies both here and abroad. Basically my work focusses on fisheries management and sustainability. There are many different areas to investigate in the conservation of fish stocks.

When I am not engaged with a problem I then go fishing, catching crawfish, ray, monk and lobster. I'm back from fishing out of Newlyn, which is the winter port. St Ives is the summer port and I'm buying a new bigger boat, having sold the two boats I was working with. I haven't named her yet.

My mother is St Ives born and bred. Her grandfather was the Harbourmaster when fishing was still good and catches were plentiful. He was one of the Jennings family. My great, grandfather was fortunate to have been fishing in the period before fish stocks were in decline.

Born in Germany. Living in Lelant.

Gary Leach – fisherman

I've been out in the catamaran *Bethshan* this morning testing some new equipment for fishing with hook and line. The new gear needs some trial runs, with different size hooks that have to be just right.

I've been fishing since I was 16. Dad and granddad were fishermen. Dad was Captain on the deep sea trawlers in Lowestoft, where I was born, but we're a St Ives family. All three generations have worked on the big boats travelling to America, Ireland, Scotland and France and skippered Newlyn Beamers. I'm back in St Ives now for the summer but if there are fish round at Newlyn it only takes me two hours to get there. In winter Stuart and Karl come aboard with me on the *Bethshan*. We work out of Newlyn and St Ives.

There are two catamarans fishing in the bay. They are powerful boats with a good turn of speed and a spacious deck with a cabin and enough room for fish, gear and men.

Born in Lowestoft. Lives in St Ives.

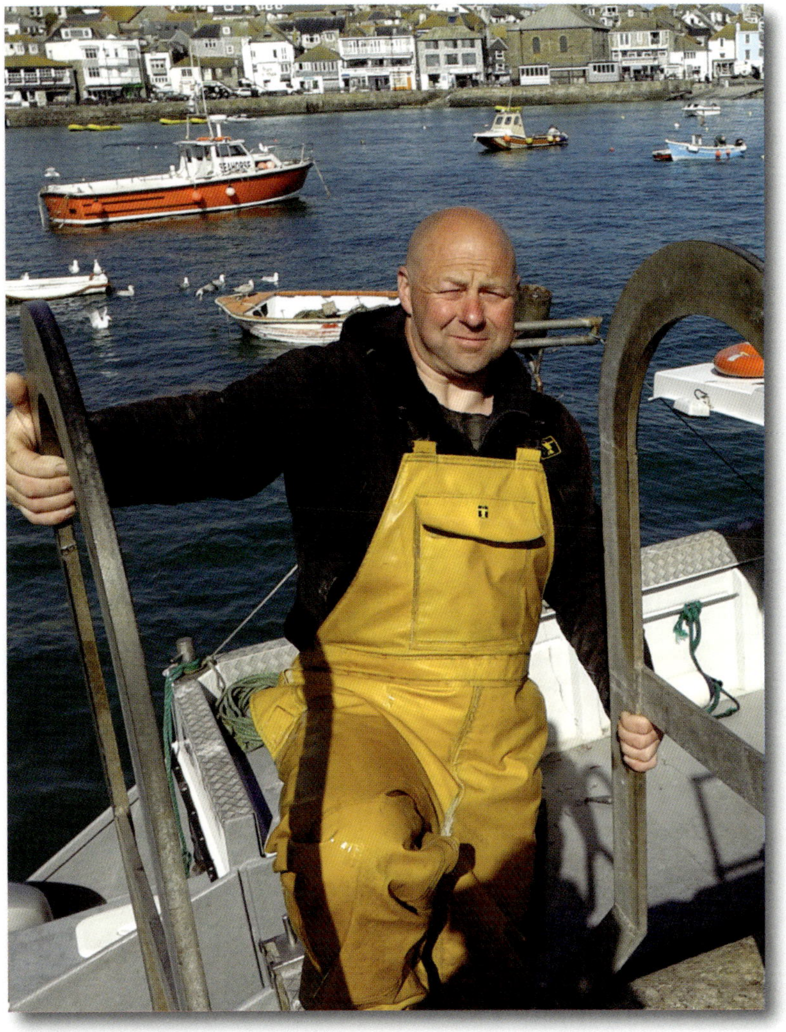

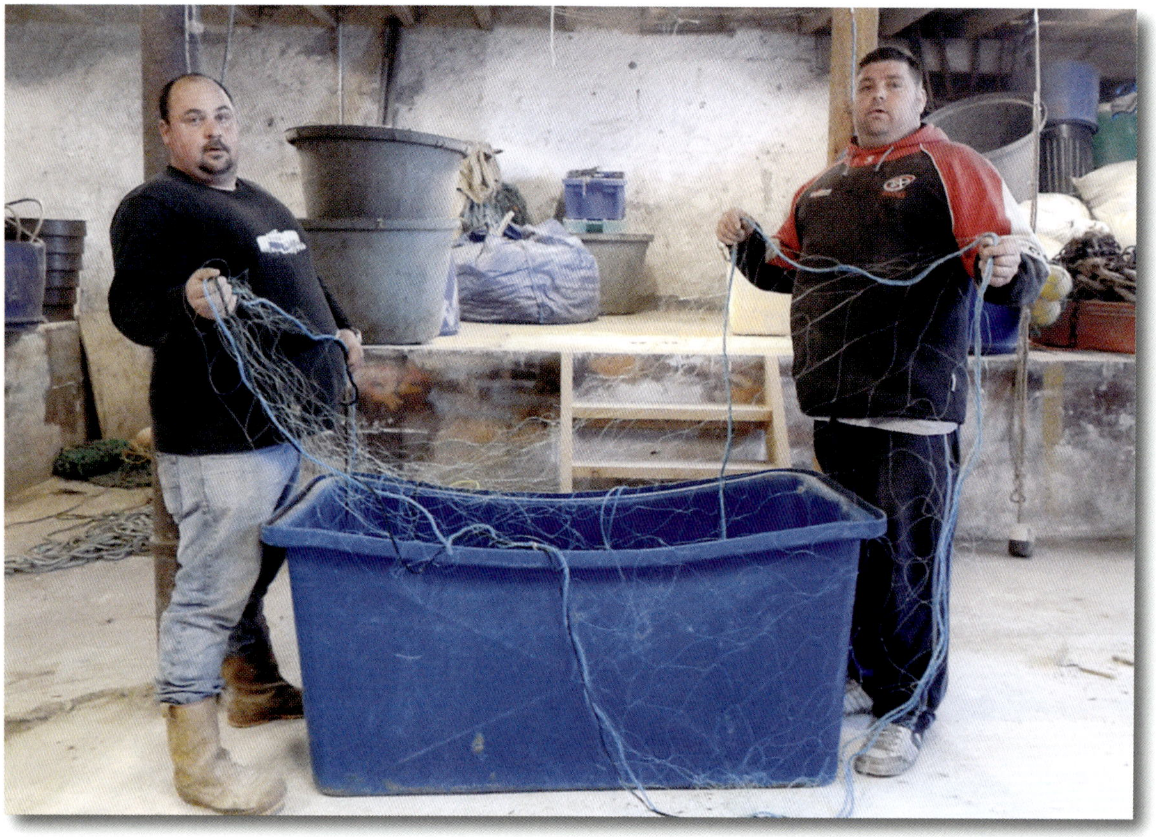

Left: P J and Raggy

Below: PJ operating the crane for unloading a catch of shark (tope), with Wm. Rowe

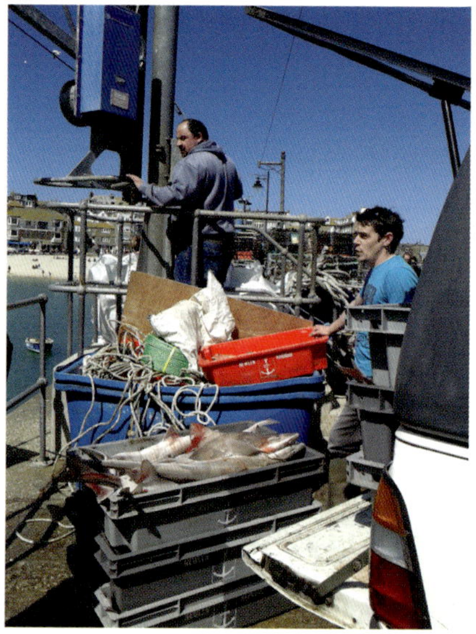

P J Godfrey – Fisherman – (PJ)

Skipper of the *Silvery Sea.* It is one of the biggest boats in the harbour. We are the last of the fishermen. When we're gone there'll be nothing. We fish with a large mesh net capable of catching the big fish like rays and monkfish. The smaller fish can easily pass through.

It is vital for me to have a Porthmeor net loft and a secure unit. It is somewhere safe and dry to work in. We now have a concrete platform with a good length of flooring to stretch the netting. I buy the net direct from the factory, but it has to be stitched to the ropes. The net John and I are working with is worth about £1,000 and the bins are £300. In having this net loft for storage I know that my tackle cannot be stolen. If I only had the pier then equipment gets stolen and it is also subject to bad weather conditions when gales and high tides toss your valuable kit into the harbour.

Born in St Ives. Living in St Ives.

John Lee – Fisherman – (Raggy)

My boat is the *Northwood.* I work out of Newlyn usually, but when I'm in St Ives I work with PJ and we sort out the nets and gear in the Porthmeor cellars, mending and preparing the nets for going to sea. In different seasons we use a variety of nets for many types of fish. We're getting ready for the summer season.

We fish fifteen to twenty miles out of St Ives and in that distance PJ will often run into the French and Belgian trawlers who are fishing for the same catch.

These Porthmeor cellars, or net lofts, are the last of their kind in St Ives. All the other net lofts have long gone, along with many of the old fishermen. This is a huge space and the equipment in this cellar is worth thousands of pounds.

We're very fortunate to have such accommodation that serves all our needs and gives us a weather proof place to work in and store everything vital to fishing.

Born in Newlyn. Living in Penzance.

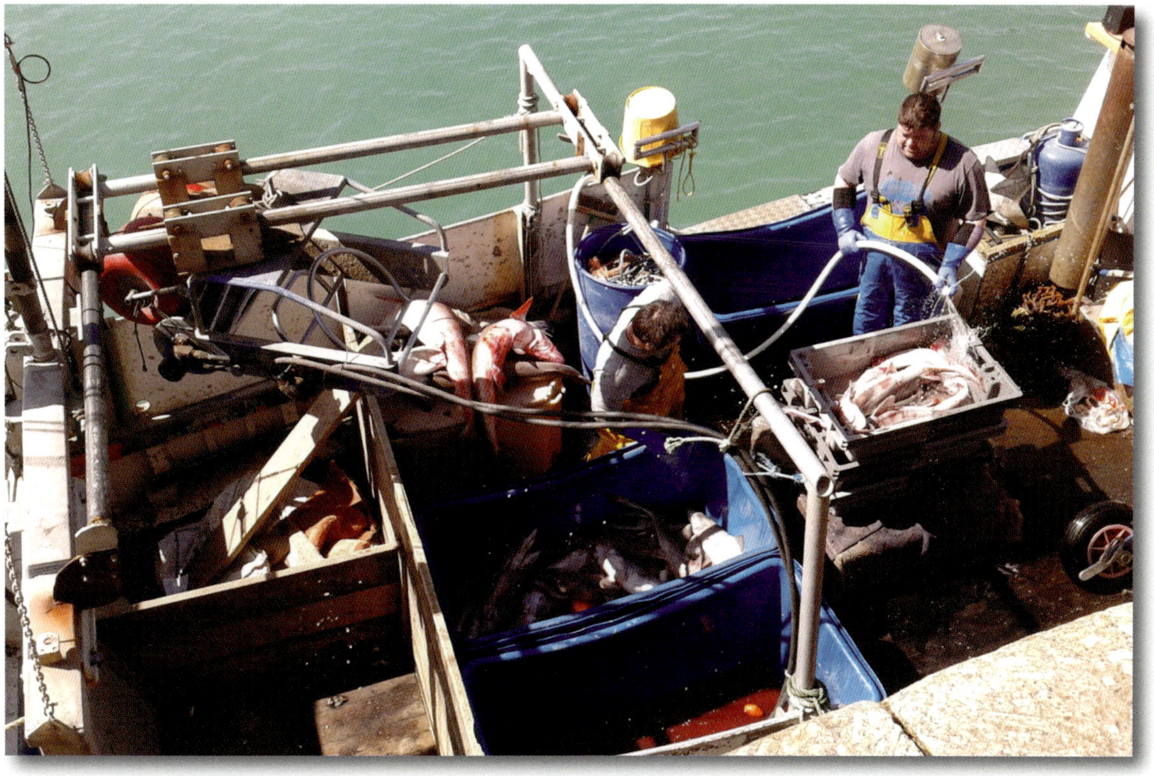

Raggy (right) hosing down the fish, working with Alex on the *Silvery Sea*

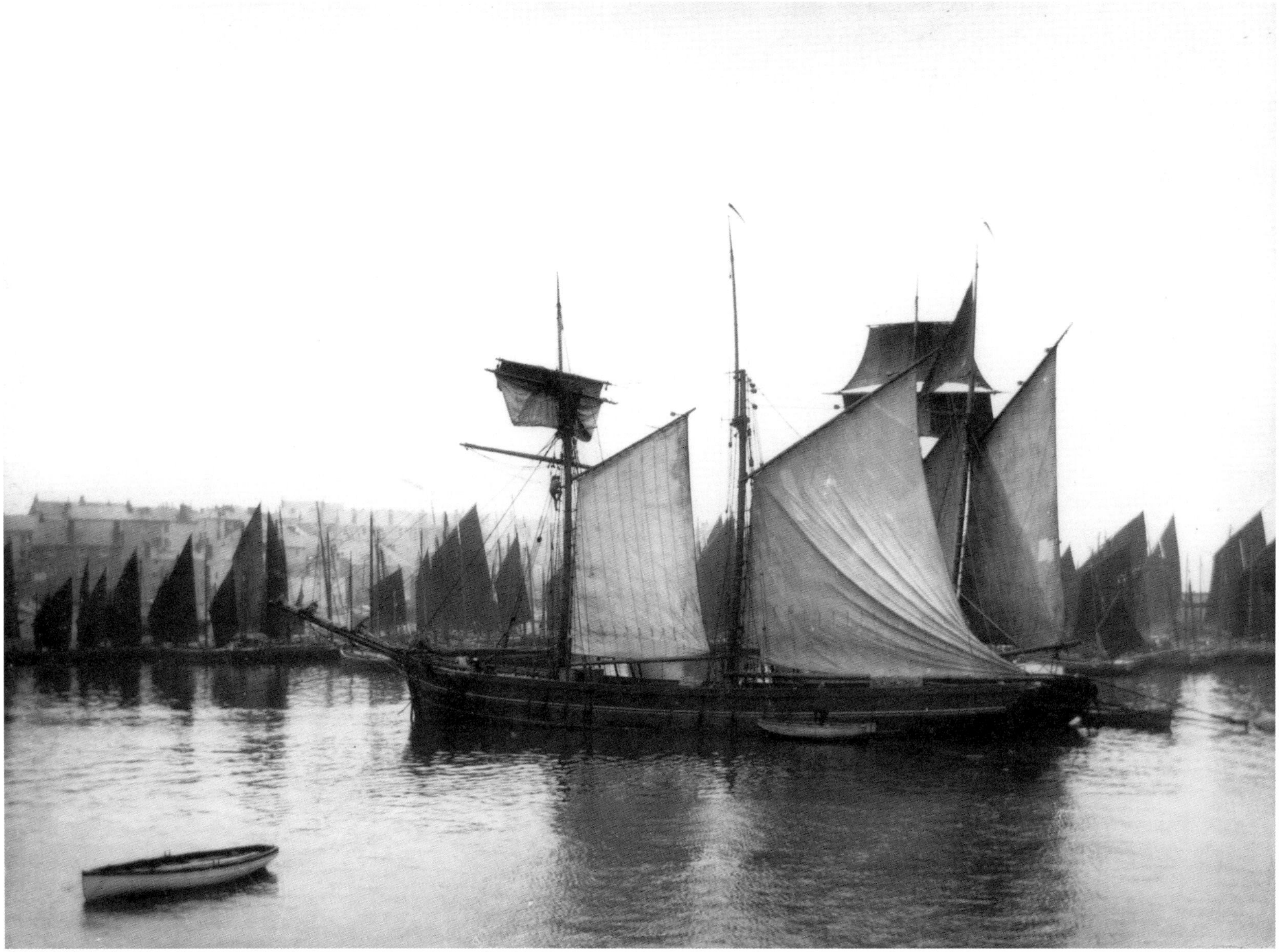

St Ives Harbour, Luggers drying sails 1900s

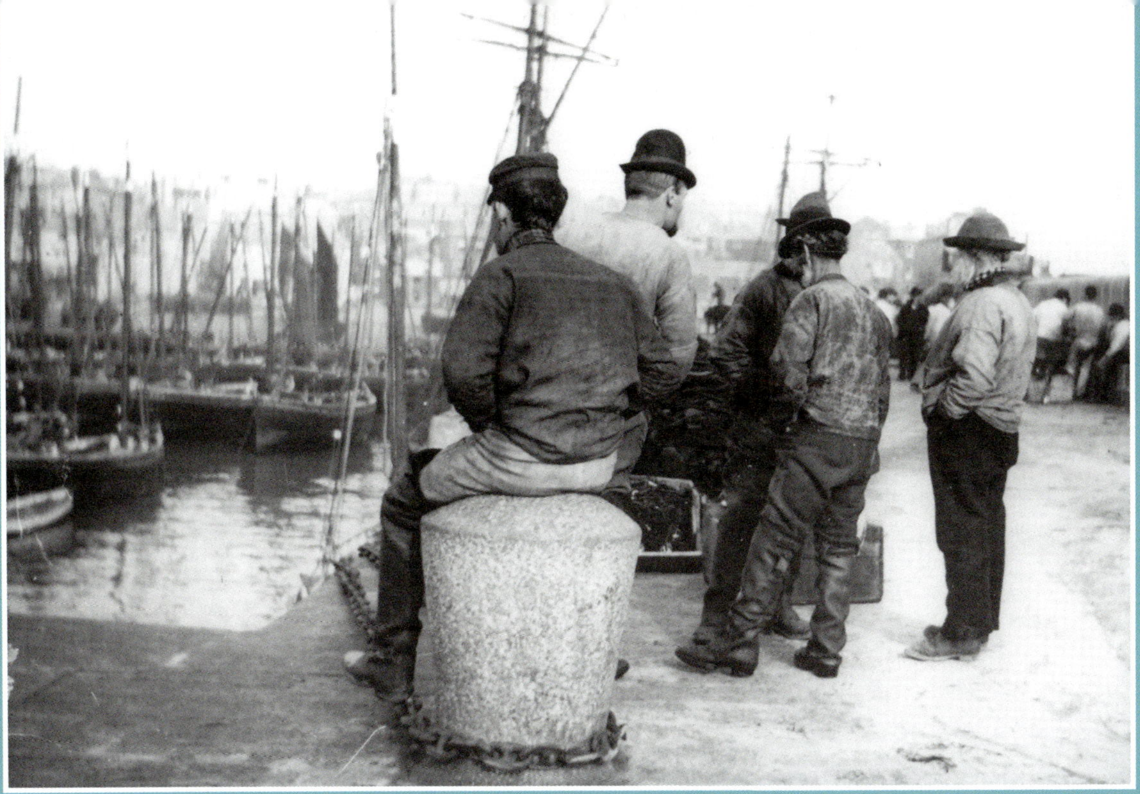

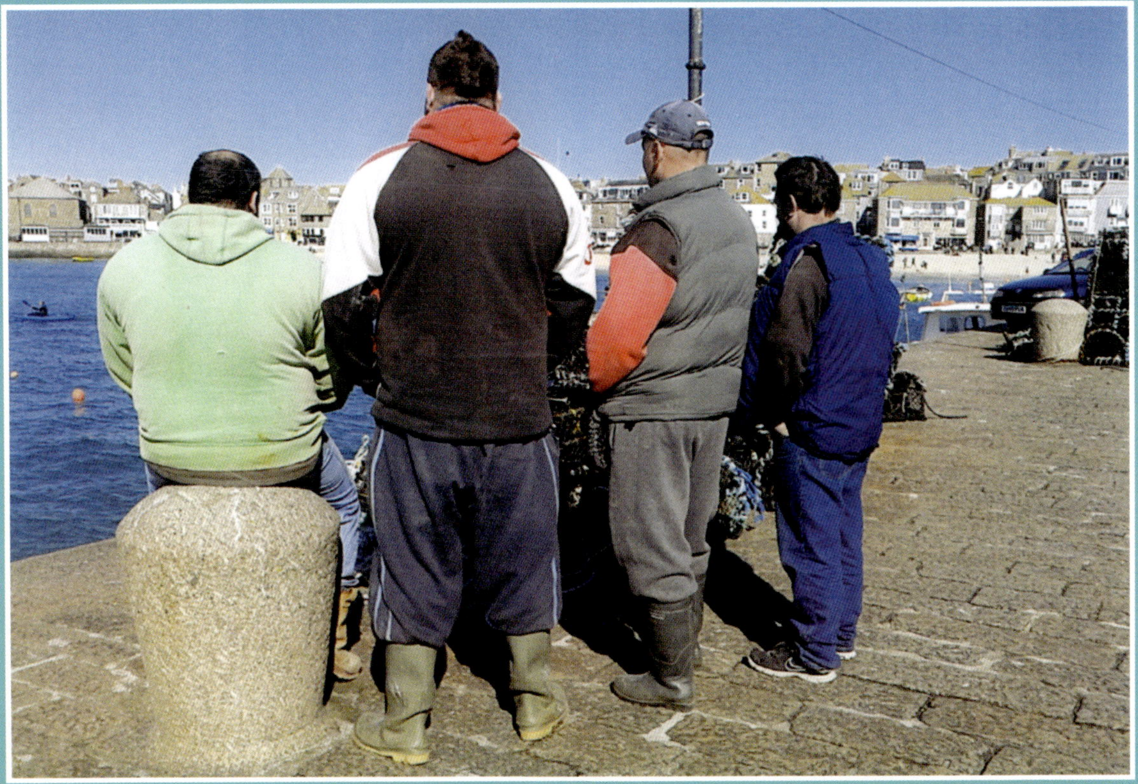

Fishermen on the Pier 1900

Fishermen on the Pier 2013. PJ, Raggy, Dave, Alex

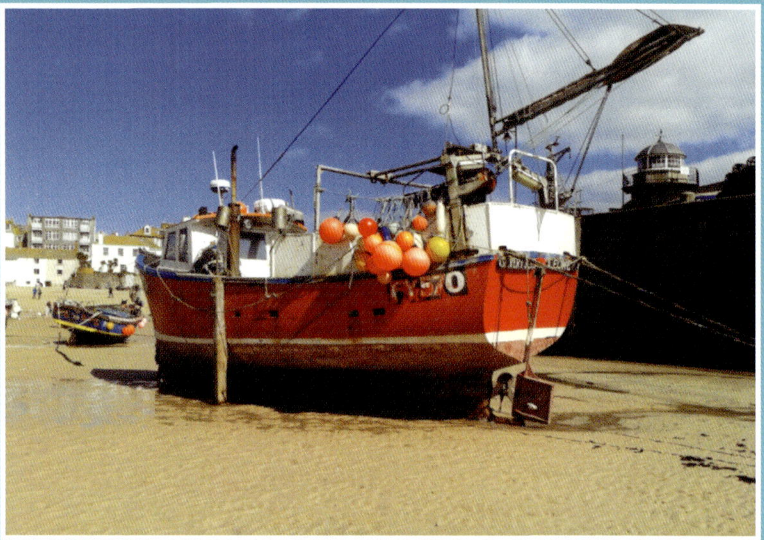

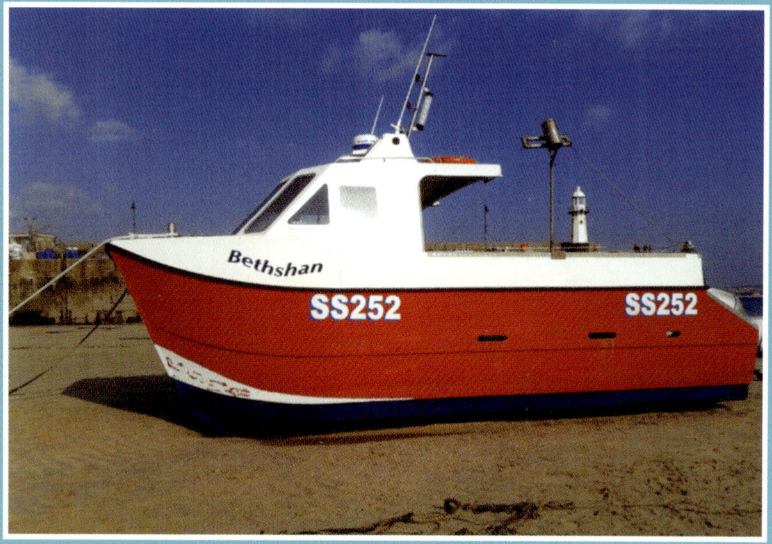

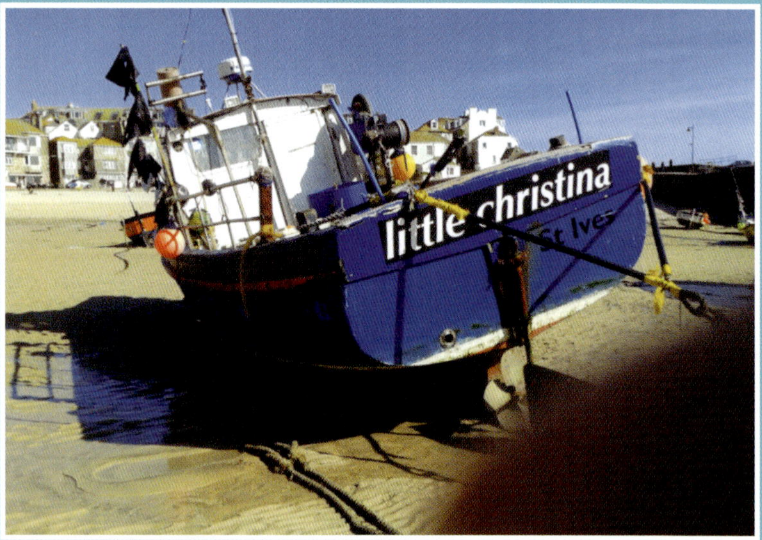

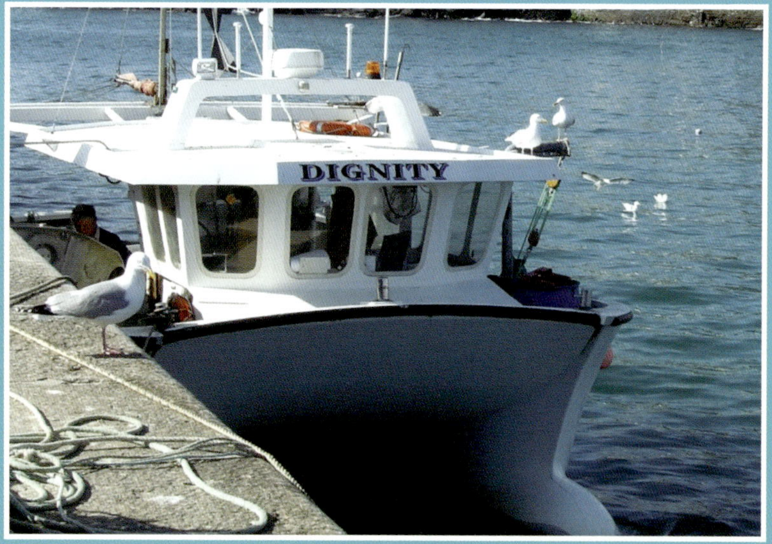

Clockwise from top left: Fy 570 *Silvery Sea PJ Godfrey*; SS252 *Bethshan* Catamaran Gary Leach, The Catamaran *Dignity* Andrew Treloar; SS80 *Little Christina* Stuart McClary

THE BUILDERS

Chris Symons Construction

CHRIS SYMONS IS a St Ives man who is sympathetic to the fishermen, many of whom were his childhood companions. The understanding of their wants was paramount. He was also mindful of the artists, being familiar with the artists and the architect within his own family. As the appointed main contractor he was able to employ local tradesmen in St Ives and throughout Cornwall and help sustain their livelihoods and the economy of the county.

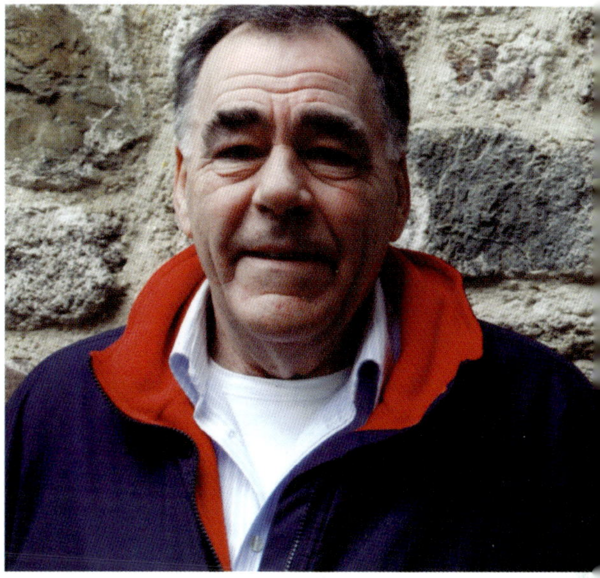

Chris Symons

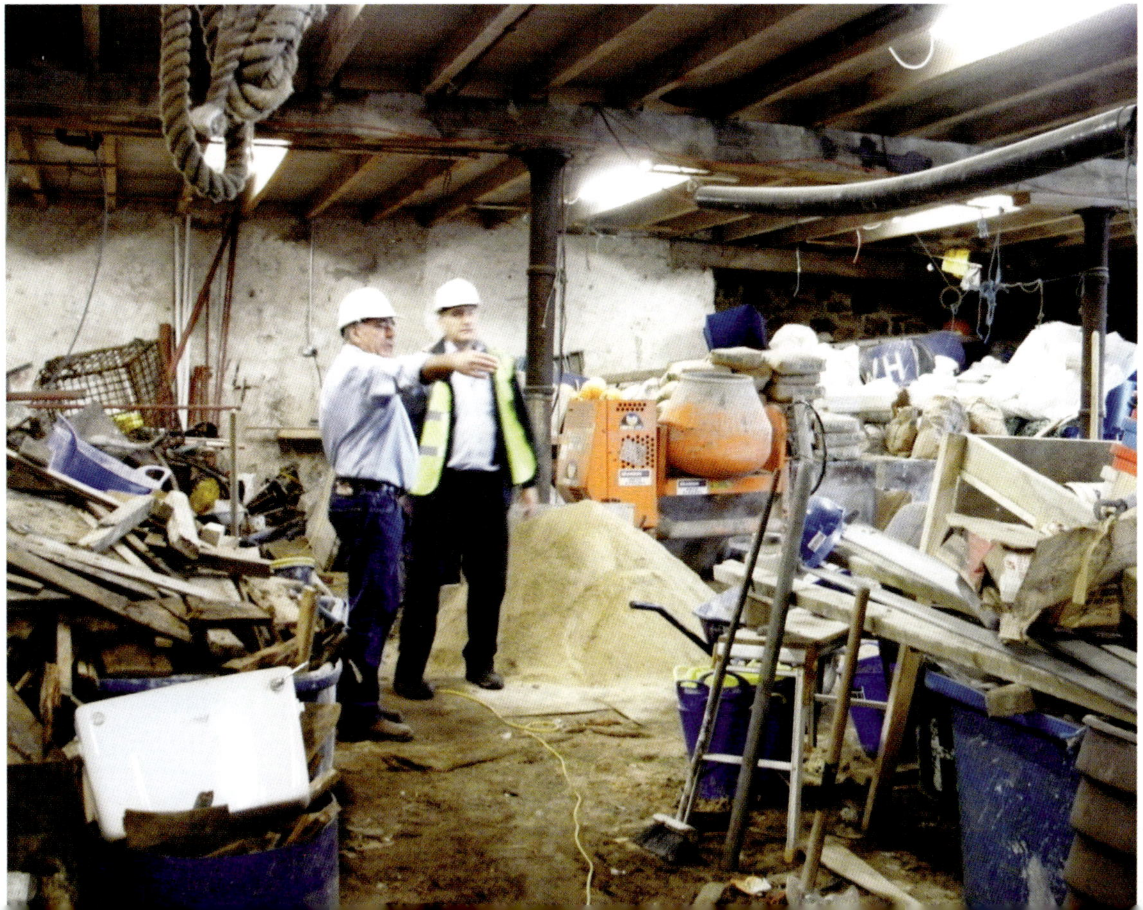

Directing operations in the fish cellar

Chris Symons I suppose we must have employed 50 men from every trade on the Porthmeor studios and cellars project. It was a challenging site because of its close proximity to other dwellings and access was a problem for loading and unloading supplies and machinery. Also, there was no local parking. It was difficult for men and materials.

The majority of the materials were sourced locally and the timber grown in Cornwall.

We were using Douglas Fir and Cornish Oak. We used new scantle slates from the Delabole Cornish quarry, the traditional slates used in Cornwall.

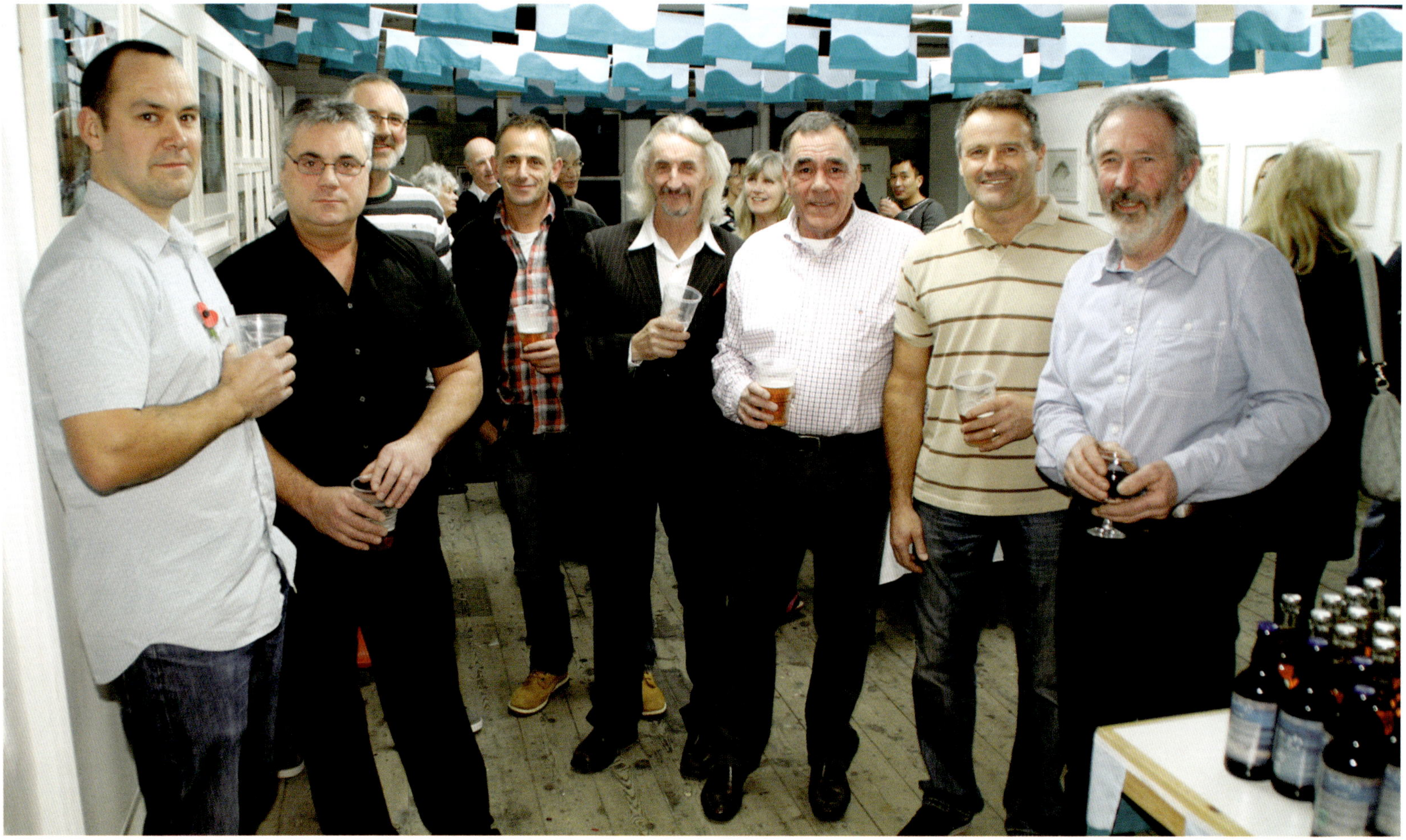

Tradesmen, Builders and Contractors who worked on the project celebrating the completion of their work on the Porthmeor Studios. Left. Ben Jeffries, Foreman; Tommy Hoskin, Plumber; Ian Hughes, Carpenter; Kevin Boas, Mason; Tony Richards, Fisherman; Chris Symons, Boss; Bradley Gibson, Joiner; John Aggart, Carpenter (and many others)

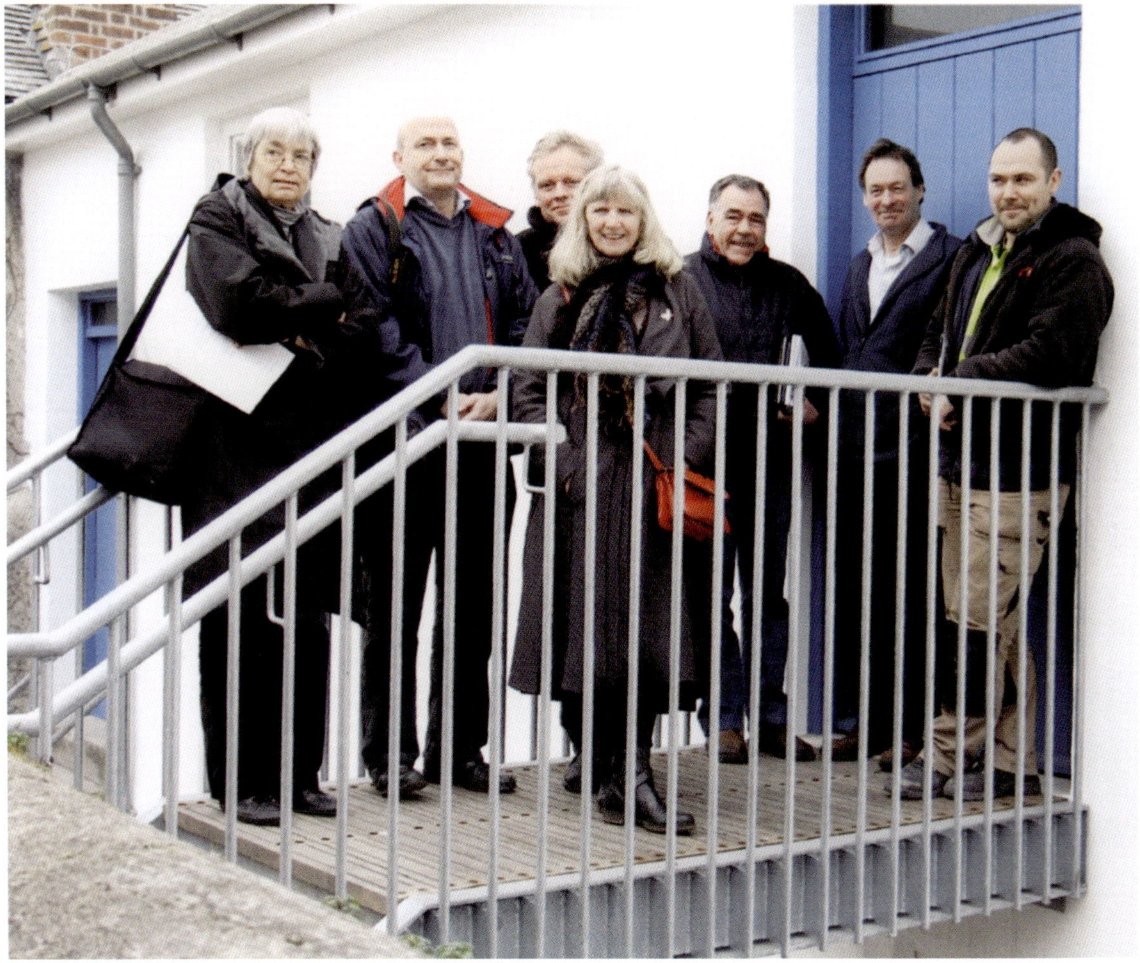

New bridge to the studios
Architect M J Long; Trevor Humphries, Surveyor; Rolfe Kentish, Architect; Chris Symons, Builder; Chris Hibbert, Trust Manager; Ben Jeffries, Foreman; Jane Val Baker, Director

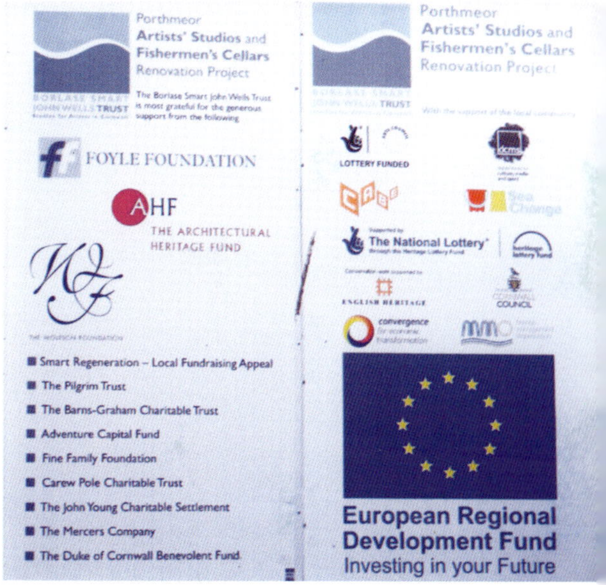

The Funders

An archaeologist came on site to look at the fish cellars. She was trying to establish the previous use of the buildings which have always been for traditional trades. One of the problems was the removal of a great accumulation of sand from the cellars. In a separate area in this huge space we put down a concrete floor so the fishermen could set their fishing nets. The project took over two years to completion. It was a tremendous challenge and commitment and everyone worked to capacity and with a real interest in the venture.

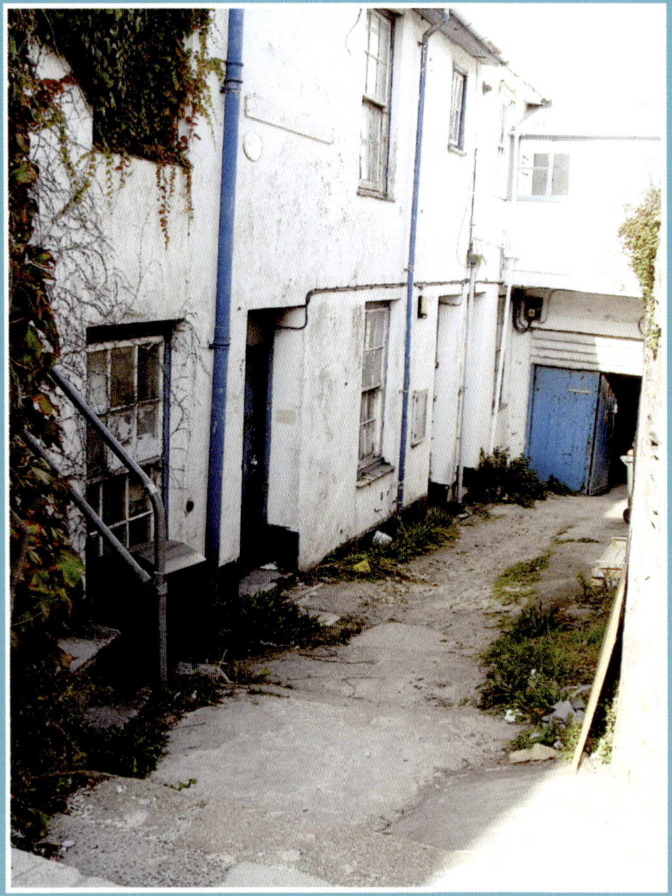

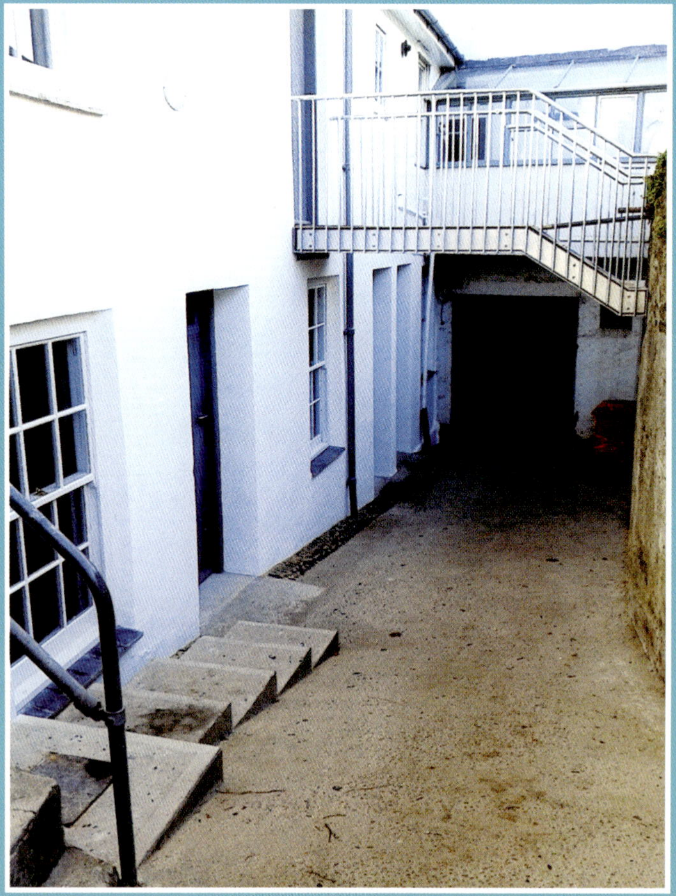

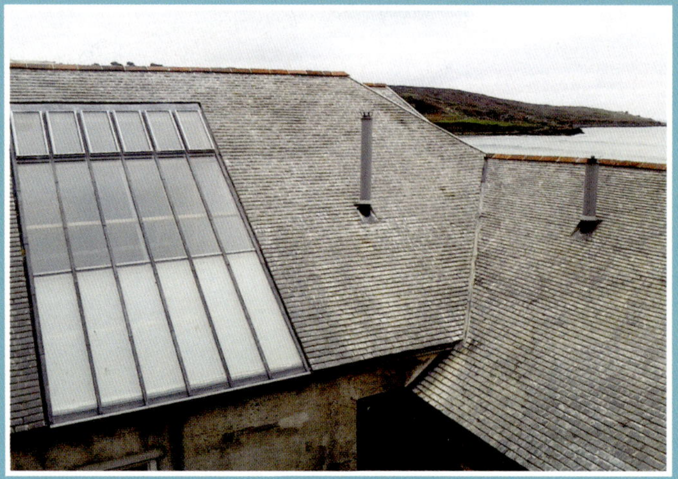

Above left: Old entrance to studios and cellars 2010

Above right: New entrance to studios and cellars 2012

Right: New roof and skylight

St Ives

Today, St Ives is largely unchanged, especially in Downalong, where the cottages used to house the fishing families. There are still fishermen in the town. They are largely men who take pride in skippering, owning and even building their own boats. Crews too are all St Ives men who grew up in fishing families. They work out of Newlyn in the winter and return for the summer to fish in St Ives Bay. They make their nets and store their gear in the fish cellars on Porthmeor beach, leaving the cottages in Downalong for rental to the tourists, who appreciate the charm of the area. It is one of those magical places that people visit and return to again and again.

Artists and writers have been attracted to this beautiful town for over a century, where a large art colony has been established and artists flourish in a town which houses studios, many of which are above fish lofts. There are old established art galleries and newer ones, and to celebrate a

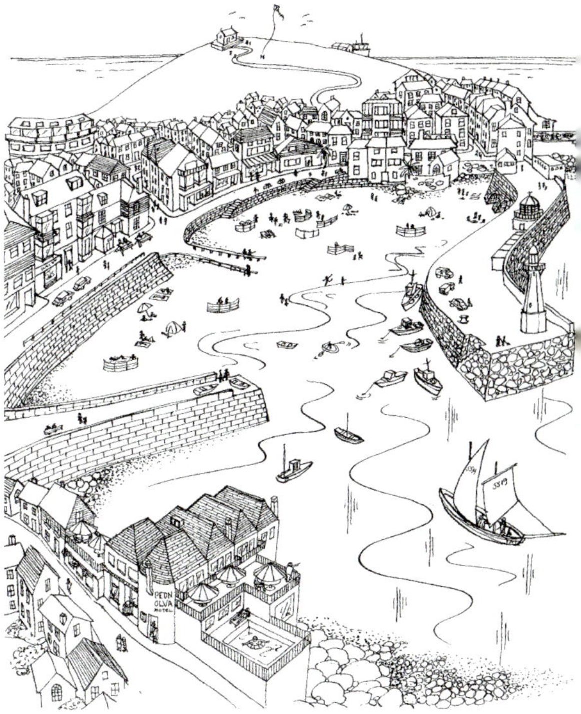

'The Harbour' by Kim Lynch

The Harbour St Ives

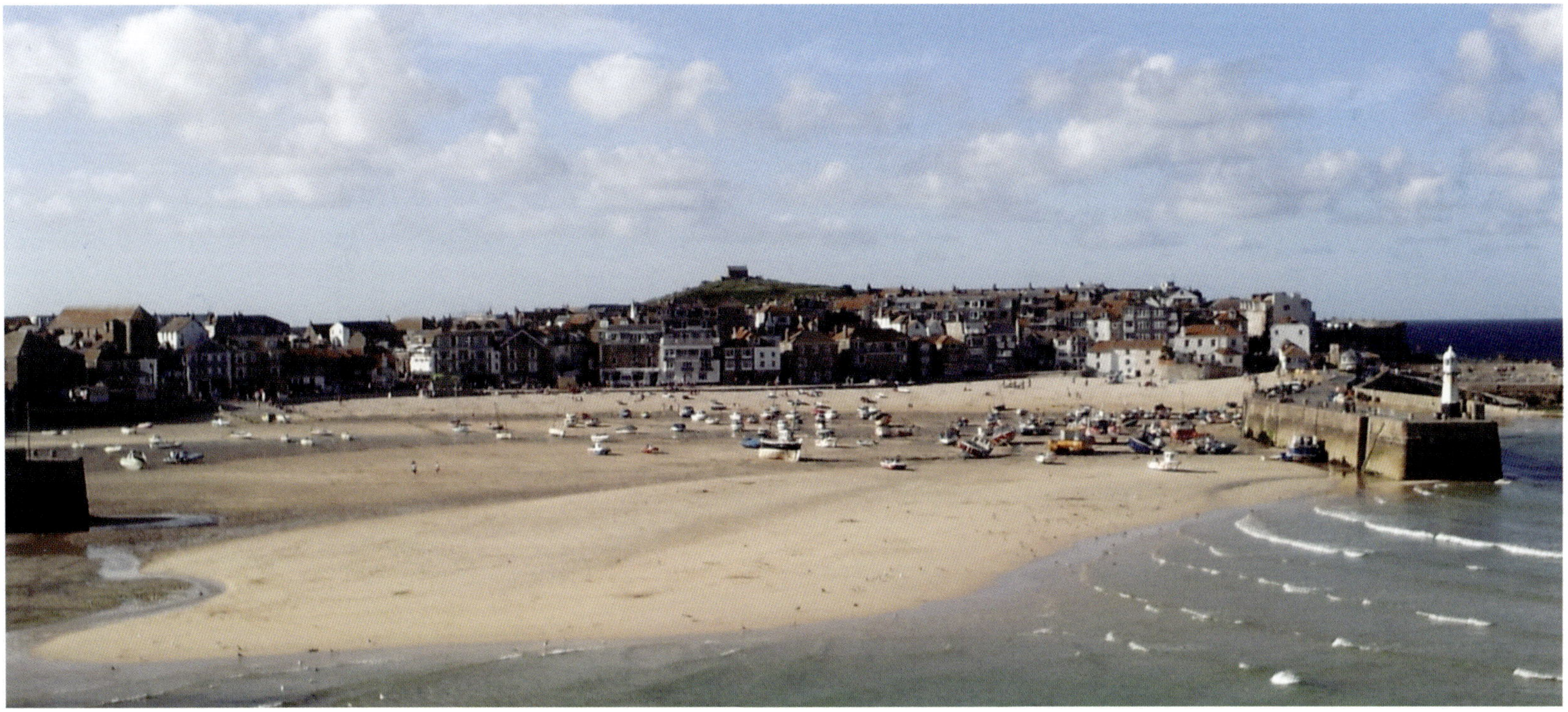

Porthminster Beach 2013

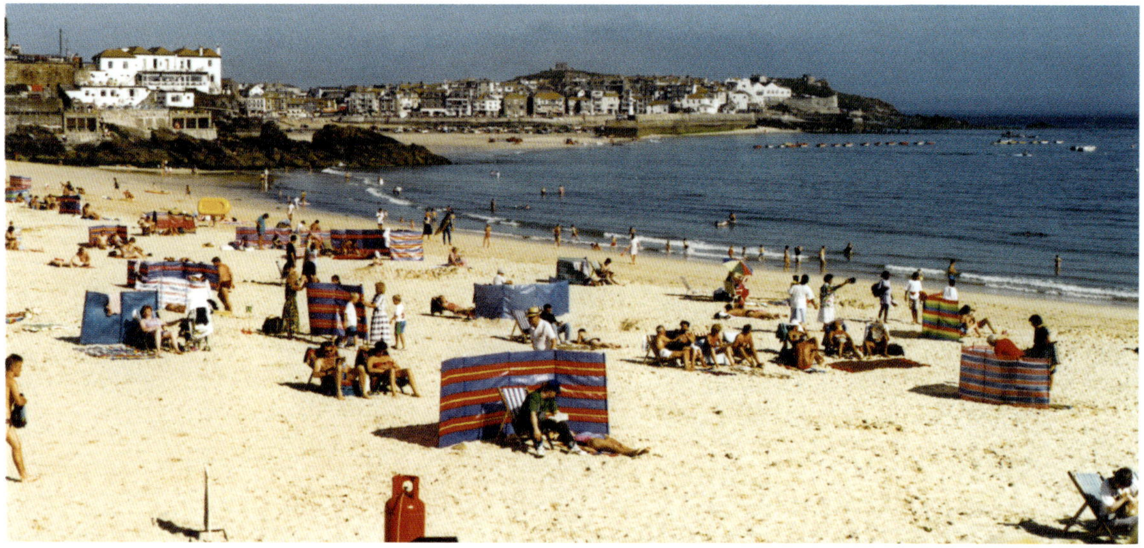

century of art history there is Tate St Ives. Creative people are pulled by a thread that lures them to Cornwall to experience that indefinable magnetic quality, and allows their artistic genes to flourish. They paint in pure light mirrored by fine white sands, unhindered by pollution. The resident writers are influenced by the landscape, the legends and its early ancient history, which inspires their writing.

St Ives is a charming place, renowned for its incredible blue seas and five sea-washed sandy beaches; its harbour and its ability to sustain credibility in various descriptions of loveliness.

Summer Boats St Ives Harbour

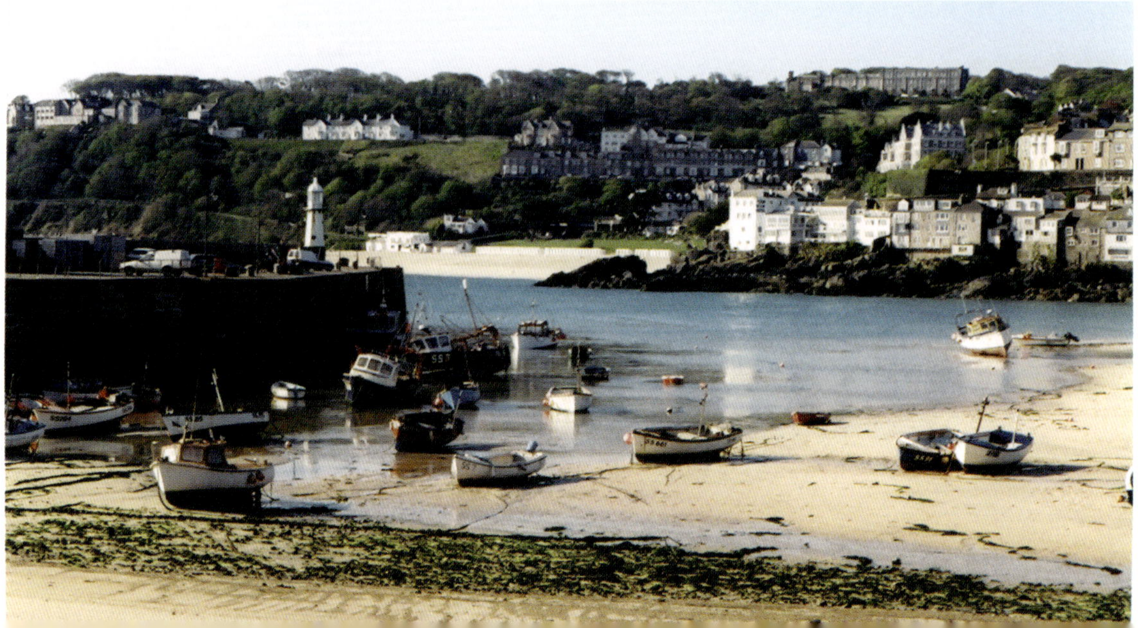

REFERENCES, ACKNOWLEDGEMENTS, PHOTO CREDITS, BOOKS

References

1 Brian Stevens

2 *The Studio*

3 *St Ives 1883-1993 Portrait of an Art Colony*

4 *Tremedda Days* – Alison Symons

5 *St Ives 1883-1993 Portrait of an Art Colony*

6 *The Studio* 1922

7 *Some Statements by Barbara Hepworth*

8 *A Pictorial Autobiography* – Barbara Hepworth

9 *Barbara Hepworth,The Plasters* – Sophie Bowness

10 *A Pictorial Autobiography* – Barbara Hepworth

11 *A Pictorial Autobiography* – Barbara Hepworth

12 *A Pictorial Autobiography* – Barbara Hepworth

Acknowledgements

As always, my husband Terry, for support and reading of the script

My daughter, Kim Lynch, for her careful reading of the script

Frank Ruhrmund for writing the foreword

Borlase Smart John Wells Trust

Millenium Gallery, St Ives

Waterside Gallery, St Ives

Sophie Bowness

Simon Butler and Sharon O'Inn of Halstar

Maureene Swenson for computer assistance with photos

Sam Foreman for computer technical help

Chris Hibbert for constantly answering my questions

St Ives Library, Jane, Florence, John, Kate, Sue

Alison Sharkey

Ann Kelley

Arwen Fitch, Tate, St Ives

Barry Sinton, Tate, St Ives Bookshop

Dr Liz Shore

Dell Castagli

Helen Dunmore

Jane Val Baker

Judie Browne

Katharine Heron

Susanna Heron

Photo Credits

Ann Kelley
Brian and Margaret Stevens – St Ives Museum ©
Brian Pierce, kernowphoto.co.uk
David Elsbury Archive
David Ward
Estate of Patrick Heron ©. All rights reserved DACS 2013
Graham Gaunt photowork
Janet Axten – archive photos
Julian Feary
Lee Sheldrake - Barbara Hepworth © Bowness, Hepworth Estate
M J Long – architect
Marion Whybrow – artists, fishermen and various
Michael Murphy, St Ives Archive
Morag Robertson
Penwith Society of Arts
Peter Garrett
Richard Waite Photography
Rolfe Kentish
St Ives School of Painting
St Ives Society of Artists
St Ives Times & Echo
Tate St Ives
Tate Britain
Tobi Carver
Toni Carver

Others

The Artists
The Fishermen
The Builders

Books

Alison Symons. *Tremedda Days. A View of Zennor, 1900-1940.* Tabb House 1992

Ann Kelley – *Born and Bred, Portraits of St Ives.* Cornwall Books 1988

Barbara Hepworth – *A Pictorial Autobiography* – extended edition, Moonraker Press 1978

Barbara Hepworth – *A Pictorial Autobiography,* Adams & Dart, Bath 1970

Barbara Hepworth – St Ives Artists, Penelope Curtis – Tate Gallery Publishing 1998

Barbara Hepworth – *The Plasters, The Gift to Wakefield*, edited by Sophie Bowness. Lund Humphries 2011

Barbara Hepworth by A M Hammacher – Thames & Hudson, Revised Edition 1987

Barbara Hepworth Centenary – Tate Publishing 2003

Ben Tufnell – *On the Very Edge of the Ocean – The Porthmeor Studios and Painting in St Ives.* Tate Publishing 2006

Colour in Space – Patrick Heron : Public Projects; Michael Tooby and Julian Feary. Tate St Ives

M J Long – *Artists' Studios.* Black Dog Publishing 2009

Marion Whybrow – *Borlase Smart – St Ives Artist – Man of Vision.* Halsgrove 2012

Marion Whybrow – *Studio- Artists in Their Workplace* 1994

Mel Gooding. *Patrick Heron.* Phaidon Press Limited 1994

Paintings by Patrick Heron 1965-1977 – Donald B Goodall, Kelly Fearing, Sir Alan Bowness, Patrick Heron, RC Kennedy. The University of Austin Texas Art Museum

Some Statements by Barbara Hepworth – Barbara Hepworth Museum 1977

Will Arnold Forster – *Shrubs for the Milder Counties* – Alison Hodge